#895

THE MAKING OF DÉTENTE

THE MAKING OF DÉTENTE

Soviet-American Relations in the Shadow of Vietnam

KEITH L. NELSON

THE JOHNS HOPKINS UNIVERSITY PRESS

BALTIMORE AND LONDON

© 1995 The Johns Hopkins University Press
All rights reserved. Published 1995
Printed in the United States of America on acid-free paper
04 03 02 01 00 99 98 97 96 95   5 4 3 2 1

The Johns Hopkins University Press
2715 North Charles Street
Baltimore, Maryland 21218-4319
The Johns Hopkins Press Ltd., London

ISBN 0-8018-4883-0

Library of Congress Cataloging-in-Publication Data will be found
at the end of this book.
A catalog record for this book is available from the British Library.

FOR PADDY

CONTENTS

PREFACE AND ACKNOWLEDGMENTS

Many of the perspectives in this book go back more than twenty years, to the time when I first realized that the Vietnam War was altering the United States in ways that were hardly noticed or discussed. Partly in response to this realization, and also out of curiosity about the effects of international violence generally, I published an edited volume in 1970 in which I traced and compared the impacts on U.S. life of the national experiences in World War I, World War II, and the Cold War. My attention was focused then on the domestic sphere, but in subsequent years I have come to recognize that war-induced internal changes can themselves transform a nation's foreign policy and that these transformations supplement those precipitated more directly by such events as victory or defeat. Indeed, today I believe that the repercussions of war, indirect as well as direct, are among the most profound determinants of a country's foreign relations.

I also believe, in this specific instance, that the Vietnam War was a major turning point in the history of the Soviet-American Cold War, the decline and end of which have now themselves become defining experiences. This is not to deny the role of other factors in policy formation that operate independently of war but merely to suggest that they are often of less importance. In this volume, I attempt to make my case with reference to the period 1969–72, when leaders of both East and West were led to create foreign policies in response to what was in large measure a postwar situation.

In the course of my writing I have acquired many debts, both institutional and personal. My foremost obligation is to the National Archives and especially to the men and women of the Nixon Presidential Materials Project in College Park, Maryland (formerly in Alexandria, Virginia), who were very helpful. I am grateful to them. I also wish to thank the librarians at the University of California, Irvine, the librarians at Lunds Universitet in Lund, Sweden, and the staff of the Institute for the Study of the World Economy and International Relations (IMEMO) in Moscow. I offer added thanks to those agencies that have assisted me with financial grants. Without help from the School of Humanities at UCI and the program in Global Peace and Conflict Studies (GPACS) at UCI I would not have been able to travel to Washington and Europe or to interview participants so widely. Without an academic quarter in Sweden as a Fulbright research professor during 1990, I would have been severely handicapped in completing the final stages of my research and writing.

Speaking more personally, I would like to emphasize how much I appreciate the cooperation of former officials who took the time to talk with me about their experiences as participants in the U.S., Soviet, British, or West German governments during the 1960s and 1970s: Georgi Arbatov, Egon Bahr, McGeorge Bundy, Oleg Bykov, Anatoly Dobrynin, Lawrence Eagleburger, Daniel Ellsberg, Philip Farley, Alton Frye, Raymond Garthoff, Noel Gayler, Dennis Healey, Richard Helms, William G. Hyland, Alexis Johnson, Spurgeon Keeny, Jack Matlock, Robert McNamara, Serge Mikoyan, George Rathjens, Kenneth Rush, Herbert Scoville, Gerard Smith, Helmut Sonnenfeldt, Immo Stabreit, Maurice Stans, Yuri Streltsov, Henry Trofimenko, and Elmo Zumwalt.

For counsel, criticism, and assistance along the way, I am immensely grateful to present and former colleagues at UCI: Spencer C. Olin, Karl Hufbauer, Jon Jacobson, Lynn Mally, Gordon Chang, Julius Margolis, Paula Garb, John Whiteley, Patrick Morgan, Kendall Bailes, and Helen Weil; and to scholars at other universities in this country and abroad: David Levering, Edith Gelles, Robert Schulzinger, Allen Greb, George Breslauer, Peter Loewenberg, Richard D. Anderson, Egbert Jahn, Galia Golan, Göran Rystad, Kristian Gerner, and Kim Salomon. Thanks are due to Georgi Arbatov for lending me the typescript of his memoirs before they were published. Let me also convey my appreciation to Wolfgang Hartenstein, Marya Vanyan, and Sergei Plekhanov not only for their time and friendship but also for their help in guiding me to important interviews.

I must add to this list my typists, Mary Duitsman and Mindy Han, who worked indefatigably in preparing this manuscript; my editor and copy editor, Henry Tom and Diane Hammond, who made ingenious and helpful suggestions for its improvement; and my tennis partner, Andrew Guilford, who read the results carefully and offered thoughtful commentary.

Finally, to the members of my immediate family: my mother, Elizabeth; my children, Scott, Lori, and Katherine; and especially my wife, Paddy, I wish to express my gratitude for their continuing and loving support. They kept the faith on what was a somewhat longer journey than we had expected.

INTRODUCTION

As we look back on the early 1970s and that substantial if brief improvement in Soviet-American relations commonly referred to as détente, a number of challenging questions inevitably come to mind. How was it possible for such an improvement to occur after the countries involved had waged a Cold War against each other for more than two decades? What factors or persons on either or both sides can be held responsible or given credit for this unexpected relaxation in tension? What were the characteristics of détente, both internationally and within the participating nations, and was the phenomenon really as unprecedented as many thought at the time? Finally, what happened subsequently to undermine and displace the attitudes and policies of détente, at least until the coming of the Gorbachev era?

To be sure, there are those who believe that the United States was tricked—that there never was a positive change on the other side during this period but only an endeavor to get this nation to let down its guard. The evidence, however, does not substantiate such conclusions. Though there may have been an element of deception and even self-deception in the process, and though each side certainly intended that in the long run détente would work to its advantage, a careful analysis of available materials demonstrates that the leadership of both countries did make a genuine if limited effort to cooperate during the Nixon-Brezhnev years. The collaboration, though modest, uneven, and suspicion-ridden at times, was real.

What changes transpired to put détente within the reach of these historic actors? The answer to this query is not simple for either America or Russia, but in the case of the United States it seems clear that at least one event was indispensable in creating the necessary preconditions—the conflict in Vietnam. In combination with other, longer-range developments—economic, military, and international—this painful and divisive war was central in producing that shortage in support and resources that ultimately led a conservative president to attempt to strengthen the status quo through accommodation with the superpower rival.

Oddly enough, though always ready to blame the "Vietnam syndrome" for the demise of détente, neither Richard Nixon nor Henry Kissinger has ever publicly recognized the contribution of the Vietnam War and the antiwar movement to the breakthrough in relations. From Nixon's perspective, "the discords of that decade and its aftermath critically weakened the nation's capacity to meet its responsibilities in the world, not only militarily but also in terms of its ability to lead."[1] Kissinger echoes this refrain. "One could argue," he says, "that Vietnam delayed adaptation to new circumstance by confusing the debate and focusing on one quarter of the globe, by polarizing the country and destroying the political center. In that sense, Vietnam was a symptom and not a cause of [the] reconsideration [of postwar U.S. foreign policy]."[2]

These two statesmen are not alone in holding such views. As the outpouring of comments on the tenth anniversary of the collapse of South Vietnam made clear, Americans in general do not see the connection between the trauma of the Vietnam War and the coming of détente.[3] The majority of this nation tends to assume that American motives and actions are essentially benign and also that others view them as benign.[4] Thus it is not the United States that has to change in order to make reasonable international compromise possible—it is the other side. There is no need (nor by implication, was there in the 1960s) for Americans to be shocked or pulled by a cataclysmic event into a different, more positive foreign policy posture.[5]

Not surprisingly, though Russian observers have been relatively clear-sighted in perceiving the Vietnam-détente relation,[6] they have been as resistant as Americans to facing the fact that their country was also being driven by internal and external circumstances toward an arrangement with its foe.[7] Granted, the Soviet Union during these years was not engaged in an overseas war (though it had of course been helping to finance and supply one). Nevertheless, despite obvious national accomplishments (particularly in the military field), the 1960s was a difficult and demanding period for the U.S.S.R., involving setbacks with regard to domestic unity, the performance of the economy, and relations with allies—setbacks that severely reduced the resources and leverage available to Soviet leaders in maintaining their existing foreign policy. In this sense, Moscow was confronting constraints analogous to those Washington was encountering.

There was also a certain similarity in the leadership of the two countries. The importance of this can be exaggerated, but it is surely significant that, as the decade of the 1960s ended, both the United States and the Soviet Union found themselves in the hands of cautious, pragmatic conservatives—relatively insecure men who could talk an ideological line of Right or Left but who, when the crunch came, generally preferred to be liked by their fellows and to buy off their critics. In any case, despite their different situations and personalities, both Richard Nixon and Leonid Brezhnev (and their closest colleagues) ultimately behaved like politicians who realized that they had overcommitted themselves to their constituencies. When neither could meet by conventional means the obligations he had incurred, each was thrown back on finding an alternative way to fulfill his commitments.[8]

In sum, then, my contention (and I feel that the scholarly literature has not reflected this sufficiently) is that the relation between the Soviet Union and the United States moved toward détente in the early 1970s as the result of developments that created a scarcity or potential scarcity in both countries of resources needed to maintain the current structures and activities of their societies, economies, and governments. Given ample means and apparent success, the natural tendency of each nation would have been to continue with existing domestic and foreign policies, even if these had meant perpetuation of the Cold War. In the face of substantial shortages, however (shortages often only partially sensed), realistically conservative leaders on both sides (i.e., leaders with little interest in radical domestic change) found themselves irresistibly attracted to making an arrangement that would reduce the demands being put upon them. This is not to say that the configurations of either the resources or the leadership in Russia or America were identical. Nor is it to argue that either Washington or Moscow was completely unaware of—or unwilling to take advantage of—the fact that the other great power was experiencing certain difficulties. On the contrary, it is to affirm both national uniqueness and situational complexity and at the same time emphasize that significant similarity did exist on each side of the interaction.

There is, after all, something of an understandable and predictable quality to what happened. Indeed, in a very real sense, détente, or (as it is generally defined) a relaxation in relations following severe, if nonviolent tension, seems to be a recurrent and almost inescapable stage in the ongoing relation between two interacting powers.[9] The recent détente may have been unusually important because it broke the momentum of a long-standing struggle involving huge nations with devastating weapons, but it was also in many ways typical of a process that has occurred on other occasions in history.[10]

What is the nature of the development we call détente? How should we comprehend its dynamics and its causes? The beginnings of an answer can be found in the fact that, despite differences and alikenesses, nation-states and even empires successively attract and repel each other in modest or decisive ways over the course of time. Their governments and their peoples do such things as assist, injure, admire, ignore, misunderstand, and compete with their equivalents in other countries. Often they carry out these actions sequentially. Sometimes they perform two or more simultaneously.

Why do nation-states act this way? Briefly, they do because they and the social groups within them find themselves confronting changing situations and therefore in possession of certain internal and external needs. At any given moment, obviously, leaders, groups, or populations may be secure, passive, estranged, frightened, ambitious, frustrated, or divided. At any given time, the international situation may be threatening, reassuring, tempting, irrelevant, or stable.

In other words, though they are infinitely more complicated than individuals, nation-states (and their constituent groups) tend, like individuals, to react in terms of their needs and the resources available to meet those needs. These realities are shaped in part by ideological perspectives, which, in turn, are created out of both historic experiences and immediate self-interest. Naturally, if there is no consensus on beliefs within a nation, or at least within a leadership, we may find indecisiveness and inconsistency in that nation's behavior. On the other hand, where consensus has been achieved, we may see remarkable continuity and inertia, even if the policy involves the continuation of war.

Faced with a problem of reconciling needs and resources, most national leaders will try to manipulate or enlarge the latter before they make a serious effort to reconsider or restructure the former. After all, the leadership's definition of a nation's needs involves not only the issue of their personal and their nation's survival but also the means by which they have come to comprehend their own significance, the direction in which they think the world is moving, and the conditions they believe are necessary to keep their role secure and their people satisfied and cohesive. These "needs" are very basic matters, and it is not surprising that it is easier for statesmen to think of adjusting the means than of altering the ends.

Moreover, there are many kinds of resource manipulation available to a nation-state. Confronted with a shortfall due to increased demands or the declining effectiveness of a domestic or international effort, national leaders may move in any one of several directions, attempting, for example, to raise the energy level of the nation's population, to render the nation's economy more efficient, to obtain foreign assistance, to acquire military advantage, or to build international alliances. If nothing else works, they can even approach their international adversaries in the hope of agreeing to limit or reduce the scope of the competition.

This last approach is not as common as we might wish, because, of course, it requires collaboration between groups or nations whose leaders have been conditioned to fear and distrust each other. Nevertheless, the history of international relations is rich with examples of situations in which long-standing enemies, often in desperation, found it possible to reach an understanding. One need look no farther than the experiences of the Protestant and Catholic princes in the early modern era, the alliance between the tsar of Russia and the French republic in the late nineteenth century, the Hitler-Stalin pact of 1939, or the negotiations between Egypt and Israel in our own era. Whether agreements such as these turn out to be long term or only for the moment depends on many factors, including the degree of ideological fixation that characterizes the protagonists and the level of stability in the larger situation. Still, it is possible that, given some consistency of need and some success in meeting it on the part of the participants, what started out as a temporary deal may grow into a surprisingly permanent arrangement.

With the Nixon-Brezhnev détente it remains difficult, even from the vantage point of 1995, to estimate how extensive, how serious, and how symmetrical the positive changes in attitude and behavior really were. Encouraging events made it relatively easy to believe that goodwill and trust were penetrating the elites and publics of both nations in a profound and almost irreversible way. The misunderstandings and problems of succeeding years, however, make it clear that the détente of the 1970s was a relatively fragile thing, a plant that had put down roots among certain groups but not among others. Having reached its greatest vigor in the period of the Brezhnev-Nixon-Ford summit meetings in 1972–74, it suffered serious and almost continuous decline from the Angola crisis in 1975 and the U.S. presidential campaign of 1976 down through the mid-1980s. Indeed, the Soviet invasion of Afghanistan and the election of Ronald Reagan apparently dealt détente near mortal blows, and though it is surely an exaggeration to say that the superpowers entered at that point upon Cold War II, who can deny that we witnessed an ominous return to the fear, threat, and unilateral actions of three decades ago?

Nonetheless, and especially since the rise of Mikhail Gorbachev, it is possible to argue that the Nixon-Brezhnev accommodation remained impressive and that, when a set of conditions arose that was in many ways similar to those of the early 1970s (e.g., an unsuccessful war, economic strain, military parity), it proved to be a valuable inspiration to both sides in achieving a return to détente.

I do not imply total symmetry in the causal sequences that brought the United States and the Soviet Union to find détente attractive. Though there are similarities in the history of these two countries, particularly in the last decades, it is also true that each possessed a distinct civilization, economic system, political structure, and frame of reference. The fact that both countries found it possible in the early 1970s to come to certain understandings clearly owes something to shared and comparable experiences (such as having lived under the threat of nuclear incineration or having invested extravagantly in their mutual competition). But it may also be in part the result of coincidence—that is, of different factors, different needs, and different motives operating by chance to achieve the same ends.

Having conceded this, however, I believe that there were remarkable parallels in the configurations of forces that impacted on Washington and Moscow. In fact, this was so much the case that in analyzing what happened it will be interesting and useful to examine the two countries jointly by subject area, taking up, in chapter 1, the behavior of each nation toward the other in the years before and during the Cold War; in chapter 2, the special problems and pressures that developed within each society in the course of the 1960s; and in chapter 3, the challenge to each country posed by new military parity and the weakening of alliance systems. These are followed by three chapters (4, 5, and 6) in which the diplomacy of the Americans and that of the Russians are discussed in terms of their assumptions, procedures, successes, and failures.

The thrust of the interpretation is that, at the end of the 1960s, analogous developments combined to persuade the leading groups in both the United States and the Soviet Union that they no longer possessed the resources required to achieve their basic objectives and that collaboration with each other was a relatively safe way to bring needs and resources into balance. Thus the decision of the leaders to pursue détente was, in effect, an effort to increase their capacities and to maximize their control without serious side effects. Indeed, the foreign factor may well have been introduced into the equation to avoid having to make more extreme and perhaps unpalatable domestic adjustments.

THE MAKING OF DÉTENTE

1

THE DEVELOPING
CONFRONTATION

Over the last two centuries, as the United States and Russia grew prodigiously in size and moved toward substantial interaction, their relation was both promising and inconsistent. During the decades following the revolutionary era a degree of friendliness developed between them— the result, apparently, of their common fear of England as well as their wide separation from each other. But these same years also brought to their relations moments of estrangement and outright hostility. During the twentieth century, despite increasingly serious conflicts of interest and ideology and an extended Cold War, the two countries experienced periods of vigorous collaboration and even alliance. External circumstances, the ideas and interests of publics and leaders and the shifting pressures of mood and development, combined to create a surprisingly changeable mix of foreign policy postures. When it was supremely advantageous for the United States and Russia to get along, their governments often found the means to do so.

The character and experience of the two peoples have been in some ways distinctly similar, in other ways vastly different. Both nations having been peripheral to and dependent on the European heartland, both having expanded consistently outward into regions not thickly populated, both having built extraordinarily vast multiethnic states, the two countries at the same time came to stand at almost opposite ends of the modern political, economic, and ideological spectrums.

The United States, the oldest major republic, evolved out of an unusually decentralized yet innovative British culture, creating a tradition that emphasized limited government and the right of the individual to speak, act, own, and venture. Russia, by contrast, organized itself in a much more defensive way, presumably because of the trauma involved in several hundred years of vulnerability to foreign invasion. The tsarist government and, after 1917, the Soviet regime remained centralized and autocratic, generally closed to outsiders and guarded with its citizens and resources. That Russia lagged in commercialization and later in industrialization (which did not get under way until 1890, roughly forty years after it did in America) and that, as a result, its middle class grew very slowly did not prevent the Russian state from presenting itself in missionary-ideological garb, both before and after the Communist revolution. Indeed, neither country was reticent about suggesting that its own political-religious creed (American liberalism, Russian orthodox Christianity and, later, Soviet Communism) was universally valid.

During the American Revolution, of course, the need for foreign assistance on the part of the former colonies constituted both an opportunity for nations like France and Russia to weaken the recently enlarged British empire and a danger to their own traditional institutions from association with a revolutionary republican movement. Perhaps as a result the balance of power on the Continent seemed much too delicate for Catherine the Great to go beyond trying to unfreeze wartime commerce by means of a League of Armed Neutrals. American efforts in the 1780s to obtain diplomatic recognition from Russia were rebuffed, and in succeeding years, as the horrors of the French Revolution unfolded before the world, the rising ideological temperature made the achievement of normal ties more and more difficult. Not until 1808, when both Russia and the United States were desperate to break out of the maritime straightjacket imposed by the British during the Napoleonic wars, was it possible for the two nations to establish formal relations.

Following 1815, the two countries found it easier to be tolerant and cooperative. Though it was clear that Alexander I sympathized with Spanish efforts to crush the new republican governments in Latin America, it was also obvious that St. Petersburg and Washington had a common interest in preserving a European balance of power that protected both nations. Thus, while Russia was ostensibly one of those states that the Monroe Doctrine of 1823 was designed to ward off, in reality Americans were much more concerned about the threat that the dynamism of Britain and France posed for the New World. Similarly, though there was resentment in the United States at the role Tsar Nicholas's armies played in putting down the liberal revolutions of 1848, there was also expressed empathy for Russia when that nation's armies were defeated by Anglo-French-Turkish forces during the Crimean War (1854–56). Within a few short years the Russians were able to return the compliment when they helped to forestall European mediation during the American Civil War and then sent their Atlantic and Pacific fleets to visit the United States in a move that was widely interpreted as signaling support for President Lincoln and the North. With the Metternichean international system now in ruins, Russia's need was greater than ever for an American counterpoise to the power of Western Europe.[1]

During the second half of the nineteenth century the factors making for cordiality between the two countries began to give way to more problematic influences. Increased travel and better communication created greater awareness in both nations of the profound ways in which their social structures differed. Moreover, as Alexander II's reform efforts of the 1860s faded and he turned to repression to cope with internal discontent, Americans were being buoyed and subtly chauvinized by the experiences and implications of their own industrial development. By 1899, American needs and expectations were involved enough in the China market for the United States to demand an "open door" when Russia and other powers began maneuvering to close off spheres of influence in that region. Such intervention, not to speak of the rapprochement between the United States and Britain (Japan's foremost ally), was viewed with suspicion in St. Petersburg, and in truth there was also a growing dislike in Washington for Russian "imperialism" in the Far East. Theodore Roosevelt's efforts to achieve a balanced peace after Russia's disastrous war with Japan should not obscure the intensifying mutual distrust, subsequently compounded by the Taft administration's attempts to enlarge trading rights in Manchuria and by the horrified reaction of the American public to the persecution of Jews in Russia after 1903.[2]

In any event, the succeeding decade was to witness two unprecedented reversals in the attitudes of Americans and Russians toward each other. Understandably, war in Europe after 1914 did not immediately transform perspectives, since growing economic interdependence and the increasing alienation of the United States from Germany worked only gradually to improve official Russian-American relations. However, in the spring of 1917, with liberal revolution in Russia and the American entrance into global conflict, the need for the two countries to be mutually supportive suddenly became manifest. They were now on the same side, fighting the same enemy, and apparently sharing the same democratic dreams. The Russian nation in particular, with its tiny middle class, incomplete and badly organized industrial system, and exhausted and ill-equipped army, was desperate for assistance of almost any kind. But the United States, too, required help, since without continued Russian participation in the war there seemed little chance of defeating the Central Powers.

Woodrow Wilson responded to the situation with both verbal and material encouragements for the new regime. The United States was the first nation to extend diplomatic recognition to the provisional government, acting on March 22, 1917. Wilson followed this up by dispatching a series of delegations instructed to identify ways in which America could assist the Russian war effort. Approximately $450 million in financial aid was made available, though only after the administration received assurances that Russia would not leave the war.

Yet this insistence on preserving the eastern front proved in the long run to be a costly mistake for America and the Allies. Having assumed that the very act of overthrowing the tsar would enable the Russians to fight more effectively, they failed to recognize that long years of war had so ravaged and demoralized the country that only peace could enable the liberal revolutionary regime to survive. As it was, the authority of the provisional government came under constant attack, particularly from the antiwar Left (Social Revolutionaries and Bolshevik Social Democrats), and grew steadily weaker throughout the spring and summer of 1917.[3] Within a few weeks the government (led now by the moderate socialist Alexander Kerensky) was compelled to accept the help of the Bolsheviks in repulsing a coup organized by a right-wing general and detachments from the front. The unforeseen result was that the Bolsheviks and their leader, V. I. Lenin, obtained a majority in the municipal soviet and quickly won over most of the military garrison of Petrograd. The Bolshevik seizure of governmental power followed, on November 7, 1917.[4]

With this, relations between the two countries, along with the ties between Russia and the rest of the capitalist West, plunged from euphoria and entente into an unfathomable void. Allied and American statesmen possessed few precedents to guide them in dealing with so radical a regime, and in any case it seemed wise to make no commitments, chiefly because most of these leaders clung to the hope that the Russian people would rise up and throw out these misguided zealots. The Bolsheviks, for their part, as "orthodox" Marxists, thought of themselves not as having assumed control of a traditional state but as having initiated a movement toward international revolution. By demanding a peace of "no annexations, no indemnities," they believed they could generate such massive, worldwide support that bourgeois governments would be compelled, in self-defense, to end the European slaughter. Unfortunately for them, the only response was from the Germans, who in negotiations at Brest Litovsk drove a bargain so hard (taking from Russia their Baltic, Polish, and Ukrainian lands) that, when Lenin felt compelled to accept it in March 1918, nearly half of the Bolshevik Party Central Committee resigned in protest.

The principal British and American effort to influence Lenin's Russia before it left the war came with the formulation of liberal war aims, announced in speeches by the prime minister and the president in January 1918.[5] But having failed with this to stay the Bolsheviks' passion for peace, and having lost the fear of forcing them into cooperation with Germany, the Allies proceeded in the spring of 1918 to a second step, with fateful implications: military intervention. Originally anti-German in objective (the hope being that an eastern front could be preserved), the intervention had, by the end of the summer, begun to take on an anti-Bolshevik coloration. Wilson attempted to limit the political activity of the contingents he sent to northern Russia and Siberia, but the British, French, and Japanese were much less reluctant than the Americans to assist elements that had begun to resist the Bolshevik regime. Their lack of success was not for want of desire, and this fact would not be easily forgotten by the Soviets.[6]

In the interim, even before the Allies freed Russia from the burden of the Brest Litovsk treaty by defeating Germany, both the Bolsheviks and the Allies began to reach out to each other. Since Lenin feared the concerted action of the capitalists almost as much as he trusted in their ultimate falling out, he made every effort to achieve an understanding with individual capitalist nations even while continuing to preach and expect world revolution. This was especially true in the case of the United States, which Lenin saw as a source of economic assistance and as a useful counterweight to Japan in protecting Siberia. Though Lenin received no direct response to these overtures, the Allied leaders at the Paris Peace Conference in 1919 did make two attempts to negotiate an end to the Russian civil war, first by proposing a conference of the various factions in Turkey and later by sending an American mediator to Moscow (the new Bolshevik capital). On each occasion the endeavor was frustrated by the intransigence of the anti-Bolsheviks and the French.[7]

By the early months of 1920 the Red Army was emerging victorious from the internal struggle and Russia was entering upon perhaps its most difficult and vulnerable period—the years of devastation that international and civil war had engendered. Sometimes described as an era of normalization, these years are better characterized as a time of impoverishment and exhaustion. Granted, the ideological impetus of the revolution remained strong enough among Bolsheviks (now Communists) to justify the propagandistic activity of the Comintern (the Third, or Communist, International), already in 1920 on its way to becoming a disciplined adjunct of the Soviet state. Nevertheless, by the end of the civil war Lenin and the party leadership had come a tremendous distance toward accepting what conventional statesmen would have called the realities of the domestic and foreign situations.

Faced with the almost total collapse of the country's industry and a catastrophic decline in living standards, Soviet rulers introduced a "new economic policy" in early 1921, which allowed a return to small-scale capitalism as a means to furthering reconstruction. They also began a noteworthy effort to entice foreign capitalists into arrangements that would make outside skills and credit available to Russia, in the process establishing commercial agreements with a number of western European governments. In 1922, when the Communist regime was invited by the Allies to attend its first international conference in Genoa, the Soviet foreign minister broke new ground by calling for multilateral collaboration on reconstruction and disarmament. This was the occasion on which the Soviet and German delegations met separately at Rapallo to sign a renunciation of war claims, an agreement with which Lenin continued his tactic of playing the capitalist states off against each other while "coexisting" (as he put it) with their system.[8]

As for U.S.-U.S.S.R. relations, it was the United States rather than the ideological Communist state that displayed the most rigidity during these years, possibly because the United States at this point needed the Soviet Union a good deal less than the Soviets needed this country (and because the United States itself was in a deeply ideological phase). Lenin and his colleagues hoped that the business-oriented administration of Warren G. Harding would see advantage in exchanging diplomatic recognition and resuming commerce, but despite repeated soundings from Moscow, Secretary of State Charles Evans Hughes held firmly to the policy of nonrecognition laid down by the outgoing Wilson administration. Yet not even restrictions on credit and the movement of gold could prevent American relief organizations from sending humanitarian aid to Russia during the extraordinary famine of 1921–22. As the decade wore on, ordinary commerce grew steadily, if unevenly. By 1930 several thousand American engineers were in Russia under corporate aid contracts, and American exports to the Soviet Union exceeded those of any other country, reaching $114 million, or 25 percent of total Soviet imports.[9]

By this time, Lenin had been dead for six years and Joseph Stalin was vanquishing the last of his political competitors as he drove the U.S.S.R. toward a simpler, more self-centered nationalism. Originally allying himself with the right wing of the Communist Party against the radicals and internationalists on the grounds that temporary stabilization of capitalism had made it necessary to build "socialism in one country," by 1928 he turned on his erstwhile allies, abandoned the new economic policy, and introduced a five-year plan to collectivize the peasantry and industrialize the economy, ostensibly because the world was verging on an upheaval that would generate "imperialist assaults" against the Soviet Union. By seeking a radical transformation of the country, Stalin in effect returned to the domestic program of the party's Old Left, but he justified this as a response to an external threat from the capitalist states.

This did not mean that Stalin lost interest in establishing relations with the United States, which was still highly respected in Moscow. Indeed, after Japan added real danger to Soviet fantasies by invading Manchuria in 1931, Moscow became so eager for a Washington connection that it cut back on commercial orders from the United States specifically to pressure the depression-wracked Americans into recognition. Herbert Hoover proved unwilling to bargain, but Franklin Roosevelt's new administration was willing and Stalin quickly responded by sending his foreign minister to the United States to conduct negotiations. The resulting agreements of November 1933 (putting off disputed debts and promising mutually loyal behavior) led to high hopes on both sides for a cooperative effort against the newly emergent militarism of Japan and Nazi Germany.[10]

Nevertheless, the next six years were to demonstrate that even a great need for physical reinforcement on the part of both countries did not lead to easy collaboration. The Soviet regime, for its part, embarked on an effort to obtain protection from those very arrangements and institutions it had denounced. It undertook an active role in the Geneva Disarmament Conference and in 1934 became a member of the League of Nations. A year later, having tried and failed to create a multilateral pact guaranteeing European borders, Stalin entered into military alliances with Czechoslovakia and France. He also directed the Comintern, at its Seventh (and last) Congress, to abandon its hostility to capitalist governments and to encourage Communist Parties to join socialist and middle-class parties in creating "popular [antifascist] fronts." Such actions abroad were supplemented by changes within the Soviet Union. Patriotism became acceptable again, as the government sponsored conferences and publications featuring Russian folklore, literature, history, and inventive genius. Industrialization was largely transformed into a program for military armament.

Ironically, however, much of the behavior induced in the U.S.S.R. by growing international tension was directly counterproductive in terms of that country's relation with the West. The Comintern's refusal to relinquish its connection with the Communist Party of the United States, for example, was badly misunderstood in Washington. Similarly, Stalin's gruesome and incomprehensible purges during this period, together with the country's increasing xenophobia and decreasing internal freedom, did much to alienate Western opinion and to raise doubts about the ultimate strength of the Soviet Union. These developments only fortified those currents of isolationism, passivity, and anti-Communism already strong in the publics of Britain, France, and the United States. The strength of these attitudes in turn inhibited these countries from opposing aggression and thus contributed directly to Western weakness and Russian frustration during Italy's attack on Ethiopia (1935–36), the Spanish Civil War (1936–39), and the German-Czech crisis preceding the Munich Conference (1938).

The ultimate and tragic consequence of these events was the diplo-matic revolution embodied in the Hitler-Stalin pact of August 1939, an understanding that reflected not only Stalin's disappointment with the West in the face of Nazi expansion but also (in its provision for Russian gains in the border region) his desperate need for, and opportunism in obtaining, additional physical strength.[11]

Hitler's attack on Poland followed almost immediately, and when Britain and France honored their recent pledges to Poland, the world was again at war. Yet it is worth remembering that World War II remained a European conflict for the better part of two years; neither the United States nor the Soviet Union bestirred itself to resist the Nazis until it was actually attacked. Repeated mistakes by Hitler and the Japanese were required to drive together the coalition that had begun to form against them in the early 1930s but that had broken apart at the end of that decade. This inability of Hitler's enemies to unite was due as much to America's sense of invulnerability and ideological bias as it was to Soviet anxiety, ambition, or unscrupulousness. The need for these nations to cooperate had been great, but the perception of need had not fully matched it.

The grand alliance finally took form under the whip of Fascist fury and despite the legacy of profound mistrust. As the Red Army reeled backward following the German attack on June 1941, Prime Minister Winston Churchill and President Roosevelt rushed to send all available war material to the beleaguered Russians. By mid-1942 the stream of assistance had be-come a river that would ultimately provide the Soviet Union with over $11 billion in armaments and food. On January 1 of that year, shortly after the Japanese attack on Pearl Harbor, representatives of the United States, Britain, and Russia had met in Washington to sign a declaration pledging to continue the war to final victory. Meanwhile, Communist Parties in Western countries abandoned their defeatist line (adopted since 1939) to become the foremost supporters of anti-Fascist mobilization. In an even greater concession to the capitalist world, Stalin dissolved the Comintern in May 1943.[12]

Admittedly, there was a serious and embittering source of dispute among the Allies throughout this period: the matter of a second front. With more than 200 German divisions in the Soviet Union, Stalin was understandably eager for a major British and American attack on Nazi-occupied Europe. FDR had rashly promised Foreign Minister V. M. Mo-lotov a second European front by the end of 1942, but transport shortages, the Pacific conflict, and Churchill's qualms led the British and Americans to decide to invade North Africa instead. Subsequently, Anglo-American involvement in the Tunisian, Sicilian, and Italian campaigns further de-layed the cross-Channel operation to the point (before it finally occurred in

June 1944) that the Russians suspected there was a deliberate Western policy to let them bear the brunt of the war. At Casablanca in January 1943 Roosevelt and Churchill reassured Stalin (and, at the same time, reduced his room for maneuver) by proclaiming their determination to fight on until achieving the enemy's "unconditional surrender." At Teheran in November 1943, the first conference of the Big Three, there were further efforts by Western leaders to pacify their Soviet colleague, particularly with regard to postwar boundaries.[13]

As the war drew to a close, the intentions of the victor nations with regard to the peace settlement became more explicit and more difficult to reconcile. As early as December 1941, Stalin had attempted to obtain British recognition of the territorial gains the U.S.S.R. had won from the Nazi-Soviet pact, but he refrained from pressing the matter after Churchill (buttressed by the Americans) refused to cooperate.[14] By mid-1943, however, with the Axis powers in full retreat, it was no longer possible to put off such issues. It was becoming clear (as a result, for example, of Moscow's breaking off relations with the Polish government in exile) that Stalin was seeking to strengthen the postwar position of the Soviet Union by achieving a return to the frontiers of 1939–41, a sharp reduction in German national power, and the installation of regimes in Eastern Europe that would be friendly to Russia.[15] The main lines of British policy were also recognizable: as the weakest of the three allies, Britain desired a favorable balance of power in Europe, a balance that could be created only if Germany and France were allowed to remain strong and if the United States continued to play an active role overseas.[16] Finally, the American approach to the postwar world was increasingly visible: convinced that general prosperity required free trade and international organization and that these in turn demanded moderation in Soviet behavior, the Roosevelt administration strove to accomplish its ends both directly and indirectly, seeking as much as possible to meet Russia's genuine security needs.[17]

Still, the fact was that by the end of 1944 the Red Army was in possession of most of Eastern Europe, and Soviet assistance for the final attack upon Japan was considered essential by the West. As a result, FDR was largely reduced to appealing to Stalin to handle the situation in Soviet-occupied Europe so as "not to offend world opinion." Churchill had earlier taken a more traditional tack with the Communist leader, proposing the division of this region into spheres of influence, but neither his initiative nor Roosevelt's appears to have had much success in altering Stalin's attitudes.[18] Though at Teheran, and again at Yalta (February 1945), Stalin promised to create "representative" governments in Eastern Europe, he later exhibited few scruples in imposing autocratic regimes upon Poland, Romania, and Bulgaria.[19]

For this and related reasons, U.S.-Soviet ties in the postwar era deteri-orated steadily. To be sure, there were factors in the major power equation that might conceivably have improved the relation: the Soviet Union, after experiencing 20 million dead and terrible destruction, was badly in need of economic assistance, and the United States was extremely weary of war-time sacrifice and ready to turn its vastly enlarged productive capacities to peaceful pursuits. On the other hand, the foreign danger that had been so crucial in bringing and holding these very different allies together was no longer present. There was now a vast vacuum of power in both Europe and Asia, and the helplessness (as well as the traditional allegiances) of these regions was bound to worry the victor nations severely and to tempt them to intervene.

In retrospect, it seems clear that, at least for the Soviet leadership, the need for national security outweighed the desire for early reconstruction, and the two objects must have seemed to be mutually exclusive. The injuries that the war had done to Russia were so severe that they surely raised grave doubts in Stalin's already fearful mind about his ability to accept help from the outside and at the same time maintain control and pursue a self-interested foreign policy. The historic result of these and other interacting factors (such as the victory-induced resurgence of ideo-logical thinking on both sides) was to be that shift from entente to uni-lateralism and hostility that we recognize as the coming of the Cold War.

Even before Roosevelt died in April 1945 the tension between East and West was obvious; after Harry Truman became president it grew rapidly. Though Truman made a genuine effort to continue Roosevelt's policies, agreeing for example to major concessions on Poland in return for Stalin's acceptance of U.S.-style voting procedures in the United Nations, the Big Three conference at Potsdam in July produced little aside from wrangling and certain provisional understandings regarding Germany.[20] If the development and use of the atomic bomb by the United States seemed to have no immediate impact on Soviet policy, the weapon did at least lead to an early Japanese surrender and a quick end to Russia's last-minute war against Japan. Nonetheless, disagreements continued to multi-ply with regard to Soviet activities in Eastern Europe and northern Iran, to the point that by early 1946 Stalin was speaking of the incompatibility of Communism and capitalism and former Prime Minister Churchill was speaking of a Russian Iron Curtain having descended across Eastern Eu-rope.[21]

By the following winter, as Europe's economy faltered badly under the impact of continuing dislocations and harsh weather, the United States was ready to act comprehensively, particularly with regard to the interna-tional commitments that Britain found itself incapable of maintaining. In

March 1947, the president, in justifying a program of military aid to Greece and Turkey, proclaimed the Truman Doctrine, a commitment to resist totalitarian aggression whenever it occurred. The following June, Secretary of State George Marshall unveiled a four-year $17 billion economic assistance plan for Europe designed to enable war-weakened nations to recover their strength and prosperity (and thereby their ability to resist internal Communist subversion and the appeal of Marxist political parties).[22]

The Truman Doctrine and the Marshall Plan elicited a surprisingly frightened reaction from Stalin, who responded in three ways: by clamping down on Western influences and ideas within the Soviet Union, by consolidating Russian power in Eastern Europe (e.g., installing a pro-Soviet government in Hungary in May 1947), and by reintroducing centralized control to the international Communist movement in the guise of a Communist information agency (Cominform).[23] None of this was well received in the West, but it was the overthrow of the legally constituted Czech government by the Communists in February 1948 that was directly responsible for the creation of a defense alliance among Western European powers and for the Anglo-American-French decision to establish a West German state. Stalin retaliated in mid-1948 with a blockade of West Berlin, which he called off only after it provided the impetus for the formation of the North Atlantic Treaty Organization (NATO) in April 1949.[24] So it went on and on, this action-reaction cycle leading to greater and greater estrangement.

The worst was yet to come. On the Soviet side, the combination of unexpected vigor on the part of capitalist opponents and an astonishing break between Tito's Yugoslavia and the Cominform produced an almost tangible paranoia that not even Communist revolution in China and Russia's development of the atomic bomb, both in 1949, could overcome.[25] Similarly, on the U.S. side, the Soviet bomb, the fall of Chiang Kai-shek in China, and finally in June 1950 the North Korean invasion of South Korea (with the quick involvement of the United States) ushered in three years of limited war and semihysteria that featured an almost indiscriminate anti-Communism.[26]

Stalin now adopted violent measures to speed up the tempo of sovietization in satellite states. He also terrorized and purged the party at home, increased investment in heavy industry, and after the United States began to rearm, expanded the size of the Soviet army.[27] Americans, despite the economic dominance of the United States, behaved with equal anxiety. The Truman administration espoused policies that involved a military draft, enlargement of the armed forces, the dispatch of troops to Europe, and the armament of West Germany—all in the context of a widespread hunt for subversives, popular frustration with the Korean War, and a turn to political conservatism.[28] This, then, was the classic Cold War, when vigorous defensive reactions on both sides drove the antagonists to a new level of hostility and at the same time unleashed the arms race.

With the presidential inauguration of Dwight Eisenhower and the death of Stalin in early 1953 the situation became somewhat less intense. The Republicans were publicly committed to "rolling back" the Iron Curtain in Eastern Europe, but as it turned out, Eisenhower was primarily concerned with ending the bloody struggle in Korea and streamlining the defense effort in such a way that a war-weary, emotionally exhausted citizenry (and future generations) would find it affordable. Able to accomplish his first objective by means of an armistice in July, the president strove to achieve the second by developing a strategic posture that relied more heavily than heretofore on atomic weaponry. Though critics found the threat of "massive retaliation" unnerving (especially with the advent of American and Russian H-bombs), the administration did succeed in using it to reduce the army, cut military costs, and substantially calm public opinion. Secretary of State John Foster Dulles, a more pessimistic man than Eisenhower, supplemented and extended the strategy (and perhaps rendered it less dangerous) by helping to organize anti-Communist alliances in both Southeast Asia (SEATO, 1954) and the Middle East (the Baghdad Pact, 1954) and by strengthening NATO with the accession of a rearmed West Germany (in 1955).[29]

More encouraging developments than these, however, were occurring in the Soviet Union. A collective leadership emerged after Stalin's death when Georgi Malenkov, the dictator's intended successor, was forced to share power with Molotov, Nikita Khrushchev, and others. This group, understandably impressed with the cost of Stalin's terror as well as its own vulnerability, recognized that it could derive political advantage from a reduction of internal tension and an improvement of relations between their country and the outside world. This insight led to such domestic reforms as emphasizing "socialist legality," emptying the forced labor camps, and improving the public's standard of living. Internationally, it produced a willingness to end the Korean War, to assist the industrialization of China, to restore ties with Yugoslavia, and to unfreeze relations with Turkey, Iran, and the Third World in general.[30]

Though Soviet movement in these directions was interrupted in early 1955 when Khrushchev, in alliance with hard-liners, exploited Malenkov's endorsement of "peaceful coexistence" in order to unseat him, by summer Khrushchev and the new premier, Nikolai Bulganin, had largely readopted Malenkov's policies.[31] Thus the year 1955 was to witness, first, a tour of India by "B and K" (with promises of Soviet foreign aid), then, a visit by the same pair to Yugoslavia, next, a Russian peace treaty with a neutralized Austria, and finally, a summit conference in Geneva at which the Soviet leaders met those of the United States, Britain, and France. If substantive progress at this summit was negligible (despite Ike's efforts to win acceptance of an "open skies" proposal), at least the cordiality—the "spirit of Geneva"—that developed among the participants seemed an indication of increasing relaxation and mutual acceptance.[32] It was on this basis, and in recognition of the economic advantage to be derived, that Khrushchev now proceeded both to reduce Soviet armed forces by more than 2 million men and (in his bid for political leadership) to undertake explicit de-Stalinization.[33]

As it turned out, Khrushchev's historic denunciation of Stalin at the Twentieth Party Congress in February 1956 was important for several reasons. It increased Khrushchev's preeminence, sketched out a different future for the U.S.S.R., established "peaceful coexistence" as a principle of Soviet foreign policy (marking a retreat from the traditional emphasis on the inevitability of war), and reinforced a centripetal process that was to have major repercussions within the Communist world. Though de-Stalinization's effects in the Soviet Union and China were not so disorienting as many expected, the consequences for Eastern European nations were much more serious. Long-time rulers in this region were discredited and cast adrift, with the result that by October 1956 political crises in Poland and Hungary had thrust less orthodox leadership into power, and by November neutralism in Hungary had led to Russian military intervention. These catastrophes in turn weakened Khrushchev's position within the Presidium to the point where the following June he was able to turn back a plot against him by Malenkov and Molotov only by a desperate appeal to the full Central Committee and the military.[34]

When the dust had settled, Khrushchev had expelled his leading opponents from the Presidium and reembarked on his attempt to find an appropriate balance among de-Stalinization, coexistence, and national growth. Yet this is not to say that he could now operate without antagonists. For all his victory of 1957, Khrushchev's position throughout the ensuing seven years of his ascendancy would remain precarious. His complex ambitions, his impatient personality, and above all, the rapid changes occurring in the Soviet Union and other countries drove him to improvisations and gambles that inspired continued concern at home and abroad.[35]

Both East and West were especially challenged by the swift collapse of the traditional imperial systems following the failure of Britain and France to bring down Egypt's Gamal Abdul Nasser in the Suez debacle of November 1956.[36] The Eisenhower administration subsequently attempted to fill the Middle Eastern void by pledging to protect the countries of that region from Communist aggression, but such a doctrine proved singularly inapplicable when a military coup overthrew the pro-Western government of Iraq in 1958 and destroyed the linchpin of the Baghdad Pact.[37] By the end of the decade, as the Soviet Union and the United States were drawn more and more into struggles over places like Jordan, the Congo, Cuba, and Vietnam, it was evident that the geographical scope of the Cold War had expanded to include the entire Third World.[38]

The attention of Washington and Moscow, however, remained primarily with the major powers, and here the crucial issues arose from the decline of bipolarity. Western Europe, Japan, and even China were becoming stronger, economically and politically, and though the United States and the U.S.S.R. were pleased to a degree with this change, both countries found the military implications extremely disturbing.[39] The Soviet Union in particular was troubled by the prospect that two nations immediately adjacent to it (strangely, one capitalist and one Communist—West Germany and China) would acquire nuclear weapons, and it was largely in terms of foreclosing this possibility that Khrushchev strove during these years to achieve the diplomatic success he needed to consolidate his power. His proposition to the United States (and hence his conceptualization of coexistence) was, in essence, this: that the Americans and the Russians maintain the military hierarchy of their alliance systems, the United States preventing the West Germans from acquiring an independent nuclear force and the Soviet Union preventing the Chinese.

The tactical problem for Khrushchev, of course, was that such an agreement was difficult to negotiate, since it was necessary for him to pursue assertive policies vis-à-vis the West (and thus pacify the increasingly suspicious Chinese) at the same time he bargained with American leaders. Moreover, his proposal was obscured not only by his anti-Western rhetoric (and penchant for indirection) but also by the fact that he was attempting after 1958 to pressure the United States with his alleged missile advantage into "normalizing" the German situation by abandoning or neutralizing West Berlin.[40]

There was some progress in developing understandings with the Americans—for example, with regard to a nuclear test ban when Khrushchev visited the United States at President Eisenhower's invitation in September 1959 (hence the "spirit of Camp David"). However, by the following summer, the collapse of the Paris summit (after the U-2 incident) and an open, if not public, Soviet break with China ended any forward movement.[41] The greatest irony of all was that when the administration of John F. Kennedy took office in 1961 it was so impressed with Soviet threat and bluster (and later so humiliated by its Bay of Pigs fiasco in Cuba) that it embarked on a crash missile-building program and introduced a strategic doctrine ("flexible response") that improved the U.S. capacity to fight limited foreign wars.[42]

Khrushchev was now faced with the fact that, in the world of missiles, his bluff had been called, but when in 1962 he attempted to redress the American advantage (and to protect Fidel Castro's regime) by installing intermediate-range missiles in Cuba, this move too backfired badly, his defeat at Kennedy's hands weakening his international and domestic standing. Thus what one historian describes as Khrushchev's strategy of seeking "détente through intimidation" was seriously flawed, his threats and maneuvers having been so confusing and frightening that they effectively misled (and provoked) the very people with whom he wished to deal.[43] The need for superpower accommodation was real, perhaps even more for the Russians than for the Americans, but the expectations and the methods (in Khrushchev's case, often the result of his attraction to both Beijing and Washington) did not fit the occasion.

Only in the aftermath of the Cuban missile crisis were U.S. and Soviet leaders to develop sufficient desire to identify and pursue an agenda of cooperation. A variety of historic changes now made this possible. On the Soviet side, the hope of restraining China's nuclear armament was finally lost, construction of the Berlin Wall in August 1961 helped stabilize East Germany, and difficulties with the Soviet economy further undermined Khrushchev's domestic position.[44] In the United States, Kennedy began to feel the pressure of a developing antinuclear movement at the very moment he was receiving increased support from the American Right for the toughness he had displayed in the Cuban crisis.[45]

Most significant of all, in both countries the brush with nuclear catastrophe (almost like the experience of war) had a markedly sobering effect. The result was a sudden rush toward détente in the summer and fall of 1963, as a number of understandings were reached that lowered the level of hostility and danger for both powers. The Americans and Russians agreed to ban nuclear weapons tests in the atmosphere, to establish a hot line between the Kremlin and the White House, to endorse a United Nations resolution outlawing nuclear weapons in outer space, and to arrange the sale of $250 million worth of surplus U.S. wheat to the Soviet Union.[46]

Feelings of relief and amiability were such during these months that some people actually speculated that the Cold War was ending. Unfortunately, however, even as the new mood was developing, the Kennedy and Lyndon Johnson administrations were being pulled ever deeper into involvement in a Vietnamese civil war that (at least in its early stages and in part because of the Sino-Soviet split and ensuing competition) would constitute a major obstacle to further progress. Unfortunately also, the response of China to the rapprochement between East and West was so angry and vitriolic that it robbed Khrushchev of much of the credit for the achievement that might otherwise have been his within the Politburo.[47] The cycle of war and peace in Russian-American relations would have to take one more turn before the mix of need and confidence on both sides would be such as to make substantial relaxation possible.

2

THE BREAKDOWN OF
OLD ARRANGEMENTS

As the endless war in Vietnam dragged on through Lyndon Johnson's administration and into Richard Nixon's, American unity steadily gave way, first to division and ultimately to frustration, disillusionment, and fatigue. The middle sixties, which saw public attitudes severely shaken by both racial unrest and antiwar protest, featured a radicalization of the reform movement and a new political polarization, but the traumatic election of 1968 and the angry demonstrations against the Cambodian invasion of May 1970 ushered in a social fragmentation that included more passive and diverse reactions. Though the "generation gap" remained explosive, though racial tension continued unabated, and though radicalism still generated reaction, these things now occurred in a milieu of growing confusion, withdrawal, and self-absorption.

It is too much to claim all of this as a direct effect of the war, even if almost everything undesirable that happened seemed in some way tied to developments caused by the war. Yet, what is undeniable is that the later war years brought a deepening public disorientation—a loss of unity, confidence, and energy—and that such a condition constituted an enormous challenge for an administration committed to maintaining a powerful and essentially traditional role for the nation in world affairs. Richard Nixon and Henry Kissinger certainly recognized this fact, though it is doubtful that even they realized how huge the obstacles were (and therefore the need for rethinking) until after they tried and failed in 1969 and 1970 to extricate the country from the war and to recreate the preexisting foreign policy consensus.

It was almost as if America had embarked on two reform programs in the 1960s—the one designed to solve age-old domestic problems of unfairness, the other designed to build a democratic regime in South Vietnam—

and had failed at both. Enhancement of minority rights was not the only objective of LBJ's Great Society, of course, but massive riots in the black ghettos from 1965 through 1968 cast a pall upon the wisdom and effectiveness of his entire reform effort. Such events, together with the assassination of the Kennedys and Martin Luther King, turmoil on the campuses, and the oppressive violence of a brutal foreign war, were increasingly perceived as evidence that something had gone wrong with America—or possibly that something had always been wrong with the way America achieved its power and success. Meanwhile, the fact that young people were central to the dissatisfaction and that they took advantage of the situation to throw off long-standing social customs was especially disconcerting to older, middle-class Americans and contributed greatly to their rising anger, embitterment, and pessimism about the country.[1]

To be sure, such phenomena as these have occurred during and after other wars as well, especially if the conflicts were long, painful, and divisive. The periods following the American Revolution, the War of 1812, the Civil War, World War I, and even World War II are notorious among historians for collapsed standards, alienation, corruption, and hedonism—all developments associated with weariness, disappointment, and the relaxation of discipline.[2] These eras have also been distinguished by a relatively high incidence of social violence, with suicide rates rebounding strongly from wartime lows, with above average homicide rates, and with serious civil strife—behavior one might expect from a society that is confused, irritable, and tired.[3]

Parenthetically, one could speculate about the historic meaning of the 1960s for America by suggesting that complex societies tend to move through long-term cycles, with such phases as the following:

1. a period of relative satisfaction and confidence, in which the majority of citizens feel capable of coping with the social change occurring within and about them;
2. a period of aggravation and anxiety, in which (perhaps because of economic depression, inflation, or other difficulty) large numbers of people lose their comprehension of societal change;
3. an initial period of dissatisfaction and aggression, in which movements are organized for purposes of domestic reform while others are mobilized in defense of the status quo;
4. a second period of dissatisfaction and aggression, in which elites are tempted to shunt domestic reform aside and unite the nation in efforts to improve its external environment through war or foreign policy;

5. a period of growing exhaustion and disappointment (unless war or an equivalent activity is surprisingly brief and successful), in which extended conflict—be it foreign or domestic—drives the populace to weariness, division, and despair regarding further group efforts; and

6. a period of recuperation and adjustment, in which the majority accommodate or reconcile themselves to the changed situation.

Following such a schema, one could argue that during the Kennedy-Johnson-Nixon years the United States moved from the third phase through the fourth phase and on to the fifth phase. According to this hypothesis, the country shifted from an effort at domestic reform to an effort at international reform and, finally, to a running down of the energies that made both these endeavors possible. The fact that these changes were superimposed upon a continuing Cold War bipolarity could only mean that the disillusionment and withdrawal at the end would also impact upon that condition.[4]

At any rate, it is clear that, in response to domestic and foreign events of the middle and late 1960s, American confidence in the existing order and its willingness to be involved in supporting it fell sharply. National ladder rankings, in which the public is asked to evaluate the present state of the nation in comparison with the past and future, reveal a marked decline in the score assigned to the present from the mid-1960s onward:[5]

	Past	Present	Future
1964	6.1	6.5	7.7
1971	6.2	5.4	6.2
1972	5.6	5.5	6.2
1974	6.3	4.8	5.8

What this index means in more specific terms is pointed up by the increasing pessimism in the responses to questions like the following: How much of the time do you think you can trust the government in Washington to do what is right? The answers, in percentages, were as follows:[6]

	1964	1966	1968	1969
Always	14	17	8	6
Most of the time	63	48	53	47
Only some of the time	22	31	37	44

That this general decline in trust on the part of the public corresponds closely to the trends in opinion regarding American participation in the Vietnam War can be seen from the changing answers to two more queries. To the question, in view of the developments since we entered Vietnam, do you think that the United States made a mistake in sending troops to fight there?, the following responses were given (in percentages):[7]

	Yes	No
March 1966	24	59
May 1966	32	49
February 1967	32	52
July 1967	38	48
February 1968	45	42
April 1968	53	40
February 1969	52	39
October 1969	57	32
January 1970	58	33
May 1970	57	36
January 1971	59	31

A second question was, what would you like to see the United States do next about Vietnam? The answers, in percentages, were as follows:[8]

	Withdraw	Escalate	Other
June 1965	11	21	68
January 1966	18	22	60
June 1966	12	30	58
January 1967	6	37	57
June 1967	7	45	48
January 1968	10	52	38
June 1968	15	40	45
January 1969	21	32	47
June 1969	31	31	38
January 1970	30	30	40
June 1970	50	29	21
January 1971	72	27	1

Thus, although it was not until the spring of 1970—more than a year after Nixon's inauguration—that sentiment for withdrawal finally and permanently outweighed support for escalation, the preference for escalation had been decreasing steadily since the beginning of 1968, one month before the Tet offensive and two months before a majority of Americans came to the conclusion that it had been a mistake for the United States to get involved in Vietnam. Originally, and in contradiction of the stereotype about "doves," it was the older citizens (over fifty years of age), the less educated, and the poor (especially blacks) who expressed the most opposition to the war. Indeed, for many months the backbone of resistance was situated in the classic left-wing alliance of the undereducated (blue-collar workers) and the overeducated (intellectuals). Only from the time of the 1968 election, as the ranks of idealists and the alienated were reinforced by the war weary, did income and social status cease to be positively correlated with sentiment for withdrawal. In electing Nixon, the American middle class was able to strike back at the "radicals" and "antipatriots," while simultaneously anticipating that the new administration could withdraw on its own terms from the apparently unwinnable war.[9]

Still, if the turn to the Republicans reflected a desire on the part of countless citizens to return to older ways, the growing fatigue and pessimism led many Americans to adopt significantly new attitudes toward international affairs. Again, this is not to suggest that the war was the only cause of these shifts in perspective, for presumably they were affected as well by such developments as the outbreak of hostilities between Russia and China and even the arrival of Richard Nixon in the White House. Yet it remains true that there was a strong connection between the public's increasing disenchantment with the war and changing popular views regarding the rest of the world—so strong in fact that it is not too much to speak of the Vietnam experience as having destroyed a previously existing foreign policy consensus. This is reflected in the steady falloff of the percentage of the public concerned about the following international issues:[10]

	1964	1968	1972	Change, 1964–72
The danger of war	90	83	66	−24
The threat of Communism	86	79	69	−17
Keeping the military strong	74	86	61	−13
Soviet Russia	75	73	61	−14

The shift also appears in the altered rankings of concerns articulated by the citizens being polled.[11] In 1964, for instance, just before the nation's massive intervention in Southeast Asia, Americans listed as their leading worries:

1. keeping the country out of war,
2. combating world Communism,
3. keeping our military defense strong,
4. controlling the use of nuclear weapons, and
5. maintaining respect for the United States abroad.

Eight years later, in June 1972, with American forces still fighting in Vietnam, Americans identified the following matters as most worrisome:

1. rising prices and the cost of living,
2. the amount of violence in American life,

3. the problem of drug addicts and narcotic drugs,
4. crime in this country, and
5. the problem of Vietnam.

Tied for twelfth place on the list, after six additional domestic issues, was "keeping our military defenses strong." "The threat of Communism at home and abroad" was in twenty-second place.

A somewhat fuller picture of what these changes mean emerges from surveys taken in 1976 and 1980, when more than 2 thousand prominent Americans were asked their opinions regarding the sources of failure in Vietnam, the consequences of the experience, and the lessons that the United States should draw from it.[12] Respondents were classified into seven categories on the basis of policy preferences expressed during the early and late stages of the war (critics, converted critics, ambivalent critics, ambivalents, ambivalent supporters, converted supporters, supporters). These seven groups not only frequently rejected the axioms regarding international relations held by American officials throughout the post–World War II era (1945–67) but, in addition, showed themselves to be in substantial disagreement *with each other* concerning these axioms. The dominant foreign policy view had not simply lost support. It had been completely fractured.

How this affected popular attitudes toward defense spending is particularly important. The impact can be shown by tracing the percentage of the public favoring an increase in monies for the military services and the percentage favoring a decrease. The late 1940s and early 1950s had been a period of unstable opinion on these issues, apparently in part because of American uncertainty as to how to cope with the Soviet challenge. Following the end of the Korean War, however, attitudes became firmer, and though the proportion in favor of more defense spending fell gradually until the Kennedy years (from 30 percent to 22 percent), it remained consistently about ten percentage points greater than the percentage favoring reductions. From 1960 to 1964 support for larger appropriations increased once again, but with the intervention in Vietnam it declined rapidly, falling to a low of 8 percent in 1970 and not rising much above that level until 1973. Meanwhile, the proportion favoring less spending jumped spectacularly after 1965, peaking at over 50 percent in 1969 but continuing at close to that percentage until 1974. For a period of almost five years, then, more than four times as many Americans wanted to lower military spending as wanted to raise it.[13]

Such public opinion is capable of influencing any government, but it is even more formidable when it is reflected, as it was during these years, in the views of the national legislature. Indeed, congressional attitudes on defense and foreign policy in the latter stages of the Vietnam War were sufficiently indicative of the popular mood that one analyst saw two distinct defense policy-making systems, one for the 1947–67 period and a second for the 1968–74 period.[14] The second system was characterized by, among other things, longer floor debates, more amendments to bills, increased lobbying and committee testimony, more involvement by secondary committees, a greater flow of information from the executive to the legislative branch, and the emergence of a congressional antidefense bloc.

The spirit of resistance first made its presence known on Capitol Hill in July 1967, when Senator J. William Fulbright (D-Ark.) introduced a resolution (implicitly critical of LBJ) stipulating that the commitment of U.S. military forces in future foreign wars must be made in accord with "constitutional processes."[15] Congressional independence became even more obvious in the spring of the following year, when during the Senate debate on the Johnson administration's Sentinel ABM proposals a number of senators revealed that they had serious reservations about the wisdom of deployment.[16] Though in 1968 the foes of the ABM never numbered more than one-third of the Senate, by the time the new Republican administration had rethought and reintroduced a modified ABM program (now called Safeguard) in the summer of 1969, the coalition of opponents had grown to the point that it came within one vote of defeating the proposal.[17] The same months saw the passage not only of the Fulbright resolution on war powers but also of two laws specifically designed to limit executive policy making: the Military Procurement Authorization Act of November 1969, which included a ceiling of $2.5 billion on the amount that could be spent in Vietnam, Laos, and Thailand; and the Defense Appropriations Act of December 1969, containing an amendment by Senator Frank Church (D-Idaho) that precluded the use of American ground forces in Laos or Thailand.[18]

After Nixon, in the guise of "winding down the war," sent American and South Vietnamese troops into Cambodia at the end of April 1970, Congress developed an even greater mind of its own. Three weeks prior to this the Senate had passed a resolution offered by Senator Edward Brooke (R-Mass.) calling upon the United States and the Soviet Union to achieve a MIRV moratorium by suspending the deployment of new strategic weapons.[19] Then, on June 30, after more than seven weeks of intense discussion, the Senate approved, 58 to 37, an amendment by Senators John Cooper (R-Ky.) and Frank Church that forbade the use of funds to maintain American combat troops in Cambodia. Subsequently, the Senate devoted itself to two more months of debate on an amendment proposed by Senators George McGovern (D-S.Dak.) and Mark Hatfield (R-Ore.) that would have cut off money for all American forces in Vietnam after December 31, 1971. It rejected this stipulation in September by a vote of 39 to 55.[20]

Meanwhile, legislators in both houses of Congress had begun to spell out their desires to set appropriate limits on the president's war-making powers. In the House this took the form of a resolution sponsored by Representative Clement Zablocki (D-Wis.) that required the president to submit a detailed report to Congress whenever he committed troops to combat. In the Senate it took shape as a bill, cosponsored by Senators Jacob Javits (R-N.Y.) and Robert Dole (R-Kans.), that listed precisely four circumstances in which the president, as commander in chief, could employ the nation's military forces abroad.[21] Though Congress was not to enact the War Powers Act until November 7, 1973, when it overrode Nixon's veto of a bill establishing procedures for notification and possible legislative limitations regarding any presidential use of force, the House and Senate kept this question alive throughout 1970, 1971, and 1972 by passing earlier versions of the 1973 law.[22] It was of course (in addition to the Watergate scandal) the president's prolongation of the American bombing of Cambodia, even after the Paris Peace Accords of January 1973, that made the final enactment of this legislation possible.[23] These air attacks also enabled (many would say, required) the House and Senate, through the process of amending the Supplemental Appropriations Act, to force the president in June 1973 to agree that the American bombardment of Cambodia would end after August 15 of that year. Thus Congress was finally able to achieve what some historians have called "the legislated peace."[24]

This overview of congressional activity in the field of foreign affairs is intended not to be exhaustive but to make clear that, during the period in which the Nixon administration was achieving détente with the Soviet Union, the federal legislature was heavily influenced by (and vigorously representative of) the mood of withdrawal from anti-Communist confrontation that was sweeping America. This is not to say that either the policy of détente or the mood of withdrawal coincided only with the Nixon era, for both obviously predated these years to an extent and continued to exist under Gerald Ford and Jimmy Carter. Nor is it to suggest that the mood caused the policy, or the policy the mood, for without much doubt the public and the politicians were participating in an interactive process along with a substantial number of other groups and factors, foreign and domestic.

In the chapters that follow I attempt to delineate more exactly the context and origins of the decisions of the Nixon and Brezhnev governments that contributed to the détente process. Suffice it here to point out that, while public or congressional opinion, if vigorously asserted, can each have an important effect upon the way an administration behaves, acting together they can have a truly significant impact upon the government's decision making.[25] Moreover, the foreign policy leaders of the Nixon government not only knew this but felt constrained by their own ideological and political convictions to take the breakdown of consensus and growing opposition at home with utmost seriousness. Note, for example, the testimony of Henry Kissinger, who complained to a British magazine in 1979 that he had been compelled to conduct foreign policy for eight years "under [domestic] conditions of near civil war":

> In the early 1970s, in the face of an ominous Soviet buildup, the administration in which I served sought to reverse this process. But under the impact of the Vietnam turmoil its defence programmes were being cut by the congress every year. Every new weapons programme we put forward was systematically attacked or dismantled. As a result, starting in 1970 our defence department was pleading with us to negotiate a freeze on the Soviets lest the disparity in numbers would continue to grow.[26]

Or observe the retrospective commentary of Gerard Smith, Nixon's director of the Arms Control and Disarmament Agency and also chief American delegate to SALT during 1969–72 in Helsinki and Vienna:

> Nothing concentrated the minds of American leaders on the advantages of SALT as much as the clear and present danger of one-sided arms control in the form of congressional cuts in US defense budgets. The changing popular and congressional mood about strategic arms was not lost on such an astute politician as Secretary of Defense Melvin Laird. His interest in SALT was, I thought, in good measure based on a concern that in the absence of agreed limitations the Congress would go for some unilateral limitation.[27]

Admittedly, such remarks are not only revealing but ironic, since few Nixon officials (and certainly not Nixon and Kissinger themselves) have ever given much credit to the antiwar movement and to polarization at home for the emergence of détente. On the contrary, Nixon and his colleagues have tended to blame the public and Congress for undermining relations with Russia by not supporting administration efforts, especially during the period 1973–76, to create what Kissinger called "incentives for responsible [Soviet] behavior and . . . penalities for irresponsible behavior."[28] Nevertheless, and despite the possibility that there is some validity to the Nixon-Kissinger interpretation of what happened in later years, there clearly would have been much less incentive in 1969–71 for the new

Nixon administration to rethink Soviet-U.S. relations along more cooperative lines if there had been no fierce and widespread public desire, growing primarily out of the war, to pull America back from its overextended international position.

Although the Soviet Union did not suffer the same convulsions and traumas that the United States endured in the latter half of the 1960s, it did experience difficulties at home and abroad sufficiently serious to render its leaders increasingly amenable to the idea of exploring détente with the West as a means to escaping their dilemmas. To be sure, the solutions to these difficulties did not point unequivocally toward international accommodation. Problems of social control in Eastern Europe and Russia, for example, were likely to become more rather than less severe as a result of any Soviet effort to improve relations with the capitalist world. Nevertheless, many of the challenges the U.S.S.R. encountered during the years 1968–71 did have the effect of making a conciliatory foreign policy attractive to the country's leadership.

Any explanation begins with a recognition of the extent to which the men who overthrew Nikita Khrushchev in November 1964 were committed to making the Soviet system work without the "harebrained" unpredictability and daring decentralizations of their boisterous and energetic predecessor. Indeed, the leading figures of this group—Leonid Brezhnev, Alexei Kosygin, Mikhail Suslov, and Nikolai Podgorny—possibly because of their largely technical background as well as their experiences under Stalin and Khrushchev, were clearly convinced that only a blend of patience, science, and system could stimulate the Soviet people to play their proper role as the cutting edge of the future.[29] Brezhnev, as party leader, was not as directly involved as were state officials in devising and implementing the "rational" centerpiece of this new mix, the economic modifications of 1965 that came to be known as the "Kosygin reforms." Yet Brezhnev, as much as the other oligarchs, was in a sense responsible for these policies and for a number of related compromises that involved investment commitments to light industry, agriculture, and the military-industrial sector as well as promises of cooperation to the intelligentsia, the party, and foreign allies.[30]

When in 1968 and 1969 evidence began accumulating that the Kosygin economic formulas were not working—producing neither the hoped-for boost in public morale nor the increase in technological innovation and productivity on which the regime's capacity to fulfill its commitments and promises depended—it became imperative for the party leadership to do something to alter and improve the situation.[31] One option, of course, was to retreat to an even more orthodox centralism in administrative control and organization. Another alternative was to move what was still in essence a command arrangement farther along the road to becoming a market-oriented economy. A third possibility—and as it happened, the one the Politburo ultimately chose, primarily in response to Brezhnev's prodding—was to avoid a challenge to domestic economic interests by seeking a détente with Western Europe or the United States as a means of acquiring abroad the credit, goods, and technology the regime so desperately needed.

This policy, which began to become visible late in 1969, was made doubly desirable to the U.S.S.R. by the necessity of counteracting the worldwide revulsion engendered by Moscow's decision of August 1968 to use force against the reform Communists in Czechoslovakia.[32] The intervention had been an outgrowth of increasing anxiety within the Kremlin, anxiety triggered by the strength of centrifugal forces and manifested in the growing Soviet tendency to cope with domestic problems by limiting dissent and mobilizing against "creeping counter-revolution."[33] Thus fear led to repression, both domestic and foreign, and repression needed to be obscured or justified. The irony was that détente with the West, while helping Russia improve its image, pacify its dissidents, and meet its economic necessities, understandably did little to alleviate anxiety among the ideological hard-liners. Moreover, it provided a vehicle for the essentially moderate Brezhnev to break down the restraints that his fellow oligarchs had placed upon each other in attempting to maintain a balance of power within the ruling elite.[34]

As we turn now to examine these developments in detail, it is important to notice that one of the increasingly potent if subtle pressures on the Soviet leadership during this period was that exercised by the public at large (and the representatives of light industry) on behalf of increasing the availability of consumer goods. To Brezhnev and his colleagues such pressure must have seemed like a genie that their predecessor Khrushchev, by his erratic actions with regard to consumer priorities, had let out of the bottle.[35] In any case, however, the post-Khrushchev oligarchy evinced little eagerness to reassert the sacredness of heavy industry and put the genie back whence it came. On the contrary, the new elite revealed itself to be sensitive to public desires and criticism, responding with promises of a better performance and with allocations to consumption of a larger share of the GNP than in the past.[36] Thus the economic reforms of 1965 included among their main objectives an improvement in the consumer sector. What is more, during 1966–70, consumer-oriented investment was allowed to grow faster than producer-oriented investment.[37] As early as 1966 the government made a stunning concession to the new consumerism when it entered into a contract with Fiat of Italy to build a $1.5 billion plant at Togliatti on the Volga that could produce 600,000 passenger cars a year.[38] By the time of the Ninth Five-Year Plan (1971–75), though the rate of growth in consumption investment was scheduled to be somewhat lower than its peaks of the 1960s, the regime had clearly committed itself to long-term increases not only in the production of consumer goods but also in income levels and social benefits.[39]

An obvious factor in prompting this enlarged support for the consumer sector was the evidence of malaise and public frustration at the end of the decade. Despite certain changes for the better, Soviet citizens continued to be victimized by recurrent shortages, inadequate quality, and an inappropriate mix of goods and services. Complaints grew, and the government had little success in quieting criticism despite repeated administrative modifications: three in 1969 and 1970 and four in 1971 and 1972 following the particularly ominous consumer riots in Poland of December 1970.[40] Meanwhile, the attitude of the Soviet public manifested itself in a peculiarly distorted pattern of demand. In the face of restricted alternatives, individuals chose not only to save most of each ruble of additional income but also to spend an abnormally large part of the remainder on alcoholic beverages and quality foods, especially meat.[41]

Such a fact serves to remind us that there was an important agricultural dimension to this problem. Like light industry, agriculture had been severely underfunded (and exploited) for decades, as Soviet rulers employed the bulk of their resources to drive their people through the painful process of industrialization. Moreover, again like light industry, agriculture had been seriously shaken and only temporarily assisted by the experimentation and innovations of the Khrushchev era.[42] Now, in the second half of the 1960s, the situation in agriculture constituted one of the greatest weaknesses in the Soviet economy. Needs and expectations had been increased without an increase in production, with the result that, on occasion, belts had to be tightened or food had to be imported at the cost of precious foreign exchange.[43]

Khrushchev, in truth, rose to power and fell from power in conjunction with the agricultural issue. In 1953–54 he mounted his successful attack on his rival, Malenkov, to a substantial extent in terms of the need for revolutionary changes in the farming sector (e.g., greater incentives for peasants, more investment in equipment, and the cultivation of the "virgin lands"). In his middle years (1955–58), as he carried out these policies (and vastly enlarged the cropland of the U.S.S.R.), his success in raising the yield in grain by almost 50 percent fortified him in his struggle to dominate the political process. Unfortunately for him and the Soviet people, however, after 1958 things in the agricultural world went seriously wrong. Not enough land had been allowed to lie fallow, too many marginal regions had been plowed up and planted, and monetary incentives had been replaced with moral exhortations and Communist Party interference. Several seasons of falling yields culminated in the drought year of 1963, an agricultural and political disaster for Khrushchev. This year also marked the first occasion on which it was necessary to import grain from the capitalist West.[44]

After Khrushchev's ouster, his successors made it clear they were as determined to improve performance on the farm as in the factories of light industry. Brezhnev took the lead, pushing through substantial systemic changes as early as March 1965, changes that included a revamped agricultural ministry in Moscow, greater autonomy for farms, lower delivery quotas, higher prices and pay scales, and most important, a doubling of the rate of government investment (from 34 billion to 71 billion rubles) over the next five years.[45] Though there were to be sizable cutbacks during 1967–69 in the monies allocated to certain areas, the overall Soviet investment in agriculture continued at an all-time high into the seventies. Brezhnev, unlike Khrushchev, would remain relatively constant in his efforts to implement his original plans.[46] The accompanying strain on the economy was therefore considerably greater.

The results for agriculture, as the decade neared its close, were only moderately encouraging. The three years from 1966 through 1968 saw harvests that averaged nearly one-quarter larger than those of the 1962–64 period and permitted some improvement in the Soviet diet as well as replenishment of grain reserves. In 1969, however, farm production declined notably, and a wave of public dissatisfaction surfaced regarding inadequate food supplies.[47] Thus pressure continued on the nation's leaders to enlarge their already substantial involvement in the transformation of agriculture.

An even more basic problem confronting the leadership related to the changing mood, morale, and discipline of the Soviet people, to its posture vis-à-vis Communism, and especially to the perspectives of its younger generation. As intangible as these matters were, they did constitute important limiting or stimulating factors with regard to the behavior of any Soviet government. On this occasion they clearly played a significant if indirect role in influencing the process by which the majority of the reigning oligarchy became proponents of détente.

The status of popular compliance and belief at the end of the 1960s gave the leadership understandable cause for concern. There had been disturbing currents visible in Soviet society ever since de-Stalinization in 1956, but by the end of the Khrushchev years many troublesome tendencies were undeniably on the rise. The most obvious category included such negative activity as "dodging socially useful labor" (a phenomenon called "parasitism"), alcoholism, crime, and "hooliganism" (a term covering lawlessness, ranging from minor theft to gang violence).[48] A second area of difficulty was less clear-cut, involving things like widespread cynicism, indifference to Marxism-Leninism, resistance to military or party service, and infatuation with "careerism."[49] This was tied to a diffuse development that had also been identified and viewed with alarm, namely the "deradicalization" of society and its "embourgeoisement," by which was meant its growing preoccupation with consumption and possessions.[50] Finally, there was a category, not unrelated to the others, which involved an increasingly wide range of dissent or lack of conformity on the part of the scientific-technical and cultural-artistic intelligentsia. This kind of activity had frequently been encouraged by Khrushchev, who sometimes found the ideas and criticisms of intellectuals useful weapons in his continuing fight for political ascendancy. But even he, as his political position declined after 1962, found it difficult to maintain an attitude of tolerance.[51]

The response of the Brezhnev-Kosygin regime to such alienation and deviation tended to be unappreciative and harsh, especially after these tendencies did not subside during a period of governmental moderation in early 1965. Soon, a number of coercive measures were enacted, including an antiparasite law permitting mandated labor, decrees strengthening the power and authority of the police, and rules enlarging party control over literature.[52] In September 1965 came the arrests of the well-known authors Andrei Siniavskii and Yuli Daniel, and in succeeding months other dissidents were legally harassed or imprisoned as waves of unrest and protest repeatedly swept their ranks.[53] Governmental repression was combined with loyalty campaigns that were supplemented by educational reforms, new recreational programs, stepped-up attacks upon alcoholism and crime, and a revised military service law.[54]

The climactic thrust of this defensive impulse came at the plenum of the Communist Party Central Committee in April 1968, when the public was urged to mobilize itself against what was described as a "subversive" effort by the West to destroy socialist society from within.[55] The implications of this for foreign policy and détente were not made explicit, but it was obvious, first, that the actions taken were as much in response to unrest in Eastern Europe as to troubles in Russia and, second, that any progress made by Moscow toward easing relations with its foreign enemies would probably complicate efforts by the party and the police to strengthen control and discipline in the satellites as well as the Soviet Union. At the same time, it was also clear (especially after the Soviet invasion of Czechoslovakia in August 1968) that a foreign policy emphasizing international cooperation could be used to gloss over or legitimize even the most autocratic of regimes, both for people abroad and for those in Russia and Eastern Europe. Which of these considerations the Soviet Politburo would take more seriously depended, obviously, on the extent to which its individual members were tied to a particular perspective or a special interest. As we shall see, by the early 1970s the majority of that body had been persuaded that the dangers generated by international détente would be more than outweighed by the advantages it brought the U.S.S.R. in domestic or foreign affairs.

One further aspect of these developments that must be mentioned has to do with their relation to the so-called nationalities question. It should not be forgotten that the Russians—though composing 53 percent of the Soviet population in 1970—were but the largest of more than 100 ethnic groups in the U.S.S.R. and that in the 1960s and the 1970s their proportion was declining at almost 2 percent a decade as the non-Slavic Soviet peoples (25% of the total and entering the middle phase of modernization) experienced a vast demographic expansion.[56] Nor should we overlook the fact—conceded by the Russians themselves in the census of 1970—that, as a result of slowing growth rates in the European areas, the Turkic nationalities of the southeast had come to constitute the primary source for major additions to the country's industrial workforce.[57] More to the point, however, is that there were continuing signs of rising sensitivity and self-awareness among the ethnic groups of the Soviet Union, despite and in part because of the "federal" system (involving fifteen republics) that Lenin had designed to pacify various particularisms while at the same time enlisting them in the cause of socialism.

Here too the Brezhnev-Kosygin group might well have blamed Khrushchev, since it was his rapid administrative and cultural decentralization, followed after 1959 by a vigorous assimilationist emphasis, that stimulated much of the new nationalism both within the southern republics and in Ukraine and the Baltic states.[58] In any event, Brezhnev and his colleagues were forced to tread warily in the late 1960s, abandoning regional arrangements and granting greater representation to the republics while simultaneously trying to systematize education and repress separatist activities.[59] Such a gradual "tightening up" thus ran parallel to the oligarchy's policy with regard to the country's dissidents, wayward youth, and unemployed. In this instance the impact on Soviet foreign policy was less ambiguous, since it seems probable that for the men in the Kremlin the Soviet nationality problem (unlike the more frightening phenomenon of nationalism in Eastern Europe) was serious enough to constitute a real constraint to external belligerence without being so grave as to make the unity of the country seem vulnerable to the process of détente.[60]

Meanwhile, if domestic ethnic tensions were to an extent working for international accommodation during this period, so, oddly enough, were the increasing demands being put on the economy and government by the proponents of an expanded Soviet military establishment. This fact was of course no tribute to those we might call Russian hawks, who continued to be a noticeable and potent group within the government (especially within the armed forces) and who remained as fearful as ever of hostile encircle-ment and aggression. Nor does it reflect credit on those Soviet strategists who, sensing that the United States was deeply preoccupied in Vietnam (and had halted the expansion of its missile forces), wished to use the opportunity to try to gain a permanent advantage over that nation in arms competition.[61] It is, on the contrary, testimony to the perceptiveness of Soviet statesmen like Leonid Brezhnev, who, though long dedicated to matching America in the building of military power, had over a period of time developed commitments to their system's civilian sector that they were unwilling or unable to relinquish. They had come to see that, while it may have been possible—through extraordinary effort—to equal or excel the United States in missile construction during particularly advantageous years, a renewed arms race featuring ABMs and second-generation ICBMs would become so endless and so expensive that it would seriously impair almost all governmental activities (even including nonstrategic military programs). And they had come to realize that, no matter what they spent, the U.S.S.R. would never be able to achieve much more than the strategic parity with the United States that it was already approaching in 1969.

If at this juncture the Russian economy had given promise of a steady growth in productivity and technical sophistication, perhaps these leaders, being the politicians they were, would have attempted to provide every Soviet group—from workers and consumers to military forces and "metal eaters" (the ever-hungry heavy industry)—with the amount and types of investment it desired and had often been promised. But as we shall discov-er, the Soviet economy did not give such indications, and as a result, when demands upon it grew precipitously, the Politburo was confronted with extremely difficult choices. That it decided to attempt to solve its dilemmas through rapprochement and greater cooperation with its foreign enemies is naturally to its credit, but in evaluating this, one should not overlook the problematic quality of the alternatives.

It remains only to sketch the development of this last and most insid-ious pressure on Soviet leaders—that on behalf of the military—during this critical period. Admittedly, such pressure had been present from the very beginning of the Brezhnev-Kosygin regime, as the new leadership necessarily responded to the fact that the Khrushchev government had never succeeded in reshaping Russian military power to support a global political strategy. This lack of fit between capacity and desire had been driven home to the ruling clique by the fiasco of the Cuban missile crisis in 1962. It has been rendered even more painful after 1965 by the Soviet inability to counter U.S. aggression in dealing with such "national liberation movements" as that in Vietnam.[62]

As I note in more detail later, Brezhnev and Kosygin adopted a strategy and intensified a number of military programs that quickly demonstrated an impressive ability to gobble up resources. The most demanding of these, although it was temporarily cloaked in secrecy, provided for the expansion of offensive missile forces from the several dozen ICBM launchers that Russia possessed in 1965 to the more than a thousand it was deploying three years later (slightly more than the United States possessed).[63] Other important and expensive areas of activity included the development of missile-bearing submarines, multiple-warhead ballistic missiles (MRVs and MIRVs), antiballistic missiles (ABMs), and an ocean-going navy and merchant marine.[64] The cumulative cost of such endeavors made successive annual increases in the military budget inevitable, the official totals mounting from 12.8 billion rubles in 1965 to almost 18 billion in 1970.[65] Even more critical, however, was the fact that Soviet defense spending was expanding at a much faster rate than the country's gross national product (GNP).[66] In proportion to its GNP, the U.S.S.R. was making a greater defense effort than the United States, which was in the midst of the Vietnam War.[67] It was clear this could not go on indefinitely.

It was ironic, though not perhaps unpredictable, that economic factors would render a policy of accommodation attractive to both U.S. and Soviet elites in the last years of the 1960s. Differing assumptions about economic reality lay at the very root of the long-standing ideological disagreement between proponents of the two regimes. Nevertheless, it was becoming increasingly clear to both sides that their competition was driving them into an extravagant expenditure of resources—an expense that robbed them of the flexibility they needed to maintain existing advantages and to accomplish future objectives. This is not to say that Cold War economics were necessarily and consistently a force making for peace. But economic developments in both the U.S.S.R. and the United States were working at this moment, with surprising symmetry, to emphasize the advantages of a policy of détente.

On the Soviet side the crux of the matter was that its economy was no longer growing as rapidly as it had in earlier times. The U.S.S.R. had reached the point in its development when it could no longer rely primarily on increases in what economists call the quantitative sources of growth: the size of the labor force, the availability of natural resources, and the stock of invested capital. In the future, Soviet economic growth would be much more dependent on whether or not the managers of the economy could find ways to raise productivity by improving general efficiency and promoting technological progress.

A continuing high rate of growth was of particular importance to the Soviet leadership. Most obviously, growth had become central to fulfilling the historic Soviet commitment to "overtaking and surpassing" the advanced capitalist countries. Indeed, Communist economic success in the face of increasing capitalist stagnation had become a proof of the correctness of Marxist convictions as well as a justification for the great hardships endured by the Soviet people in the years of revolution and industrialization.

Beyond this, however, growth had become crucial simply because the Soviet Union was attempting to match the military power of the United States, the world's foremost industrial nation, at a time when the Soviet per capita GNP was less than half that of the American.[68] This meant that the weight of the military establishment for the rest of the economy was roughly twice as great in the Soviet Union as in the United States. No nation in history not actively engaged in war had carried so large a burden of defense over such an extended period.

Not surprisingly, the pressure to increase output and to reduce this burden was considerable and became greater as the demands of and promises to other sectors of the economy grew more significant. As long as the post-Khrushchev leadership could anticipate that the economic reforms it had introduced in 1965, the so-called Kosygin reforms, would actually solve the problem of a declining growth rate, there was no imperative to explore alternative arrangements. But when, in the years 1968 and 1969, it became clear that there had been no basic improvement, and that productivity trends had actually gotten worse, the incentive to find a more successful economic policy increased substantially.

The United States, meanwhile, was experiencing productivity problems strangely similar to those of the U.S.S.R. Granted, whereas the Russians were dealing with declining growth in productivity from the standpoint of a nation that was just catching up with its opponent, Americans were approaching their own falling rates of growth from the perspective of a people that had long been dominant economically. Still, both economies were overcommitted, and the American experience of long-standing dominance was itself a part of the problem. World War II, by destroying the United States' competitors and stimulating its industry to immense exertions, had left the country with an industrial plant that was far more powerful and efficient than any other in the world. The result was that Americans had taken upon themselves a number of roles that no other people could have assumed in the 1940s and 1950s, roles that provided the world outside the Soviet orbit with its economic rules of the game and with indispensable portions of its food, manufactured goods, credit, and defense against outside threat.

This liberal world order, built upon the foundations of free trade, a powerful and convertible dollar, heavy American investment overseas, and an efficient U.S. economic machine, might well have survived in its existing form almost indefinitely had its proponents understood it better. What was needed to preserve it, and what it did not get, was a series of adjustments (both in this country and outside) to compensate for the return of America's natural economic competitors—capitalist nations disabled by World War II that by the 1960s were regaining their strength and utilizing advanced technology to offer better (and cheaper) consumer goods than America produced. Thus the United States went on as before, proud and overconfident, carrying a disproportionate load of military costs, ignoring crucial research and development (R&D) as well as the international export market, and allowing its multinational corporations to manage their competition by investing overseas rather than at home.

Small wonder that the country, particularly after lengthy involvement in Vietnam, began to show signs of economic noncompetitiveness as its infrastructure and plant wore down, its people came to prefer foreign products, and its balance of trade and payments fell into negative figures, with a consequent outflow of gold and growth in dollar balances abroad. In the end, with business hurting and foreign policy constrained, there understandably developed both a mounting demand for direct assistance to industry (usually in the form of tariffs and investment incentives) and a sharpening interest in the expansion of American markets overseas.

Let us now examine the Soviet economy in detail, taking up the significant trends and relevant events of the period from 1965 to 1970. From the onset of the country's second industrialization in 1928 until the late 1950s, Soviet growth was unusually vigorous, peaking in the years 1950–58, when national income climbed at the rate of 7.2 percent a year. Then came a dramatic change, as the annual increase fell off to an average of 5.3 percent during the period 1958–64, reaching a low of 2.8 percent in 1963.[69] The explanation, according to Western analysts, is as follows: whereas from 1928 to 1958 over 70 percent of Soviet growth was due to quantitative increases in productive factor inputs, by the late 1950s the possibilities of continuing that strategy began to disappear.[70] The "virgin lands" brought under cultivation by Nikita Khrushchev were virtually the last large unfarmed areas available for exploitation. Excess agricultural labor and the female working force had been substantially absorbed, and the rate of population growth had declined drastically.[71] There could be no return to growth rates like those of the 1950s without qualitative improvements, such as better equipment, more highly skilled labor, or more efficient organization.

It was to achieve such objectives that the Kosygin reforms were introduced in the autumn of 1965. Having previously revoked Khrushchev's economic decentralization of 1956, the new leadership now returned to a system of centralized ministries for industrial management, combining this with changes in established procedures for administrators at all levels. In place of the directives of a command economy, the reformers proposed to develop a limited version of those economic levers—prices, profits, market demand, interest, and incentive funds—the West uses to regulate and control production and distribution.[72]

The results were on the whole disappointing. For two years, thanks in part to good harvests, there appeared to be some recovery from the sluggishness of the Khrushchev era (the growth rate jumped to 5.8%), but by 1969 it was evident that the improvement in the economy had fallen off once again.[73] The first hint of trouble came in March 1968, when it was announced that the government had made downward revisions in the schedule of investment in light industry.[74] This was followed in October 1968 by a number of modifications in those areas of the original reforms that related to priorities, pricing, and research.[75] Then, during the autumn and winter of 1969–70, there were numerous indications of official displeasure at the way the economy was performing. Brezhnev, who turned sharply against Kosygin and his ideas during this period and was pushing himself forward, delivered "an unusually frank report" at the plenum of the Central Committee in December 1969 in which he was highly critical of economic reformism and called for a new campaign to generate discipline, hard work, and thrift.[76] Meanwhile, there were repeated delays in the publication of the outline for the Ninth Five-Year Plan (1971–75), which was promised by August 1968 but could not be agreed upon by the leadership until almost two years later.[77]

There was a fair amount of uncertainty in the spring of 1970 both as to the extent of Brezhnev's personal primacy and the nature of his policy, but by midyear it was evident not only that he had worked out certain arrangements with his colleagues but also that he had achieved a clearer notion of his own economic priorities.[78] The Kosygin reforms were definitely not to be repudiated, and the sacrifices that had been called for over the previous few months were not forgotten. But Brezhnev identified two factors as indispensable from this point onward: technological innovation and modern administrative technique. As he put it in a speech in June, the secret of future growth lay in the "management of science" and the "science of management."[79]

Appealing to science and technology for solutions was not, of course, a new thing on the part of either Brezhnev or his countrymen. Some historians have even seen in Russia's past what one scholar calls "a pattern of periodic forays into the international economy"—at the beginning of the 1700s as well as in the 1890s and 1930s—to find and acquire the most advanced technology of the day.[80] Khrushchev himself after 1959 had made major purchases of foreign patents, licenses, and even factories (primarily chemical plants) in an attempt to enlarge the productive capacity of the Soviet economy.[81] Though his successors at first curtailed imports of technology, within a few months they became impressed enough with domestic inertia that they reversed themselves and negotiated the contract with Fiat of Italy to build an automobile factory in Russia. And the deal with Fiat was only the beginning; Soviet buyers quickly began to appear all over Europe and Japan.[82]

The Russian economy, however, has generally proved almost as unsuccessful at incorporating foreign technological advances as at generating improvements of its own. Until the 1980s the centrally administered Soviet apparatus possessed no mechanism to stimulate or disseminate new discoveries in the way the profit-seeking market does. New techniques and products were introduced by deliberate actions of administrative bodies, and attempts to coordinate the process among interrelated enterprises were rendered difficult by the absence of a realistic pricing system, genuine feedback from customers, or effective rewards for managerial innovation. One study of Soviet industries concludes that foreign machinery took considerably longer to be assimilated in Russia than in Western Europe and that the number of workers employed was on the high side while output levels were on the low side.[83]

Nevertheless, in 1969–70 a tremor of insight and concern with regard to the technological imperative swept through the Soviet elite. The summer of 1969 was the occasion of the American landing on the moon, an event that we now know had a substantial impact on the attitudes of Soviet scientific and military observers.[84] Indeed, the following March an appeal for action by several well-known Soviet scientists to party and government leaders was published in the official press:

> When we compare our economy with that of the United States, we see that ours is lagging behind not only quantitatively, but—and this is the saddest part—also qualitatively. The more novel and revolutionary the aspect of the economy, the wider becomes the gap. . . . We are ahead of the United States in the production of coal but behind in the production of oil, gas, electric power, ten times behind in chemistry, and immeasurably behind in computer technology.[85]

Emphasizing the importance of computers to the "system of production," the scientists went on to point out that "the first men to set foot on the moon were Americans . . . one of the outward signs of an essential and ever-growing gap between our country and the West extending through the whole spectrum of scientific-technological activity."

Given this context, Brezhnev and his colleagues realized they had to redouble their effort to obtain that infusion of Western technology critical to Russian growth and competitiveness. No longer was the general secretary as ambivalent about imports as he had been in March 1968, when he noted that many "clearly underestimate the achievements of scientific-technical thought in our country and . . . are inclined to overestimate the achievements of science and technology in the capitalist world."[86] By late 1970, and especially by the Twenty-fourth Party Congress in the spring of 1971, Brezhnev had singled out scientific-technical achievement as the key objective for the future, describing it as an "organizing concept" for trade between the Soviet Union and the outside world.[87] Premier Kosygin stated the matter even more explicitly the following November in a speech to the Supreme Soviet:

> With [our changeover] to the practice of [making] long-term agreements . . . consideration can [now] be given to mutually beneficial cooperation with foreign firms and banks in the working out of a number of important economic problems connected with the use of natural resources . . . the construction of industrial enterprises, and the search for new technologies.[88]

It is helpful in understanding the meaning of these events to notice what was occurring simultaneously in the economic relation between Russia and its Eastern European allies. To be sure, during the first decades after World War II the relation had been largely exploitative, as the Soviet Union took advantage of its political and military power to reorient the trade of the region and obtain extremely favorable prices for its imports and exports. By the 1960s, however, the increasing costs of the fuel and raw materials that the U.S.S.R. had contracted to supply its neighbors transformed the situation; now, Soviet economists complained that their own country was being victimized.[89] Thus, with Russian leaders coming under greater and greater pressure to find additional resources for their nation's economy (as well as to provide an alternative to protoliberal reforms in Eastern Europe), it was to be expected that they would attempt to institute a reorganization of relations within the socialist camp.

The process was initiated at the Twenty-third Meeting of the Council for Mutual Economic Assistance (generally CMEA, sometimes Comecon) in Moscow on April 23–26, 1969, when the heads of party and government of the member states instructed the organizational secretariat to work out a new framework for "integrating" previously divergent national interests. The resulting agenda, the so-called complex program, was developed over the next two years and formally adopted at the Twenty-fifth Meeting of CMEA on July 27–29, 1971, in Bucharest.[90] The complex program was fully in accord with the spirit and objectives of Brezhnev's new emphasis on trade and technology as the answer to the Soviet Union's and the Eastern bloc's problems. As the secretary of CMEA put it on March 23, 1970: "In these days of peaceful coexistence, economic cooperation amongst Socialist countries will facilitate the victory of Socialism over Capitalism, particularly in the decisive arena of this rivalry—in the sphere of scientific and technical progress."[91]

In returning to the American side of these matters, I must emphasize again just how much the United States dominated the world economy in the years after 1945. America's war-born advantage was such that in 1947 almost half of the world's manufactured goods were made in the United States. In that year alone the nation's export surplus was $10 billion, and by 1949, despite the Marshall Plan, its holdings of the world's gold supply had mounted to 70 percent of the total. The United States, with 6 percent of the earth's population, was the global leader in trade, energy, and productivity.[92]

This, of course, was bound to change. By 1955 Western Europe and Japan were recovering vigorously from the war. From 1955 to 1960 manufacturing output grew 35 percent in France, 50 percent in West Germany and Italy, and more than 100 percent in Japan. In the next seven years the Japanese increased their industrial product by 100 percent again. Such accomplishments, coming at a time when American output was growing less than half as fast as that of France, were bound to revolutionize the international economic situation.[93]

In fact, during the period of U.S. dominance it had acquired habits and policies that reduced its competitiveness. For example, Washington continued to guide and smooth its relations with its allies by bearing an excessive share of military expenses. Almost 15 percent of America's income between 1950 and 1960 went to defense spending, while the comparable figures for NATO countries ranged from 6.5 percent in Britain to 2.8 percent in West Germany.[94] Since this expenditure was combined with Americans' higher propensity to consume (in 1960 individual savings in the United States averaged 4.9% of individual disposable income, as opposed to 8.5% in West Germany and 17.4% in Japan), a relatively smaller proportion of the American GNP was being invested in civilian sector plants and equipment, as these figures from 1960 demonstrate:[95]

Japan	30.2%
West Germany	24.3%
France	20.2%
United States	17.6%
United Kingdom	16.3%

Meanwhile, in a supreme irony, America's liberal trade doctrines were making it possible for multinational U.S. corporations to invest billions of dollars each year in lucrative overseas operations rather than in improving efficiency at home. Management's preoccupation with short-term profits and with avoiding, by generous wage concessions, such difficulties as the 116-day steel strike of 1959 (which tipped the American steel trade permanently into deficit) did not help the problem.[96]

As one might expect, by the 1960s the cumulative impact of these tendencies began to show up in a small and declining annual rate of increase in American productivity. Among capitalist powers, the United States was next to lowest, exceeding only Britain in productivity growth during the years 1950–65. In the next eight years America slipped again and fell far behind even Britain:

	1950–65	1965–73
Japan	7.2%	9.1%
West Germany	5.2%	4.3%
France	4.7%	4.5%
United Kingdom	2.2%	3.3%
United States	2.4%	1.6%

What this meant was that American businessmen were simply not matching their competition, particularly in industries like textiles, steel, electronics, and automobiles, where the Japanese and Germans were concentrating their energies.[97]

This in turn was reflected by the shifts and turns in the American balance of trade. Throughout the 1950s and into the 1960s the United States had been able to maintain (as it had since the 1890s) a favorable and consistent trade surplus, varying from $7.8 billion in 1957 to $2.4 billion in 1959 and $6.8 billion in 1964. After the mid-1960s, however, a significant weakening in the American trade position became evident, the balance dwindling from a $3.8 billion surplus in 1967 to a $660 million surplus in 1969 to a $2.8 billion deficit in 1971.[98] The situation was made worse by protectionist and discriminatory policies on the part of Japan and the new European Economic Community, especially with regard to agricultural products.[99] Other negative factors included a growing American trade deficit in petroleum items as well as price increases resulting from domestic inflation and Great Society reform legislation.[100]

The ultimate barometer of economic health, to be sure, is balance of payments, not balance of trade, and in this area the United States was also skating on thinner and thinner ice. Accustomed in the 1950s to think of itself as so strong that it could virtually ignore its balance of payments, America in those years acquired the habit of running a negative balance of payments even with a positive balance of trade. Thus, in every year but 1957 the sums of money privately invested overseas, spent by the military abroad, and made available through foreign aid were considerably greater than the dollar surplus produced by American commercial exports.[101] The differences, which were made up largely by transfers of gold, were substantial enough that Western Europe and Japan doubled their gold holdings between 1952 and 1959, by which time they had accumulated $22 billion of a world total of $57 billion.[102] By 1961 the incoming Kennedy administration was so troubled by the outflow of gold in the three previous years that it formulated an explicit if modest program to increase exports, discourage investment abroad, and ease the run on American reserves by countries with payments surpluses.[103]

For a time, the pressure on the dollar slackened somewhat, but with the coming of the Vietnam intervention in 1965 new destabilizing forces were set in motion. Both the war-induced economic boom (which stimulated purchases of foreign products) and the expenses incurred in Southeast Asia worked to the disadvantage of the American balance of payments; and although this was masked in 1967 and 1968 by short-term flows of capital, with the economic slowdown of the next year it became clear that something was seriously amiss.[104] Even in a recession, Japanese sales to the United States did not fall off (the U.S. trade deficit with Japan grew from $345 million in 1967 to $1.2 billion in 1970), and the overall American trade surplus had become so anemic that the nation's overseas expenses had driven its balance of payments to an all-time low of minus $9.8 billion.[105] Nor did things improve in 1971. The economy limped along, with inflation inching downward (from 5.5% to 4.4%) and unemployment edging upward (passing 6% in January 1971), while America's export surplus disappeared for the first time since 1893, and protectionist pressures mounted in Congress.[106]

In August 1971, faced with a gold drain of alarming proportions and an economy in the doldrums, President Nixon felt compelled to act. Aside from solving the immediate crisis, of course, Nixon's most pressing need was to stimulate the economy in such a way as to eliminate the recession and high unemployment before his run for reelection in 1972. Yet he and his advisers realized that, if they were to increase aggregate demand by means of tax breaks, lower interest rates, or preelection transfer payments, they would also fuel inflation and push the balance of trade and balance of payments into even more negative figures. Their answer to this dilemma was a cleverly balanced package of measures they called the new economic policy: a tax credit of 10 percent to spur business investment, mandatory controls on prices and wages to put a lid on inflation, a temporary import surcharge of 10 percent to make foreign goods less attractive to Americans, and the suspension of the convertibility of the dollar into gold at $35 per ounce ("closing the gold window").[107] This last action was particularly significant, for by breaking the fixed relation between the dollar and gold (and thus making continuing devaluation possible), the administration was abandoning one pillar of the Bretton Woods system, that set of financial arrangements established after World War II by the United States and its allies to foster the development of a world order based on liberal ideas and free trade.[108]

Though the domestic impact of Nixon's program was highly stimulating for several months, internationally this "Nixon shock" (as the Japanese called it) ushered in a lengthy period of financial turmoil. Throughout the autumn, as the dollar floated downward about 6 percent relative to other currencies, the major trading nations tried to work out a new monetary system. At length, in December, their representatives met at the Smithsonian Institution in Washington and agreed upon a set of interrelated exchange rates involving an average American devaluation of about 10 percent. This understanding lasted about a year, until massive flows of capital led early in 1973 to what came to be called the "second devaluation" of the dollar. Even this did not suffice, however, and by March 1973 the larger countries had abandoned any pretense of fixed exchange rates for their currencies. At that point, the dollar had lost about 15 percent of the value it had possessed in June 1971. Nevertheless, due to realignment time lags and resurgent inflation in the United States, its trade deficit climbed to almost $7 billion in 1972. It was not until 1973 that the benefits of the devaluation began to show up in healthier balances, although this improvement was overwhelmed later that year by the dramatic revolution that OPEC engineered in the price of petroleum.[109]

Meanwhile, it is of immediate relevance to our study that all through this time of troubles Americans were becoming more interested in improving the economic situation by means of direct trade with the Communist world. At this point, the Western strategic embargo of Eastern Europe, Russia, and China had been in place for over two decades, having come into existence after passage of the U.S. Export Control Act of 1949 and the creation of a Coordinating Committee (CoCom) within NATO.[110] In the late 1950s CoCom restrictions were simplified, but it was not until after the Cuban crisis of 1962 that there was any relaxation in the rules, first with President Kennedy's $140 million wheat sale to the Soviet Union and then with the decontrolling of trade between non-Communist nations and independent-minded Romania. Subsequently, the Vietnam War intervened, and Congress actually raised the barriers to East-West commerce; but following American disillusionment with the war and the economic slowdown, attitudes shifted again, propelled in large part by official worries about the balance of payments and business and labor concern that America's allies were gaining an insurmountable lead in trading with the East.[111] Congressional hearings in 1968–69 made it clear that this was indeed the case—that the American share of CoCom exports to Communist nations had shrunk to below 5 percent—and this information helped to spur the passage of the Export Administration Act of 1969, subjecting export controls to executive discretion.[112] President Nixon was thus given much more power to deal with this issue than any of his predecessors.

Many people in the Nixon administration were eager to take advantage of this opportunity. Even before the passage of the revised law—as early as April 1969—Secretary of Commerce Maurice Stans recommended to the president that more East-West trade be encouraged.[113] As Henry Kissinger remembers it, "The Commerce Department's view was . . . interesting because it reflected the surprising attitude of much of the American business community. Business leaders are, of course, vocally anti-Communist. . . . But when it comes to trade their attitude changes."[114] Indeed, during the next months commerce and state departments returned to the charge again and again.[115] In November 1970, for example, in a meeting with the president, Secretary Stans strongly urged "a relaxation of the limitations on trade with Eastern Europe." Stans believed that "the USSR wanted to buy $12 billion worth of goods" and that American industry was unnecessarily "missing those markets."[116]

Nixon and Kissinger were not easily persuaded to expand trade without a "political quid pro quo." The president had, in the first weeks, offered Soviet Ambassador Anatoly Dobrynin increased trade but only in return for "help on Vietnam," and when that assistance was not forthcoming, Nixon refused to approve any sales to Russia at all. It was only with difficulty that Kissinger, who in general agreed with Nixon's position on these matters, was able to convince him in May 1969 that the U.S. list of restricted exports should be brought into line with the somewhat more liberal CoCom list. The president was more relenting with regard to trade with China and later Romania but, again, only because this policy fit with his political strategy.[117]

Nevertheless, with each passing year the economic forces pushing the

Soviet Union and the United States toward policies of cooperation would become stronger. Interestingly enough, the pressures on both sides were rooted primarily in problems having to do with falling rates of growth in productivity (hence declining relative efficiency). Staggering under the costs of the Cold War, the United States needed new markets to absorb the goods that its more and more efficient competitors were driving out of markets (foreign and domestic) that American industry traditionally dominated. The Soviet Union, on the other hand, needed to import foreign technology to meet increasing demands on its productive capacities and to remain competitive with the West in a strategic sense. Among the many ironies of the situation, perhaps the greatest was that the Russians were now turning for technological assistance to a nation that was no longer on the cutting edge of technological innovation, though certainly this was more true in the realm of consumer goods than in the field of military technology.

3

NEW MILITARY PARITY AND
THE DECLINE OF BIPOLARITY

At the end of the 1960s, an unusual juxtaposition of achievements and needs with regard to the armaments of both sides in the Cold War contributed an added impetus to the developing U.S.-U.S.S.R. détente. The period of the Vietnam War had finally seen the Soviet Union equal the United States in the number and power of strategic weapons, accomplishing this after a six-year crash program of missile building and more than twenty-five years of strenuous military effort during which the U.S.S.R., largely for defensive reasons, had maintained larger conventional forces than its antagonists. Yet even with strategic parity at hand, Soviet leaders were concerned that America might respond to the new situation (as it had eight years before, at the time of the alleged missile gap) with a surge of military productivity that the Soviet Union would find hard to match. The United States had already demonstrated that it possessed the industrial capabilities to create and preserve an impressive military dominance. On the other hand, with the public embittered by the Vietnam War and questioning the wisdom of pouring its treasure into a never-ending arms race, the American leadership had grave doubts that the nation was physically able to regain strategic superiority or even to support an ambitious military program. Thus, the governments of both superpowers were being driven to find a way to escape high military spending.

World War II had left little doubt which of the two nations was militarily the most powerful of the victorious alliance. The United States had not only vastly outproduced all of the belligerents during the war (manufacturing more weapons than the Soviet Union and Great Britain combined) but by the end of the conflict had almost as many men under arms as the Russians (more than 12 million), had the world's largest navy and air force, and had the atomic bomb.[1] Though American forces pulled out of Europe rapidly after Germany's surrender (many being transferred to the

Pacific) and though demobilization was relatively quick and comprehensive (3.03 million remaining in the armed services on June 30, 1946, and 1.6 million a year later), there was little question that, given time, the United States could match or overwhelm almost any military power brought against it. In the interim, if its armies at home and abroad (in Germany and Japan) were modest in size, it could protect itself with its air arm and atomic weapons, threatening the homeland of any foe with immediate and devastating destruction.[2]

In the face of such American power, while ostensibly minimizing the significance of the nuclear factor, Stalin chose to respond primarily in two ways: by doing everything possible behind the scenes to speed the development of the Soviet bomb and by providing a counterweight to American weaponry with disproportionately large Soviet ground forces in Russia and Eastern Europe. The Soviet nuclear program, we now know, had been under way since 1942, and progress had been so rapid that by November 1947 Foreign Minister V. M. Molotov could announce to the world that the U.S.S.R. "possessed the secret of the atomic weapon."[3] Nevertheless, the Soviet government maintained its postwar military establishment at a strength of 3–4 million men and stationed close to thirty divisions, or about 600,000 troops, in Eastern Europe, the majority in occupied Germany.[4]

There were, of course, a number of reasons from Moscow's perspective why it made sense to do this. The most important was that the presence of a sizable Soviet army on the border of Western Europe provided the U.S.S.R. with a counterthreat to any American effort to practice nuclear intimidation. In addition, powerful forward forces not only constituted a continuing influence in Western European politics (where Communist parties were maneuvering for advantage) but also facilitated the political transformation of Eastern Europe and prevented defections. Finally, after 1949, these Soviet military units helped build and train the national armed forces of the satellite countries, which Moscow had decided to establish and which, by the mid-1950s, would number over 1.5 million men.[5]

As the Cold War heated up, and particularly after the Soviet Union exploded its first atomic bomb in August 1949, both sides in the struggle strove to expand their military capabilities. For Americans this endeavor was particularly vigorous during 1950–53, driven by the new logic of deterrence (the bomb no longer deterred an invasion now that the Russians could retaliate) and by the nation's involvement in the Korean War. In these years the United States more than doubled its armed forces (from 1.5 million to 3.5 million) and quintupled its combat strength (from one to five divisions) in Western Europe, where NATO was being established and where many thought a Soviet attack was imminent. The same period witnessed an increase in the American defense budget from $13 billion to $44 billion annually, the development and testing of a thermonuclear (hydrogen) bomb, and the growth of the Strategic Air Command (SAC) to more than 500 bombers (B-47s) capable of reaching the U.S.S.R. from overseas bases.[6] According to NSC 68, an analysis and definition of American security policy adopted by the Truman administration in 1950, the United States needed to be capable of wielding appropriate military force whenever and wherever Western interests were threatened.[7]

In the meantime, the Soviet Union continued to improve its general military posture (even though theater warfare in Eurasia still took precedence over intercontinental considerations). If we can believe Nikita Khrushchev's retrospective statistics, the Soviet army and navy grew gradually, "under Western provocation," until by 1955 they totaled over 5.7 million men.[8] Russian forces in Eastern Europe were apparently not increased in number, but they were reinforced by Eastern European national armies and coordinated with them after 1955 in the organization of the Warsaw Pact.[9] Beginning with the Korean War, serious attempts were made to modernize the equipment and structure of Soviet forces by motorizing their transport, strengthening their armored elements, and increasing the number of surface ships and submarines. As for atomic weapons, though a thermonuclear device was exploded in 1953 and attention was devoted to the development of heavy bomber aircraft (such as the Bison and the Bear), the principal effort in the early 1950s went into building medium-range bombers—that is, planes capable of nuclear delivery—around the periphery of the Soviet Union.[10]

When the Eisenhower administration took office in 1953, the nuclear stalemate had not yet emerged with sufficient clarity to render the usefulness of atomic weapons suspect. Faced with the political need after the Korean War to reduce military spending, the president and his advisers chose to place an increased reliance on nuclear response. This meant that, while American strategic forces (which by 1955 included about 1300 aircraft capable of reaching Russia) continued to supply a long-range deterrent, American ground forces (like those in Europe) were provided with tactical nuclear weapons that radically enlarged their firepower. It also meant that, as a means of deterring aggression, the United States held out the possibility that it might respond "massively," even to relatively limited Communist actions.[11]

Such a retaliation, to be sure, never occurred, but the prospect was real enough that, together with the end of active fighting, it allowed the Eisenhower administration to reduce the size of the military establishment from 3.5 to 2.4 million men during the 1950s.[12] The savings, however, were never as substantial as had been expected, largely because advances in the Soviet Union's nuclear capabilities soon threatened to undermine the credibility of massive retaliation.[13] One result was the administration's decision in 1954 to strengthen continental defense by means of a distant early warning (DEW) line and a semiautomatic ground-environment (SAGE) control system.[14] Another repercussion was Eisenhower's reluctant agreement in the summer of 1955 to a major expansion in the production of the new B-52 bomber.[15] A third result was the president's commitment, late in 1955, to an intensified program of missile development, a program that was growing rapidly by August 1957, when Moscow announced that the Soviet Union had conducted the first successful test of an intercontinental ballistic missile (ICBM).[16]

These were eventful and complicated years for military planners in the Soviet Union. By the time Khrushchev came to power in the mid-fifties, the U.S.S.R. could have embarked on an all-out endeavor to overtake the United States in strategic bombers. But apparently because he believed that missiles offered a better way to overcome the American advantage, Khrushchev opted for a less ambitious effort at bomber building, roughly one-third the size of the U.S. B-52 program.[17] The fascinating thing, however, is that Khrushchev subsequently made the same kind of decision with regard to strategic missile forces, which (Americans were later astonished to discover) from the time of the first test launching through mid-1961 were permitted to grow only modestly. In this case, technical difficulties may have been important, but it is hard to escape the impression that economic pressure was the decisive factor, perhaps reinforced by the long-standing Russian habit of holding Europe hostage.[18] (Moscow did continue to build substantial numbers of medium-range bombers and intermediate-range ballistic missiles during this period.) It would seem that Khrushchev was confident enough of essential deterrence (and American intentions) that, for the sake of other ends, he was willing to accept a position of strategic inferiority and to gamble on U.S. uncertainty about how strong Russia was (hence his "missile rattling").[19]

This interpretation is buttressed by what we know of Khrushchev's actions with regard to Soviet conventional forces, particularly after 1960, when he found himself engaged in a running battle with his military advisers over his attempts (vaguely reminiscent of Eisenhower's earlier efforts in the United States) to pare down and reorganize the military establishment in accord with the technology of the nuclear age. Khrushchev was jumping the gun, of course; he was trying to emphasize strategic retaliatory power in a context of superpower inequality. This fact may explain why his struggle with the army ended in compromise. Nonetheless, from 1955 to 1964 he was able to cut back the overall strength of the armed forces by approximately one-half—from 5.7 million to roughly 3 million men. After 1960 Khrushchev was also able to "nuclearize" the army's theater (general purpose) forces, assigning tactical nuclear weapons down to the division level and streamlining the units for fast-moving operations under nuclear conditions. Warsaw Pact forces were reequipped and modernized as well; they were furnished with missile delivery systems although not with nuclear warheads.[20] The Soviet air defense system had been reorganized earlier; surface-to-air missiles were installed to protect cities from air attack, and major research was undertaken on the development of antiballistic missile systems.[21] The navy underwent a number of changes, including expansion of destroyer and submarine fleets (now supplemented with nuclear-powered craft) and improvement of antisubmarine (ASW) capabilities.[22]

The technological transformation of Soviet military power was to have a number of ironic consequences, but perhaps the most stunning lay in its impact on the thinking and plans of the incoming Kennedy administration. Concerned by what they saw as the enfeeblement of America's deterrent powers in general, President Kennedy and Secretary of Defense Robert McNamara agreed that they must establish an advantage for the United States in the strategic arms race (thereby closing any "missile gap") while at the same time providing it with enlarged nonnuclear capacities. They would thus create a variety of potential responses to crises, making it possible not only to maintain strategic stability but also to conventionally deter actions that were not serious enough for nuclear obliteration. In addition, they were persuaded that reliable nonnuclear forces, by allowing nations to avoid the use of tactical atomic weapons, would reduce the risk that nuclear war would happen inadvertently, through escalation. In a world balanced by terror, a doctrine of flexible response was seen as both more effective and safer.[23]

In implementing these ideas, the Kennedy administration, and especially the influential McNamara, made decisions that seriously affected the quality of the country's defense and the character of the arms race. By calling for a sharp expansion of the new Polaris and Minuteman missile programs and a cutback in building more costly and vulnerable weapons (e.g., the B-47 and the large-payload Atlas and Titan ICBMs), the Kennedy leadership in effect determined that for the next two decades U.S. strategic forces would be primarily composed of small-payload missiles deployed aboard submarines or in hardened silos. Moreover, although these policies were formulated while the new administration was still unaware how great the U.S. strategic superiority was, it is understandable that, combined with decisions to put the Strategic Air Command on increased alert and to improve early warning and command and control systems, they engendered considerable anxiety in the Kremlin.[24]

This must have been especially the case in January 1962, when the administration submitted a budget to Congress that funded 800 Minuteman missiles within the next fiscal year in addition to continuing the Polaris program and completing modest changes involving the Atlas and Titan. Indeed, the following two years were to witness budgets that brought the authorized strength of American strategic forces to 1,000 Minutemen, 54 Titan IIs, 41 Polaris submarines, and 600 B-52 bombers. The rationale for this immense arsenal was obscure; originally, McNamara's preference for "counterforce," or "no cities" targeting, had justified the numbers, but by 1963 he was talking about "mutual assured destruction," that is, precluding a first strike by leaving cities on both sides unprotected from a second strike. There could be no doubt that, as far as strategic forces were concerned, the United States was sprinting to a position of real superiority.[25]

While this was going on, Kennedy and McNamara also improved U.S. conventional military capabilities. Inspired by the idea of flexible response and prompted by Khrushchev's support for "wars of liberation" and his actions in the Berlin crisis of 1961, the administration requested and obtained funds to increase and diversify the armed forces, acquire non-nuclear equipment for combat arms, and expand airlift and sealift capacities.[26] In consequence, the number of combat-ready army divisions was increased from eleven to sixteen and total military manpower by more than 200,000 (42,000 of whom were assigned to units in Europe). Army and marine divisions were reorganized so that tactical nuclear weapons were no longer assumed to be a normal part of ordnance. Seventy vessels were added to the active naval fleet and a dozen wings to the air force. By means of these and other changes the administration was able to achieve the strength necessary for what it called a "two-and-a-half war" strategy, that is, enough forces to wage, simultaneously and conventionally, a defense of Western Europe, a defense of South Korea or Southeast Asia, and a minor operation elsewhere.[27]

Khrushchev and his government responded to the American buildup (and the exposure of their own country's weakness) in a number of ways. The most obvious reaction was their decision, in the fall of 1962, to counter U.S. strategic power by placing intermediate-range ballistic missiles (SS-4s) in Cuba. This was a gamble, of course, but it must have seemed reasonable to Khrushchev at the time, first, because the same missiles had long been deployed against Western Europe and, second, because the missiles did not threaten the United States in any way different from the way U.S. missiles in Turkey and elsewhere threatened the Soviet Union. Furthermore, Khrushchev's intention was almost certainly to create a bargaining device that he could later use (perhaps after the Russian ICBM program was further advanced) to obtain either a favorable settlement of the Berlin problem or the withdrawal of American missiles and bombers from their so-called forward bases in Europe.[28]

The Kennedy administration proved extraordinarily sensitive to (and willing to risk war to prevent) any explicit Soviet intrusion into the Western Hemisphere, and since American strategic power was preponderant, Washington was able to compel the Russians to back down.[29] Nonetheless, the humiliation of the Cuban missile crisis for Khrushchev and his colleagues was so severe that it left them with but one real alternative if they wished to avoid being dealt with similarly in the future: to build an intercontinental ballistic missile force as strong as that of the United States.[30]

This, then, was exactly what they proceeded to do. Working at a vigorous pace, especially after Brezhnev and Kosygin came to power in November 1964, the U.S.S.R. increased its strategic forces by almost 300 new missiles (SS-9s and SS-11s) a year, reaching a total slightly larger than that of the United States (i.e., 1,060 missiles) in September 1969. Though the intensity of this buildup might have been somewhat less had Khrushchev remained in power, according to careful estimates, the original production decisions were made by the Presidium before Khrushchev was overthrown.[31]

While the expansion of its ICBM arsenal was clearly the most important of the measures taken to strengthen the Soviet strategic position, there were others as well. In 1968, for example, the Russians unveiled a Y-class missile-launching nuclear submarine, comparable to the Polaris in size. They also inaugurated a construction program that promised seven to eight of these submarines annually. The same year, Moscow tested a multiple-warhead ballistic missile (MRV), a predecessor of the MIRV (a launcher with multiple independently targeted warheads) that the Soviet Union would develop later and that, in its American form, the United States was already testing. As early as 1966 the Soviet leadership made the decision to begin construction of an ABM defense—deploying the Galosh missile in the vicinity of Moscow and a second system (Talinn) in northwestern Russia. Though Soviet ABM technology was reported to be relatively primitive, the Galosh system was at least partly operational by 1969.[32]

In the same period, perhaps largely out of concern with American intervention in Vietnam, the Soviet regime also strove to increase its ability to project conventional power into distant areas. Airlift capacity was enlarged by the introduction of a new heavy transport and, with it, new air-landing methods and techniques of supply. Airborne operations in Eastern Europe and air resupply activities in the Middle East tested Soviet equipment and led to important modifications in its design. On the naval side, though emphasis continued to be placed on expanding the Soviet submarine fleet, there was a noteworthy increase in cruiser and destroyer construction as well as a steady growth of merchant tonnage (Russia's carrying fleet by 1969 was among the five largest in the world). Helicopter carriers were added to the navy, and tank and troop landing ships made their appearance when the Soviet fleet established a permanent presence in the Mediterranean at the time of the 1967 Arab-Israeli war. Soviet sea power was venturing farther afield, becoming a significant instrument for the support of national interests in every part of the globe.[33]

America, in the meantime, had become completely preoccupied with its effort to save South Vietnam from Communist revolution. In the process, and perhaps partly as a result of the irrelevance of additional missiles to the problem at hand, American strategic doctrine and power were substantially modified. By 1963, as I have noted, Secretary of Defense McNamara had reached a theoretical position roughly midway between simple deterrence (requiring the force necessary to retaliate) and all-out superiority (requiring the force necessary to destroy the enemy's weapons before they could be fired). Within a few months, however, his concern about the human costs involved led him to give priority to deterrence—or in the vocabulary of the time, the capability to inflict "assured destruction." This was defined, in retaliating against Russia, as the potential to incapacitate 25–30 percent of the population and two-thirds of the industrial areas, and in responding to China, as the ability to destroy at least fifty urban centers.[34]

Assured destruction was directly dependent on the power, accuracy, and survivability of American weapons as well as the effectiveness of Russian defenses, but deterrence clearly did not demand the quantities of weaponry needed to achieve superiority. Indeed, McNamara's commitment to deterrence plus the fact that in the mid-sixties Soviet weapons and defenses were still of problematic quality (and quantity) allowed the Johnson administration to shift considerable resources from strategic programs to what were seen as more pressing needs (e.g., financing the war in Vietnam). Thus, although the overall defense budget rose from $50.9 billion in 1964 to $66.1 billion in 1966 and $75.2 billion in 1968, the strategic weapons budget declined from $9.2 billion to $7.8 billion over the same period, and the number of land-based missiles was held steady (after 1965) at 1,054.[35] Moreover, when pressure began to mount after 1967 for an increase in the number of Minuteman missiles and for deployment of an ABM, McNamara held firm on both counts by arguing that American weapons were still sufficient for deterrence (and for some damage limitation too) and could be rendered even more effective by certain qualitative changes, such as MIRVing.[36]

These were the very years, of course, in which the United States, despite a growing antiwar movement at home, was sending greater and greater numbers of military forces to fight in Vietnam. Interestingly, though the Kennedy and Johnson administrations improved the mobility of the army and its reserves considerably (and created the possibility of a genuinely flexible response), President Johnson, when actually confronted with a limited war, was so fearful of popular reaction that he chose to rely on the draft, not the reserves, to augment the armed forces (which climbed from 2.65 million in 1965 to 3.58 million in 1968).[37] As a result, not only were many army divisions in Europe and the United States stripped of experienced personnel to provide support for the new units, but an essentially draftee army was created in Southeast Asia, where a difficult and interminable war rendered it increasingly vulnerable to problems of morale.[38] As the numbers of Americans in Vietnam rose from 33,500 in 1965 to more than 550,000 by mid-1968, and as American casualties soared from 2,500 to 130,000 in the same period, neither the experience gained nor the equipment tested could obscure the fact that the enterprise was both costly and unsuccessful.[39]

As the 1960s ended, then, there was understandable concern in both Moscow and Washington about the military factor and its relation to foreign policy. For Soviet leaders, having finally achieved a rough parity with the United States in strategic weapons, the obvious worry was whether they could stay even, especially if the Americans now turned to high-technology programs like MIRV and ABM. The U.S.S.R. had almost caught up with the United States in basic strategic power at the time of the original breakthrough to missile technology, but it had subsequently fallen considerably behind. Would this happen again?

For American officials, anxiety grew out of the fact that the war in Vietnam had been debilitating and confusing. Part of their concern derived from a new uncertainty about the practicality of flexible response and the realism of U.S. military involvement in the revolutions of the Third World. But a second element of concern arose from their surprise at what had happened to the American strategic advantage in the course of the war. It was as if the United States had glanced away from its primary foe to deal with Southeast Asia and, when it looked back, found that the Russians had stolen a march. Could it regain its superiority? Or would it now have to struggle simply to stay abreast of its antagonist?

The latter was the question that Secretary McNamara sensed had become the more appropriate. It was largely to escape the waste, frustration, and danger of an endless arms race that McNamara persuaded President Johnson at the end of 1966 to propose that representatives of the two superpowers meet to discuss "means of limiting the arms race in offensive and defensive nuclear missiles."[40] Only after the Soviet government, having agreed in principle to strategic arms limitation talks (SALT), refused repeatedly to set a date did McNamara and Johnson decide (in September 1967) to recommend to Congress the deployment of a light ABM system (Sentinel) and to proceed with the testing of MIRV.[41] Even then, however, McNamara, in order not to challenge the Russians directly, insisted on describing Sentinel as a system to protect the nation from a "Chinese" attack.[42] He also continued to use the existence of MIRV technology as an argument not to increase the numbers of launchers in the basic ICBM force.[43] From his point of view, it was clearly time to begin arms control negotiations.

I have noted the extent to which the conflict in Vietnam was having a destructive effect upon the consensus in the United States that had supported and driven the U.S. side of the Cold War. Yet other, less traumatic, and even constructive developments in international affairs were also altering the capacities and calculations of the leading nations. If these changes were not identical for the two sides (either in cause or in effect), they were nonetheless similar in many ways and to an extent mutually reinforcing. The simple, bipolar world of the classic Cold War was coming to an end, and as power became more dispersed among nations, the alliance systems of the capitalist and Communist blocs were being seriously weakened. There was a real possibility of opposition from or defection by an ally and of interference by an enemy within one's own sphere of influence.

What were the factors, the processes, that played a role in this growth of multipolarity—or polycentrism, as it was often called at the time?[44] The most important and obvious, surely, was the recovery of political and economic strength by formerly powerful nations that had been ravaged and disoriented in World War II. By the late 1950s Western Europe and Japan were surpassing prewar production totals and venturing with increasing success into international trade. The European Common Market had been organized, West Germany had been integrated into NATO, and the Fifth Republic had been established in France, enabling that country finally to put its colonial wars behind it. In Asia the Chinese Communist regime had been able to stabilize its vast nation to a surprising extent. Thus large areas of the world were regaining the vigor that civil and international conflict had cost them. As a result, the superpowers lost a measure of the political and economic dominance that they, and especially the United States, had enjoyed immediately after 1945.[45]

A second and related aspect of the apparent dispersal of power was the differential rate of development among the nations with large economies. This became clearer as the 1960s progressed and as first Germany and then Japan improved their technological and industrial position relative to the United States and to the place in the international economy they held before the war. (China also was strengthening its position vis-à-vis the Soviet Union, although the accomplishment was obscured after 1965 by the confusion of Mao's Cultural Revolution.) The change occurred more rapidly than might have been expected because America now began to experience a slowdown in its productivity growth rate as well as the effects of increasingly adverse balances of trade and payments. Clearly, both Russia and America were suffering direct economic disadvantages as a result of carrying a relatively larger proportion of the costs of the arms race than many of their allies.[46]

Meanwhile, the development of intercontinental weapons systems during the 1960s was allowing the superpowers to wage or deter war independently of these same allies. For Russia and America, the value of allies began to decrease and their cost to rise; for the allies, doubts began to grow regarding the wisdom of the nuclear giants and regarding their loyalty in the event that one of their allies should be attacked. Such anxieties were at the root of the British desire to remain a nuclear power and, later, of the French and Chinese decisions to acquire nuclear weaponry. Nuclear autonomy weakened these nations' ties to the superpowers and sometimes put them in direct opposition to their nonproliferation policies.[47]

As time went on, as the opposing economic systems continued to coexist, and as evidence of new moderation began to appear (especially in post-Stalinist Russia), a certain ideological erosion took place on both sides of the Iron Curtain. The Manichean (black or white) images of the Cold War faded considerably, and the group cohesion they provided faded as well. In the process, both liberal and Communist ideologies were heavily impacted by skepticism and national particularism, not only within the developed world of East and West but also among the many new states of the previous colonial world. Nationalism seemed well on its way to becoming the most vigorous and powerful emotional force on the contemporary scene.[48]

All of these factors—and others more unique (like the Vietnam War)—helped to create a situation in which certain allied nations chafed at the constraints of the military-political systems of which they were a part. On the Western side, the country most uncomfortable and most willing to experiment with new relations was France, and particularly during the presidency of Charles de Gaulle (1958–69), there was frequent tension between Paris and Washington regarding policies toward the East. In the late 1960s, West Germany also began to explore new approaches, and American statesmen watched with some concern as the Kurt Kiesinger and Willy Brandt governments pursued an accommodating form of *Ostpolitik* with Russia and East Germany.

In the Communist world there were analogous strivings for independence, especially in the wake of de-Stalinization; first Hungary, then China, discovered itself at odds with the policies of the dominant power. Hungary was crushed in 1956 for attempting to withdraw from the Warsaw Pact, but China continued to voice its displeasure with Soviet behavior throughout the 1960s, ostensibly because Moscow had become too conservative and cautious in its foreign policy. By mid-decade other Communist nations were being fortified by the Sino-Soviet dispute and began groping their way toward greater self-determination. Albania broke with the U.S.S.R. completely, Poland and Hungary were involved with major economic innovations, and Romania embarked on a variety of direct connections with the West. When China and Russia clashed in military encounters along their mutual border during 1969, even American observers were ready to concede that the Communist bloc had lost its monolithic character.

Although France's independent foreign policy is primarily and understandably associated with the era of de Gaulle, the roots of French discontent with the Atlantic alliance go back to the Fourth Republic. The leaders of that regime were deeply chagrined, for example, that despite their NATO connection neither their war effort in Indochina nor their struggle in Algeria received the whole-hearted support of the Truman and Eisenhower administrations. Indeed, American opposition to the Franco-British intervention at Suez in 1956 (which for France was largely prompted by Egypt's support of the Algerian rebels) was a clear signal that Paris could not count on its opinions being received sympathetically in Washington. The anger that resulted showed up in a number of ways, most notably in the decision of the last pre-Gaullist government to schedule the testing of a French atomic bomb.[49]

When Charles de Gaulle came to power in April 1958, he brought a more potent dimension to French foreign policy. This derived in part from the fact that, as a result of the situation in which his recall to office had occurred, he had been able to rewrite the constitution and to centralize unprecedented authority in the presidency. It was also a function of his extraordinary personality, a charismatic blend of energy, ego, aspiration, and conservatism. This combination of power and vision allowed him to play a central role in Western diplomacy throughout his tenure and, in the process, to make a unique contribution to the coming of East-West détente. It also allowed him to respond to the emotional needs of the French people, who at this point (in an interesting preview of the American experience somewhat later) were exhausted and emotionally depressed after a full decade of unsuccessful colonial war.[50]

In terms of foreign policy, the eleven years of de Gaulle's presidency fall into four relatively distinct periods, each initiated by a major strategic turn on the part of the French leader. The first phase, from 1958 through 1961, was introduced and characterized by the new president's memorandum to the American and British governments proposing the transformation of the Atlantic alliance into a three-power oligarchy, an arrangement he deemed in keeping with France's international rank and interests.[51] Though de Gaulle may have anticipated the negative responses he quickly received to this suggestion, he continued to press for its acceptance, not allowing it to drop until John Kennedy showed as little interest in it as Eisenhower had. In the meantime, de Gaulle pursued, with impressive success, the settlement of the Algerian war, the internal stabilization of France, and the construction of a modern armed force equipped with nuclear weapons.[52]

By 1962 the French president was ready to offer a new alternative to the Atlanticism of the Kennedy administration (which Gaullists saw largely as a cover for American domination), entering upon a period in which he argued and worked for a "European" Europe independent of the United States. Having been turned back in earlier efforts to deprive the Common Market of its supranational, integrationist character, he now attempted to use a bilaterial understanding with Konrad Adenauer of West Germany both as a model for European confederation and the nucleus of a European security system separate from NATO. Simultaneously, he acted to block Britain's entry into the Common Market, ostensibly because he feared that London was too closely tied to Washington to be a genuine European partner. If continental Europe could organize itself effectively, de Gaulle believed, it could utilize its growing economic strength to challenge the hegemony of the superpowers and increase the chances for a genuine East-West settlement in both that region and the world.[53]

West Germany under Ludwig Erhard, however, was not prepared to forgo its ties with the United States, and as a result de Gaulle, after 1964, took a different approach. This involved, on the one hand, the withdrawal of France into military isolation and, on the other, direct French dealings with the Communist powers on behalf of a less bipolar world. Irritated by the unilateralism he saw manifested in Kennedy's doctrine of flexible response as well as in American behavior in the Cuban missile crisis and test ban negotiations, and irritated too by what he viewed as unnecessary American intervention in Vietnam, the French leader was not about to be constrained by the caution of his fellow Europeans. Thus he attempted to establish an independent, balancing role for France by distancing himself from NATO and offering Moscow his mediation in improving Soviet relations with China and Europe.

The opening move on the latter front came in January 1964, when de Gaulle extended French diplomatic recognition to Communist China. Shortly thereafter, France and Russia initiated a lengthy series of reciprocal visits involving high government officials. In the meantime, Paris was edging toward a break with NATO, withdrawing military units from the alliance's exercises on several occasions in 1963, 1964, and 1965. The decisive moment came in February and March 1966, when de Gaulle announced that all French forces would be withdrawn from NATO commands and that NATO would be asked to remove its headquarters and bases from France. This followed by eight months his decision to boycott the institutions of the European Economic Community until other member states agreed not to implement a decision that allowed majority (instead of unanimous) voting within the Council of Ministers.[54]

Such manifestations of independence helped prepare the way for the most successful phase of de Gaulle's collaboration with the Russians, which began with his state visit to the Soviet Union in June 1966. This journey was unusually extensive, involving the French leader in a tour beyond the Urals, substantial contact with the public, and even an inspection of a Russian missile site. Though the political results were less impressive (with little achieved on either German unification or arms control), a number of agreements were initialed providing for technical and economic cooperation and for a communications link and regular meetings between the two governments. Moreover, Franco-Soviet relations continued to be close and cordial for almost a year. In December 1966 Premier Alexei Kosygin visited France for ten days; in April 1967 the two countries signed a statement regulating maritime commerce; and in June they lined up together (and apart from the rest of Europe and the United States) on the Arab side during the Israeli-Arab Six-Day War. Meanwhile, having obtained Russia's approval for direct approaches to its Eastern European allies, France proceeded to work out trade accords with every state in that region except East Germany.[55]

Yet by mid-1967 the Franco-Soviet rapprochement had started to lose its thrust, as a new government in Bonn and the Johnson administration in Washington began to experiment with their own policies toward the Communist world. West Germany and the United States had more to offer the Soviet Union than France did in terms of technology, commerce, arms

control, and diplomatic acceptance, and as their leaders bestirred themselves to achieve better relations with Eastern Europe and (in the case of
the Americans) a nuclear nonproliferation treaty, they began to push de
Gaulle from the center of the East-West stage.

Moreover, in the spring and summer of 1968 de Gaulle's position and
strategy were badly shaken by two unexpected developments. The first
was the rioting, strikes, and student protests in May, which not only
weakened the French economy (and led to significant cuts in the defense
budget) but also undermined the Gaullist regime's international standing
and the plausibility of its claim to be the spokesperson for Europe.[56] The
second development was the invasion of Czechoslovakia in August by
Warsaw Pact forces, which raised grave doubts throughout the West regarding the ability of the Soviet leadership to tolerate any dissent or independence in Eastern Europe.[57] Indeed, this double shock led to a certain
disillusionment, on the part of de Gaulle, with activism—a change reflected in his decision to return France to a limited involvement with both
the EEC and NATO. By the opening months of the Nixon administration
(and the last months of de Gaulle's own tenure), the French president
became receptive to Britain entering the Common Market, and the French
army's chief of staff publicly recommended the coordination of French and
NATO nuclear strategies. By 1969, then, the period of détente and special
intimacy in Franco-Soviet relations appeared to be nearing its end.[58]

Nonetheless, what de Gaulle had accomplished with the Soviet Union
was proving to be a powerful inspiration to the West German government
and public in defining their attitudes toward the East. Having moved more
slowly than the French during the 1960s in the development of a new
Ostpolitik, the West Germans by mid-decade had begun to sense how
much potential for constructive change was implicit in the French president's approach. As a result, first with the Ludwig Erhard government,
then with the Grand Coalition under Kurt Kiesinger, and finally with the
chancellorship of Willy Brandt, they displayed a greater and greater willingness to accept and deal with the realities of the Communist world—and
to do this with some independence. Though the Soviet Union proved at
first to be remarkably uncooperative (apparently suspecting a plot on the
part of Bonn to isolate East Germany), Moscow's difficulties with Czechoslovakia and China during 1968–69 ultimately worked a minor revolution in Russian attitudes toward the Federal Republic. Within months
after Brandt's accession to power in October 1969, the Brezhnev regime
was pressing to take advantage of the new opportunities for agreement.

Ludwig Erhard, of course, had not become head of government in
1963 with the intention of pursuing spectacular initiatives toward the
East. The most obviously pro-American of all the post–World War II West

German chancellors ("I love President Johnson," he said, "and he loves me"), he found himself not only out of sympathy with the earlier Adenauer-de Gaulle collaboration but also unhappy with de Gaulle's opposition to British entrance into the Common Market and the establishment of a multilateral force (MLF).[59] Still, with France and Britain manifesting increasing interest in trade and exchange of visits with Communist states, Erhard felt compelled to embark upon trade diplomacy as well, though it was suitably limited by the stipulation of the Hallstein Doctrine that there could be no formal recognition of a state that recognized East Germany. In 1963 and 1964 his government exchanged commercial missions with all Eastern European countries except Czechoslovakia. In March 1966 Erhard enlarged his activity with a proposal to Eastern European states that they join West Germany in renouncing the use of force in the settlement of international disputes. Such a suggestion signaled a considerable shift in Erhard's thinking, though it was far from enough to save either his government or the alliance between the Free Democrats and the Christian Democrats from collapse the following autumn, in the face of mounting public dissatisfaction with his management of the economy.[60]

The foreign policy of the Grand Coalition (Christian Democrats and Social Democrats) that brought Kurt Kiesinger to the chancellorship and Willy Brandt to the foreign ministry in December 1966 was clear evidence that West Germany's two major political parties had begun a serious reevaluation of the country's international position. The new government adopted two attitudes not seen before in Bonn: first, a willingness to approach Eastern European nations with the intent of achieving a thorough normalization of relations and, second, the determination to conduct any such approaches within the general framework of a Western search for détente.[61] The Kiesinger-Brandt partnership began to weave together a style and themes from several sources: (1) long-standing Social Democratic demands for an opening to the East, (2) Kiesinger's record as a good European and an effective conciliator, (3) the precedents and objectives established by de Gaulle, and (4) President Johnson's suggestion that it was time for "bridge building" with the East. West Germans were responding to Washington's and Paris's urgings to become active in their own cause.[62]

Progress, however, was difficult to achieve. Eager as the Kiesinger-Brandt government was for international change, it was handicapped in establishing relations with Eastern Europe by its insistence on the need for German reunification and therefore on the provisional quality of East Germany (the German Democratic Republic, or GDR). These stipulations imposed no special strain on such maverick Communist states as Romania and Yugoslavia, with which diplomatic relations were initiated in January and December 1967, but they did enable East Germany and the Soviet Union to mobilize the remaining nations of the Warsaw Pact (Poland, Hungary, Czechoslovakia, and Bulgaria) in opposition to further diplomatic normalization.[63]

The Russians, meanwhile, having initially responded with some interest to Brandt's overtures on behalf of a renunciation-of-force agreement, turned a colder and colder shoulder toward the Bonn government during 1967 and 1968.[64] In explaining the sources of this reserve, Brandt later recognized

> the probability . . . that Moscow was swayed by regard for the GDR leaders. [Walter] Ulbricht and his team, with their national hostility to the Social Democrats and particular prejudice against the Grand Coalition, lived in dread of being isolated by our Eastern policy. They not only undertook political action and agitation against us . . . but evolved their [own] counterpart of the Hallstein Doctrine.[65]

Unfortunately, he concluded, West Germans "underestimated the influence of the GDR when we persisted in refusing to treat it as a country of equal standing." As a result, aside from the new diplomatic openings to Romania and Yugoslavia, the Kiesinger-Brandt *Ostpolitik* produced little but a few economic contacts with Czechoslovakia and Poland, and it led to a frustrating rejection by East Berlin of Bonn's proposals for humanitarian, economic, and cultural cooperation.[66]

Then, in quick order, following the Soviet invasion of Czechoslovakia in August 1968, the entire situation began to change. Having demonstrated its power to control the rate of decompression in Eastern Europe, Moscow now apparently felt secure enough (and perhaps morally naked enough) in that region to be able to dispense with its West German bogeyman. What is more, the intensification of the Sino-Soviet conflict, and especially the violent border warfare of March 1969, created so much strategic anxiety in the U.S.S.R. that the Soviet leadership became unusually eager to establish positive relations on its European flank.[67] This occurred at a time when de Gaulle was losing much of his allure for the Russians and also when the election of a new and more conservative (and apparently more anti-Communist) president in the United States was casting a problematic light on Soviet-American relations. The net effect was that during the winter, spring, and summer of 1969 the Russians made a number of moves to improve their ties with Bonn, de-escalating a potential Berlin crisis in March, briefing the chancellor and foreign minister on Chinese and Eastern European developments, suggesting a renewal of negotiations on the renunciation of force, and entering into a number of contracts with West German firms.[68]

When the West German election of September 1969 resulted in a majority for (and an alliance between) the Social Democrats and the Free Democrats, ending the Grand Coalition and catapulting the socialist Willy Brandt into the chancellorship, the stage was set for substantial modifications in the diplomatic status quo. Indeed, the new chancellor made it clear in his very first governmental declaration that his *Ostpolitik* would go farther than that of the preceding government to meet the concerns of West Germany's eastern neighbors. Declaring his readiness both to explore a renunciation-of-force agreement with Moscow and, in a major concession, to sign the new Russian-American nuclear nonproliferation treaty, Brandt went on to propose negotiations with both Poland and East Germany, the first to address all outstanding problems (including that of the Oder-Neise boundary), and the second to work out new forms of cooperation. Though he clung to the notion that there could be no de jure recognition of East Germany, Brandt acknowledged the reality of what existed by speaking of "two states in one nation," and he implied that East Berlin's cooperation could eventually help end its isolation vis-à-vis the West.[69] Obviously, Brandt's *Ostpolitik* went far beyond the point of underestimating the East Germans.

In any case, this was enough for the Russians. In the ensuing months, negotiations on the renunciation-of-force agreement proceeded with Andrei Gromyko at a fairly rapid pace, undertaken first by the West German ambassador, then by Brandt's confidante and adviser Egon Bahr, and in the days before the treaty's completion by Foreign Minister Walter Scheel. When the final treaty emerged in August 1970 it was obvious that hardheaded realism had won the day. The two contracting parties pledged "to maintain international peace and [to] achieve détente . . . and in so doing [to] proceed from the actual situation existing in this region."[70] They also announced their acceptance of all present frontiers, qualifying this only with the reservation that a future peace conference could still produce mutually agreeable changes.

Bonn, for its part, expressed a willingness to conclude similar accords with East Germany, Poland, and Czechoslovakia, and to treat East Germany as a second German state within German territory. Moscow, by implication, agreed to pressure East Germany into accepting something less than full diplomatic recognition, making a concession that ultimately required the Russians to arrange for the replacement of the uncompromising Walter Ulbricht as East German leader during the spring of 1971. The Soviet government also acceded to the West German stipulation that the treaty would not be submitted to the Bundestag for ratification until a satisfactory result had been achieved in the four-power negotiations begun in March 1970 on the status of West Berlin.[71]

This stipulation was demanded by the Brandt government as a way to reassure both the West German public, which was anxious that something be done to improve the situation in the former capital, and the Western allies, who were concerned that they have the ultimate say with regard to West German affairs.[72] Still, there is considerable evidence that it did not prevent nervousness—especially in Allied countries—about the West German–Soviet détente. Conservative elder statesmen like Dean Acheson, Lucius Clay, and John J. McCloy were dismayed by what Acheson called an "insane race to Moscow".[73] So too were such contemporary leaders as British Foreign Secretary Michael Steward (who conveyed a strong word of caution to Bonn)[74] and Nixon's national security adviser, Henry Kissinger (from whom Brandt had gained the impression that "he would rather have taken personal charge of the delicate complex of East-West problems in its entirety").[75] To many of the participants in this extended drama, America seemed to have lost much of its control over its most important allies.

It was perhaps fortunate that roughly analogous things were happening in the international relations of the Communist East. There too a process was under way that could be loosely characterized as the breakdown of an earlier unity. The Communist monolith (or Soviet bloc, as it was still commonly called in the United States) had long since ceased to be a historic actuality. The disciplined and coordinated empire that Stalin had built in Eastern Europe (and to an extent in Asia) during 1947–53 had, by the end of the 1960s, given way in several stages to a fragmented and bitterly divided system.

Though Stalin had pursued a comparatively restrained course in the Balkans and Eastern Europe in the first months after the war in Europe ended in 1945, by 1947 he had begun to impose the uniformity that converted the nations of this region into genuine satellites. Existing political parties either were forced to merge with the Communist Party or were outlawed. Popular assemblies declined into impotence, and power was shifted to party committees which in turn were ruthlessly subordinated (often by bloody purges) to the national party leaderships and to Stalin. The Soviet Union became the model for economic change: agriculture was collectivized, industrialization was stepped up, and five-year plans were developed for each country. Finally, joint stock companies were organized that permitted Moscow to exploit local resources and to extract almost $20 billion from the economies of Eastern Europe in the decade following 1945.[76] The system was frighteningly centralized, and only Yugoslavia and China were able to escape its centrifugal force during these years—in both cases because World War II and the ensuing revolutions had given the

Communist leaders in those countries independent sources of political and military power.[77]

The first crack in the unity of the Soviet empire (and an indication of things to come) actually occurred in 1948, long before Stalin's death, when the Yugoslav leader Tito severed his nation's ties with the U.S.S.R. The immediate cause lay in Stalin's attempt to replace Tito with a rival as party secretary, but behind this development lurked Stalin's fear that Tito had become too ambitious and too completely the master of his own house. In any case, though Titoism did not constitute a formal doctrine at the time of the break, by 1950 Yugoslav theorists began to describe Stalin's version of Marxism as "revisionist" and to argue for a much less regimented and autocratic alternative.[78] Thus by its assertion of independence—and more important, by the continuing success in its defection—Yugoslavia under Tito laid the ideological and psychological basis for the later development of polycentrism in the Communist world.

A crucial event in this process, of course, was the demise of Stalin in March 1953. Whatever the beliefs of his political heirs, none of them was capable, or perhaps even desirous, of employing the terror he had used to hold the Soviet bloc together. As a result, the new leadership, under first Malenkov then Khrushchev, was thrown into a variety of adjustments, three of which were particularly powerful stimuli to the development of national Communism: (1) the liberalization of the so-called new course, (2) the rehabilitation of Tito, and (3) de-Stalinization.

The "new course" for Communist economies was introduced as early as August 1953 and was designed to reduce popular unrest in Eastern Europe and the Soviet Union by easing quotas and taxes and by increasing consumer goods production. Inaugurated in East Germany, it was applied differently in each country and with widely varying effectiveness (the programs in Hungary and Poland failed badly), exposing in the process the fallibility of the Communist Party and the need for further recognition of national differences.[79]

Tito's return to respectability occurred with equally stunning speed. Khrushchev and Nikolai Bulganin journeyed to Belgrade in June 1955 and, in an effort to rebuild the Soviet-Yugoslav relation, conceded there that specific forms of socialist development were exclusively the concern of the peoples involved. Subsequently, after Khrushchev endorsed the idea of "many roads to socialism" at the Twentieth Party Congress in February 1956 and also (ironically and successfully) exerted pressure on satellite governments to reverse their earlier anti-Tito policies, it became clear that the repercussions of this rapprochement would be immense.[80]

The most significant and ultimately most subversive of the new policies, however, was the campaign of de-Stalinization that Khrushchev launched at the Twentieth Party Congress. Intended not as an abandonment of party primacy but rather as a means to achieve an acceptable basis for it, this vigorous attack on Stalin and his policies was carried out both inside and outside the U.S.S.R. and led to substantial changes in Eastern Europe. In the course of this transformation, old-line Stalinists were removed from power, and party leaders identified with a more popular national line were elevated.[81]

Nevertheless, and in large part because such measures whetted the public appetite for more changes, reformist pressure in Poland and then Hungary grew to the point that in October and November of 1956 crises occurred in the relations of those countries with Russia. In Poland, because local party leadership was united at the critical moment and was focused primarily on domestic affairs, Khrushchev and his colleagues reconciled themselves to the return of Wladislav Gomulka, a national Communist who as party secretary during the next fourteen years would pursue such innovations as the decollectivization of agriculture, the nationalizing of the Polish armed forces, and the creation of a role for workers in factory management.[82] In Hungary, on the other hand, because the new leaders made the mistake of trying to restore a multiparty system and to end the Soviet alliance, Moscow, in rage and panic, opted for military intervention, overthrowing the rebellion. In the short run, this was a severe defeat for national self-determination.[83]

It was at this moment, following the stunning events of 1956, that Sino-Soviet relations became problematic. At first the Chinese gave every indication of loyalty, lending vigorous support to Khrushchev's actions in Hungary and even sending a delegation (headed by Mao Zedong) to Moscow in November 1957 to endorse Soviet leadership of the Communist camp, thereby conceding a point for which Russia had paid "insurance" in October with a promise of assistance to China in developing nuclear weapons.[84] In 1958, however, the Chinese Communists embarked upon the Great Leap Forward, an effort to speed up their nation's modernization and strengthen its independence by the creation of communes that combined small-scale industry with agriculture, an effort reflecting in large measure Chinese disillusionment with, and anxiety about, Khrushchev's de-Stalinization campaign. Chinese estrangement was given further impetus by Soviet caution in supporting China during the Quemoy crisis (1958), by Khrushchev's willingness to pursue "peaceful coexistence" with President Eisenhower, and above all, by the Politburo's decision in June 1959 to abrogate unilaterally its two-year-old military aid agreement with China.[85]

By April 1960 Beijing was angry enough to make public its feud with Moscow, although until the end of 1962 both sides preferred to criticize each other indirectly, the Chinese attacking "revisionists" in general and the Yugoslavs in particular, the Russians directing their ire at "dogmatists" in general and (after Albania sided with China in 1961) the Albanians specifically. Chinese spokesmen, arguing that China (and therefore not the Soviet Union) was the true standard-bearer of the Leninist tradition, warned against trusting the imperialist powers and took issue with Khrushchev by citing Mao to the effect that the socialist world should not fear war. The Russians, making every effort to rebut these contentions, became increasingly frustrated with the exchange, to the extent that in mid-1960 Khrushchev abruptly canceled the Soviet economic assistance program in China, recalling over 2,000 engineers and specialists from that country.[86]

The conflict soon became more intense and explicit. Khrushchev's increasing rapprochement with Tito, his "capitulation" to President Kennedy during the Cuban missile crisis, and his tacit support of India during the Sino-Indian war of 1962 confirmed Beijing's suspicions about Soviet weakness and prompted the Chinese to criticize Moscow's foreign policy severely. In June 1963, after the Russians made clear their intention to sign a nuclear test ban treaty (and on the eve of talks in the Soviet capital designed to bridge Sino-Soviet differences), China's party leadership dispatched a letter of protest to the Soviet party's Central Committee that was unprecedented in its directness and harshness. Charging Moscow with betrayal of the revolution, the Chinese accused Soviet leaders of abandoning the Third World to the imperialists out of the mistaken belief that "peaceful coexistence is mankind's road to socialism."[87] The Soviet reply of July, published as an open letter, was equally outspoken and tough. The Chinese rulers, it said, were gravely damaging the radical cause by perpetuating the Stalin cult, casting doubt on the ability of socialism to defeat capitalism in peaceful competition, and underestimating the danger of thermonuclear war.

In the following months, Sino-Soviet differences ranged across the entire spectrum of their relation. Ideological clashes now included charges of internal and external deviation. Beijing made territorial claims to large parts of Siberia, claims that allegedly originated with the nine "unequal" treaties forced on China by the tsars.[88] Trade itself became more difficult, declining from a peak of over $2 billion in 1959 to only $45 million in 1970, as China sought systematically to reduce its dependence on the Soviet Union.[89] Though relations did improve somewhat in the winter of 1964–65 after the new Brezhnev-Kosygin regime made several conciliatory gestures, by mid-1965 the developing war in Vietnam helped to drive the Communist giants apart again. Indeed, as the Russians initiated an ominous military buildup along China's northern frontier (perhaps inspired in part by China's having exploded a nuclear device), and as Mao and his followers embarked upon that experiment in militancy and xenophobic isolationism, the Cultural Revolution, relations between the two great Communist powers reached a nadir of hostility and mutual contempt.[90]

The Soviet Union, to be sure, had tried and would continue to try to overcome the disintegrative tendencies within the Communist world. Following the death of Stalin, for instance, when it became clear that extreme centralization did not function effectively, Moscow attempted to create a less onerous substitute by establishing the Warsaw Treaty Organization, a multilateral security alliance involving those Eastern European states within the Soviet orbit. Together with the Council for Mutual Economic Assistance, which dated from 1949 but which was activated only after Stalin's death, the Warsaw Pact was intended to ensure political and economic cohesion while conceding some autonomy to member regimes. If for a period after the Hungarian intervention not even the Russians provided much support to the Warsaw Pact, by 1961–62 rising tensions over Berlin and between China and Russia led Khrushchev to enlarge Eastern European military capabilities and strengthen consultative and coordinating mechanisms.[91] The multilateral framework was buttressed with a growing network of bilateral agreements between the Soviet Union and other Communist governments. There was also a marked increase in the number and frequency of international congresses and conferences involving Communist party leaders.[92]

Nevertheless, in spite of Moscow's efforts to hold the "socialist commonwealth" together, the steady deterioration of the Sino-Soviet alliance and the transition in leadership from Khrushchev to Brezhnev virtually ensured that the mid-sixties would become a golden age for experimentation and divergence in Eastern Europe. Albania, supported economically and ideologically by Beijing, continued to defy the U.S.S.R. while implementing a "cultural revolution" (1964–69) that rivaled China's.[93] Romania also gained from the Sino-Soviet split, asserting its independence by refusing to de-Stalinize or to abandon its industrialization (1960), declining to support the Soviet line against China (1964), opposing Brezhnev's proposals for changes in the Warsaw Pact (1966), and establishing diplomatic relations with West Germany over Moscow's objections (1967).[94] In 1966 Hungary decided upon economic reforms patterned much more on the Yugoslav than the Soviet model, featuring decentralization, reliance on the market, and increased Western trade and tourism. In addition, in 1968, Hungary and then Czechoslovakia took steps toward political liberalization: reducing the involvement of the Communist Party in nongovernmental affairs, limiting the activities of the secret police, relaxing censorship controls on press and radio, and enlarging the scope of parliamentary choice and power.[95] In Czechoslovakia, of course, these changes snowballed to such an extent during the Prague Spring that Soviet leaders felt compelled to use military force to restore the Czechoslovak Communist Party to power and to preserve stability in other parts of the socialist camp.[96]

Yet even after the Czechoslovak experiment was crushed in August, and even after a certain sense of limits was established in Eastern Europe by Moscow's intervention in Czechoslovakia, the Soviet Union was still confronted with an unprecedented array of forces and factors pulling in various directions within the Communist bloc. In fact, Brezhnev's new "doctrine" of limited sovereignty so greatly alarmed Beijing (since it offered a rationalization for Soviet intervention in China) that Mao and his supporters now embarked upon a substantial reassessment of their nation's foreign policy, a reassessment that would lead them, in the short run, to tentative overtures toward the United States and, ultimately, after armed clashes on the Sino-Soviet border in March 1969, to a basic reorientation of Chinese attitudes concerning relations with the major capitalist powers.[97]

Meanwhile, in Eastern Europe, as Czechoslovakia lapsed into silence and Hungary continued its experimentation, Yugoslav-Soviet relations turned cold again, Romania set about strengthening its national defenses, and Poland, laboring under an increasingly unpopular regime and ineffective economic program, lurched toward the ominous consumer riots of December 1970.[98] As the decade ended, it was clear that, despite everything Russia had done to resist, the fragmentation and alienation in the world socialist system and the Communist movement had reached very serious proportions.

4

SEEKING AMERICA'S ESCAPE
FROM VIETNAM

The coincidence of the superpowers' economic, political, and strategic needs that developed by the end of the 1960s was so extraordinary, and the simultaneity of the impact on both countries so unusual, that the situation itself became a crucial factor in Richard Nixon and Leonid Brezhnev's surprising breakthrough from hostility to cooperation. One nation's weakness without the other's would almost certainly not have sufficed to generate this change, and in fact such one-sidedness might well have caused a serious intensification of the Cold War. But the combination of need and opportunity constituted a powerful inducement for creative, conservative statesmen to achieve a number of mutually beneficial arrangements and, in so doing, to transform the entire international mood.

Most assuredly, no individual statesman was indispensable to this process; other American presidents or other Soviet rulers, given these or somewhat similar conditions, might have done as much or more to improve the bilateral relation. Still, this should not minimize the contribution of either Nixon or Brezhnev. The nature of their leadership played an important role in defining the way in which the two nations responded to each other—and ultimately in the way their understandings unraveled.

The central problem for Nixon and his administration was how to extricate the United States from Vietnam without forfeiting its credibility as a great power, which he considered essential to the maintenance of peace. Indeed, almost every foreign policy move Nixon made during his first four years in office was related to his desire and need to get the country out of Vietnam. Yet, understandably, the way he went about accomplishing this was an outgrowth of his particular conservatism and of his conceptions regarding the domestic scene and international relations. Thus, in seeking solutions to Vietnam and related problems, he tended to explore those areas in which, according to his ideological predilections, he could find additional resources. Since on this occasion he could not obtain the required political and economic support either from domestic sources or from foreign allies, he necessarily (in addition to scaling down the U.S. military effort in South Vietnam) turned to America's most powerful enemy in the hope of dividing, limiting, or exploiting its capacities for action. This maneuver had the added advantage that, even if it did not bring about a quick end to the Vietnam War, Nixon could at least garner credit with the American electorate for having moved toward a reduction in the demands and dangers that the international situation was generating for the United States.

For Brezhnev and the Soviet government two problems in particular were paramount: the slowdown of growth in domestic productivity and the increasing tension between Russia and China. The latter in fact rendered the former more serious because, at a time when the regime's economic reforms were proving inadequate, the Soviet leadership was confronted with the drain upon its resources involved in maintaining an Asian military presence (not to speak of the forces committed to pacifying Eastern Europe). In addition, these demands arose when there was growing danger of a renewed arms race with America and when, as Moscow was increasingly aware, it had lost much ground to the West in terms of the new technological revolution.

If the Soviet Union was to meet its internal and foreign commitments and to retain the parity in strategic weaponry it had worked so hard to achieve, radical changes were almost certainly necessary. Brezhnev and the party leadership, however, though ideological Marxists, were politically cautious men, unwilling to accept significant alterations in the centralized structure of their economy and state. It is not surprising that an improved relation with West Germany or the United States had its attractions for them, since such a détente would enable them to reduce competition in weapons and obtain Western credits and technology for Russia while at the same time saving face and retaining the domestic status quo.

It may be helpful at this point to explain what is meant by *ideology* and how the concept is relevant to the present story. As the term is used here, it has no judgmental or derogatory connotation but refers simply to an individual's world-view, that is, to the values, assumptions, and hypotheses that a person blends into a framework, or operational code for an interpretation of reality. Moreover, although there are endless varieties of ideology, it is clear that most Western versions fall into one or another of three great and continuing ideological families, usually identified by historians as the conservative, liberal, and radical traditions. The conservative tradition has its roots in medieval times and in a two-class, premodern society. It begins with pessimistic assumptions about human nature and proceeds from them to justify a belief in tradition, hierarchy, and community. The liberal tradition, on the other hand, has been the ideology of the middle class from the early modern era to the present. It is built on more optimistic foundations and emphasizes the extent to which human beings are rational and capable of functioning as free, self-sufficient individuals. The radical (or Marxist) worldview, the most recent of the great ideologies, arose with the industrial working class of the nineteenth century and maintains that humanity, though potentially capable of genuine rationality and community, can achieve this only after the destruction of liberal property rights and the class system that private property makes inevitable.[1]

Conventional usage of the words notwithstanding, Americans from the beginning of their history have tended to identify with the liberal ideological camp, and even today our political parties can most appropriately be described as "right liberal" (those who fear government) and "left liberal" (those who fear concentrated wealth).[2] This does not mean, however, that individual American statesmen like Richard Nixon or Henry Kissinger cannot possess classic conservative attitudes, or a conservative-liberal mix, or that they cannot pursue conservative policies (i.e., policies that would be recognized as such by conservatives of another age, like Edmund Burke or Otto von Bismarck). Within a culture there is inevitably a spectrum of personality types and political tendencies, any one or several of which can be installed in authority by the shifting of public moods or the play of events, especially international events. Indeed, my hypothesis is that it was in part the genuinely conservative inclinations of Nixon and Kissinger (combined, to be sure, with a certain respect for liberal values) that made them sensitive to, and able to profit from, the opportunity for international bargaining that they encountered at the end of the 1960s.[3] What is more, it seems clear that there was an element of conservatism in Brezhnev, which attracted him to the possibility of an agreement with the Americans.[4]

Hence, the odd fact is that, in what was ostensibly an encounter between a liberal, "freedom-loving" American statesman (Nixon) and a radical, "Communist" Russian statesman (Brezhnev), it was the essential conservatism of both that was crucial to their making the kind of arrangement they did. In the same situation, LBJ too might have cut a deal with the other side, but (despite certain similarities of personality with Nixon) being somewhat more liberal than his successor, he would probably have done it without attempting so consciously to manipulate and then freeze (to America's advantage) the international balance of power.

Not all of the shortfalls and necessities that came together for the Americans and the Soviets in 1969 were new. Some of them had been developing for a number of years, and some had played a role in the progress that had been achieved in East-West relations since the mid-fifties. Public and elite concern regarding the growing costs of the arms race and the increasing dangers of accidental war, for example, consistently helped offset and contain Cold War antagonisms and prodded statesmen to search for more rational alternatives.[5] Such pressure was reinforced on occasion by popular anxiety regarding nuclear weapons testing and by troubled reactions on the part of decision makers to crises between the superpowers.[6] A combination of strategic, political, and economic factors in 1962 resulted in the frightening confrontation between the United States and the Soviet Union regarding Cuba and, subsequently, during a surge of relief and guilt, in the limited détente of the hot line and partial test ban agreements.[7]

The years of Lyndon Johnson's presidency saw a certain renewal of hostility but some movement toward cooperation as well. Though the momentum of the post-missile-crisis détente was quickly eroded as a consequence of deepening U.S. involvement in South Vietnam, it is also true that, as the president became more and more committed to intervention in that area, he strove to establish his peace credentials and to blunt the criticism of his Asian endeavors by pursuing a cooperative policy in his dealings with the Soviet Union. As early as February 1964 Johnson used America's surplus of fissionable material to persuade Khrushchev of the wisdom of mutual cutbacks in the production of uranium for atomic weapons.[8] By the middle of 1965 (prompted by the advent of the Chinese atomic bomb in 1964), he embarked upon a campaign that would lead within three years to the signing of a nuclear nonproliferation treaty with the U.S.S.R.[9] Along the way, his administration renewed the Soviet-American cultural exchange agreement (February 1964), entered into a consular convention (July 1964; "the first bilateral treaty between the United States and the Soviet Union," bragged the president,[10] who was nevertheless unable to prevent the Senate from taking more than two years to ratify it), and began the negotiations that ultimately resulted in the inauguration of air service between New York and Moscow (July 1968).[11]

Such agreements were part of an idealistic and continuing effort by the Johnson administration to open up contacts and trade with the Communist East, though economic self-interest and the desire to exploit the breakdown of authority within the Soviet alliance were also involved. The difficulties in the American economy were not as visible as they would become later, but business groups were pressing the government to lift Cold War restrictions on trade and to allow them to compete with foreign companies that were taking advantage of the developing opportunities in Eastern Europe.[12] LBJ, frustrated that presidential authority did not permit him to go as far as he wanted in "building bridges to the East," in February 1965 appointed a Special Committee on Trade Relations, under J. Irwin Miller, to study the commercial situation. Two months later the Miller committee produced what the president called "probably the most definitive report on East-West trade relations made up to that time"[13], a report that recommended strongly that most-favored- nation status be extended to Eastern European countries.[14] Opposition in Congress, reinforced now by the Vietnam War, gave Johnson pause for some time, but in January 1966 he spoke out for new trade arrangements in his State of the Union address, and the following May he asked for the power to dismantle all "special tariff restrictions" on trade with the Communist world. Though the president's request was ultimately denied by both the Eighty-ninth and Ninetieth Congresses, he continued to work toward his objective by removing commodities from the strategic control list that limited commerce with Eastern Europe.[15]

In the area of arms control, the administration began in 1964 with a great show of activity but slipped gradually into a lethargy which it threw off only in 1967 and 1968. In his first year of incumbency, LBJ endorsed and at least briefly championed a number of proposals: a comprehensive test ban (which he subsequently hobbled with demands for rigorous on-site inspection); a verified freeze on offensive and defensive weapons (which, not surprisingly, the Russians rejected because it would have consigned them to permanent inferiority); the scrapping of medium-range bombers (which, in Moscow's view, amounted to little more than the destruction of obsolete weapons); and reductions in the defense budgets on both sides (which Khrushchev himself had suggested but which was rendered problematic by lack of clarity as to what the Soviet budget really was).[16]

As American commitment in Vietnam became more massive, however, LBJ and his government seemed to lose interest in arms control—and faith in its very possibility. In 1966, the president told Glenn Seaborg, the chairman of the Atomic Energy Commission, that he was not really convinced of the importance of a comprehensive test ban and in fact doubted the entire value of the Arms Control and Disarmament Agency.[17] During the next two years the only significant accomplishment was a treaty in January 1967 outlawing the placing of nuclear weapons in outer space (an action that neither the United States nor the U.S.S.R. was seriously contemplating),[18] though it is noteworthy that the two superpowers continued doggedly to maintain the negotiations that would one day produce a nonproliferation treaty.[19]

At the very end of 1966, when it became apparent that the United States, by devoting itself so single-mindedly to war in Asia, was in danger of losing its lead to the Russians in the strategic arms race, Washington began to develop a new interest in arrangements to limit or preclude competition in ballistic weapons. Here the crucial person was Secretary of Defense Robert S. McNamara, and the crucial factors were the uninterrupted Soviet buildup in ICBM strength (which was still somewhat underestimated) and Soviet deployment, beginning in 1964, of an antiballistic missile (ABM) system around Moscow and perhaps in other areas.[20] McNamara was convinced that the point of diminishing returns had been reached in the expansion of American offensive forces, and he was also very opposed to an arms race in defensive weapons, but he was under increasing pressure from Congress in 1966 to match the Russian ABM deployment. LBJ, of course, was concerned about his pending campaign for reelection and so was sensitive to the political implications of such pressure. In desperation, McNamara turned to diplomacy, persuading LBJ in December 1966, against the wishes of the Joint Chiefs of Staff, to hold off on ABM until there had been an opportunity to explore the possibility of an agreement with the Soviet Union on a limitation of strategic arms.[21]

Subsequently, the president pushed the Russians hard (both publicly and at the Glassboro Conference with Kosygin in June 1967) to agree to bilateral discussions, but the response from Moscow was so ambivalent and slow that in September 1967 Johnson and McNamara felt compelled to proceed with the deployment of a "thin" ABM system (Sentinel), ostensibly designed to be nonprovocative to Russia and to protect American missile bases from Chinese attack.[22] The truth is that the Soviet leadership did not display real enthusiasm for strategic arms limitation talks (SALT) until the spring of 1968. This was after the nonproliferation treaty had been agreed upon (and West Germany's Brandt was hinting that he might endorse it); after Russia was approaching parity with the United States in ICBM strength; and after the Johnson administration had announced its intention to deploy Sentinel as well as its readiness to deploy a new offensive weapon, the multiple independently targeted reentry vehicle, or MIRV.[23]

Unfortunately, and perhaps through no coincidence, Moscow's confirmation of a specific beginning date for SALT did not arrive at the White House until August 19, 1968, hours before the Politburo's decision to send Russian military forces into Czechoslovakia to crush the reform government in Prague. The invasion thus necessitated the postponement of the scheduled meetings, and by the time the two sides could renew contact after the presidential election in November, not even their apparent eagerness could compensate for the fact that Johnson was a lame duck and

Nixon was unwilling to proceed until he formally took the reins of power.[24]

The U.S. presidential campaign and election of 1968 had been an important factor in shaping the new Nixon administration. Long, violent, and exhausting, the campaign began almost a year before, when George Romney, the Republican governor of Michigan, announced his candidacy and Senator Eugene McCarthy (D-Minn.) stunned the country by announcing that he would oppose the president for the Democratic nomination, running on a peace platform. In ensuing months, Richard Nixon and Governor Nelson Rockefeller of New York surged past Romney in the Republican competition, while the Democratic picture became complicated and confused, first by Senator Robert Kennedy's entry into the race, then by President Johnson's withdrawal and Vice President Hubert Humphrey's declaration of candidacy, and finally by the assassinations of Martin Luther King in April and Robert Kennedy in June.

Turbulence and dissension plagued the campaign continuously, particularly on the Democratic side, as antiwar protesters made clear their unhappiness with Humphrey's loyalty to the Johnson administration. The nominations of Nixon and Humphrey by their respective parties in August left the antiwar movement leaderless and perplexed, while the nation at large was badly divided by the brutality that erupted when city police and national guardsmen battled protesters in the streets of Chicago during the Democratic convention. The candidacy of former Governor George Wallace of Alabama on the reactionary American Independent Party ticket only compounded the tension.[25]

As far as the international issues of the campaign were concerned, Nixon was somewhat more forthcoming than Humphrey. Though the Democratic candidate emphasized that "we must go far beyond where we've been—beyond containment to communication; beyond the emphasis of differences to dialogue," and although he spoke out for the nonproliferation treaty and for "finding the . . . means to control and reduce offensive and defensive nuclear missile systems," Humphrey was rather vague about the Soviet Union and about what he called "the necessity for peace in Vietnam."[26] Nixon, by contrast, spent a good deal of time spelling out his views on foreign affairs. Pledging to end the war in Southeast Asia by applying more diplomatic, economic, and political pressure, especially on the Soviet Union, Nixon also called for a change "from a relationship of conflict to one of cooperation" with the Russians. In any case, he contended, negotiations with Moscow would have to start with a policy of strength, since this is what the Soviets understand. What was required, he said, was not a weapon-by-weapon arms race with the Soviet Union but merely an improvement in the overall power of the United States aimed at ending the "security gap" that the Democrats had created. Such power would help to move us away from confrontation into a new era, "the era of negotiations."[27]

Immediately after the nominating conventions in August, Nixon jumped to a sizable lead in the polls, but as the race continued, his advantage narrowed, and when the election was held, it was one of the closest contests of the century. Nixon received 31.7 million votes, or 43.4 percent, Humphrey 31.2 million, or 42.7 percent, and Wallace 9.9 million, or 13.5 percent. These results—and the violence of the campaign—showed that the electorate was deeply and bitterly fragmented. The voters' clearest message to the candidates was that they were extremely weary of the war.[28]

During the three months between the election and the presidential inauguration, Richard Nixon proceeded to shape the structure, make the appointments, and establish the tone that would define the foreign policy of his administration. Basic to this endeavor was Nixon's long-standing interest and involvement in foreign affairs and his determination to be a president who made his own policies, that is, who required that the essential strategic decisions be made in the White House. These attitudes reflected his deep and continuing distrust of the governmental bureaucracy, which he considered to be by its very nature hopelessly at odds with itself and, worse, in the hands of his political enemies. His attitude also reflected a distrust of people in general and especially those in the communications media, who "informed" the public of what they considered "news." Nixon intended to be an innovative, even a reforming president, and he did not want to be hamstrung by the bureaucracy, the media, or the public.[29]

To achieve his objectives, Nixon needed a person at his right hand who shared his perspectives and could accept his style, a person who could help him conceptualize and articulate the policies he envisaged. He found that individual in Henry Kissinger, the brilliant and unorthodox Harvard professor of political science whom he appointed national security adviser in early December 1968. At Nixon's direction, Kissinger and his staff were able within a few weeks to develop procedures within the executive branch that centralized foreign policy authority, as never before, in the National Security Council (NSC) and the national security adviser. The new arrangement gave Kissinger the power to direct the State Department and other agencies to prepare and submit option papers (national security study memoranda, or NSSMs) to the NSC on specific subjects. It also allowed him to promulgate the president's policy decisions, which were usually made in private after a meeting of the NSC and took the form of highly classified directives (national security decision memoranda, or

NSDMs). Thus Nixon and Kissinger between them controlled the policy-making apparatus of the government and could literally bypass even such highly placed officials as Secretary of State William P. Rogers, American ambassadors, and the chiefs of the intelligence gathering agencies.[30]

At its root this was very much a matter of personality and ideology. Nixon was a loner by history and by preference. A bright, serious, and sensitive man, he compensated for his insecurity with a preference for privacy, intense industriousness, and aggressive problem solving. Still, he remained essentially pessimistic, even cynical about the world around him and about his acceptability in it. Ideologically, his personality manifested itself in strong conservative tendencies, obscured and camouflaged to an extent in the clothing of the liberalism dominant in America. In other words, Nixon's thought about the social scene was structured largely in terms of power and power leverage. His sense of international relations was of nation-states that were self-interested, competitive entities, perpetually condemned to amassing power and seeking advantage over each other. The most natural (and safest) international order, therefore, was explicitly hierarchical; or if necessary, hierarchical on each side of bipolarity; or failing that, organized with nation-states and alliance systems clearly ranked by power.[31]

Henry Kissinger was quite compatible with the president in terms of personality and ideology. Traumatized as a boy by his family's flight from the persecutions of Jews in Nazi Germany, Kissinger grew up with a strong sense of the world being constantly on the edge of disaster, with order and disorder in continuing struggle. His responses have been described in terms of the depressive personality, typified by alternation between insecurity and arrogance and by self-doubt, extreme ambition, suspiciousness, industriousness, flexibility, and manipulative skill.[32] His concern about chaos and his passion for order led him naturally into conservative thinking and into a high regard for statesmen who, as intelligent activists (like Bismarck, for example), utilize power effectively to regulate our species' irrationality and propensity for violence.[33]

More specifically, however, what did the Nixon-Kissinger collaboration mean in terms of the nation's foreign policy orientation? Kissinger has written more systematically than Nixon about the implications of his beliefs, but there is sufficient evidence of the president's thinking from this period to demonstrate that the two men agreed on diagnosis and prescription. Kissinger suggested, for example, that a "durable structure of peace" requires nation-states that are "legitimate" (that is, nonrevolutionary) and leaders that are "statesmen" (as opposed to "prophets" or "conquerors"). Nixon argued that stability demands a substantial cooling of passions.

One is struck by the fact that both Nixon and Kissinger were convinced that a new situation was developing with regard to the principal opponents of the United States—the Soviet Union and Communist China. Or to put it another way, both men, and especially the president, were persuaded that Russia and China, driven by their disagreements and mutual fear as well as the increasing cost of the Cold War, had ceased to be genuinely revolutionary powers and had reached a point where they would be prepared to deal.[34] This was an especially hopeful sign for Nixon and Kissinger, because their belief system necessitated that the leading opponent be central to their foreign policy (in part because they assumed that the opposing side would tend to be organized hierarchically).

A second significant factor was Nixon and Kissinger's sense that the United States as a nation had been seriously weakened—that, as a result of Johnson's policies and the Vietnam War, the country had lost its strength and direction. With their sharp instinct for power, they felt keenly the lack of domestic consensus, that is to say, the absence of national unity, which in their opinion a statesman needs if he is to have a constructive impact on world history. They concluded that, as a result of the fragmentation of opinion, the United States was badly overextended internationally. Thus, if some remnant of America's former hegemonic role was to be preserved and if a durable peace was to be achieved, three things were essential: (1) the conflict in Vietnam needed to end, (2) the nation's involvement and potential involvement overseas needed to be cut back so that they matched the U.S.'s military, economic, and political power, and (3) understandings with America's principal opponents needed to be achieved so these opponents would identify their national interests with the existing international order (and as a result, reduce their threat to its arrangements).[35]

Just how the Soviet Union—and for that matter, China—were to be fitted into the new international structure was not clear. It is tempting to conclude that Nixon and Kissinger simply decided to give the two Communist giants a stake in the system, first, by increasing the economic, political, and cultural ties of mutual interdependence and, second, by arranging the balance of power so as to impose costs on any state that attempted to destabilize the international order. At the time, however, the president and his adviser were not as explicit or as confident about this as they would later become. According to William Hyland, one of Kissinger's advisers, "initially at least neither [individual] saw much prospect for more than a narrow, limited accommodation with Moscow. . . . Eventually, they hoped, a broader and more general improvement might take shape, and it was to this end that they devised the tactic of linkage: making progress in some areas dependent on progress in others."[36] But in the beginning there was hardly more to the new world structure than the possibility of better relations with China and the promise of arms control negotiations with Russia.

At any rate, the first order of business for the new administration was getting America out of Vietnam, and this remained of central importance for Nixon's entire first term. Though Nixon later denied that he had devised a "secret plan" to end the war (he had hinted at such a plan during the campaign), the truth is that he not only possessed fairly definite ideas about how this could be done but also was optimistic about the prospects for ending American participation quickly.[37] His intention was to proceed on two tracks at once, (1) strengthening America's ally in South Vietnam and withdrawing American troops from the region while (2) negotiating a settlement with North Vietnam that achieved a pullback of its forces and permitted only the National Liberation Front (the southern insurgency) to participate in a new southern government. He hoped to facilitate his efforts with the threat (and then the reality) of escalated air war and with increased pressure on Moscow and Beijing to persuade Hanoi to come to an agreement.[38]

Nixon and Kissinger wasted no time in beginning. Only a few days after the inauguration, having devoted the first meetings of the National Security Council to the war in Southeast Asia, they transmitted a proposal to the North Vietnamese delegation in Paris calling for a mutual and simultaneous military withdrawal from South Vietnam.[39] Soon thereafter, on March 18, 1969, they supplemented this with an unannounced "signal" to Hanoi—an intensive bombing of North Vietnamese staging areas in Cambodia and Laos—intended to emphasize American will and determination.[40] Then, on April 14, Kissinger initiated what would become a series of attempts, utilizing the "back channel" that Nixon had directed him to set up with Soviet Ambassador Anatoly Dobrynin, to obtain Moscow's support for a compromise solution to the Vietnam War. Informing Dobrynin that the administration was "prepared to make progress in U.S.-Soviet relations on a broad front" but that the Vietnam War was a "major obstacle," he went on to ask for Soviet assistance in ending the conflict and hinted that, failing this, the president might have to escalate American military activity in Southeast Asia.[41]

Meanwhile, in another overture, Nixon asked President Charles de Gaulle to convey to Chinese leaders not only that he desired friendlier ties with Beijing but also that he intended "to withdraw [U.S. forces] from Vietnam, come what may."[42] The American president was trying to establish a situation in which he could bring both Chinese and Russian influence to bear in Vietnam. Even though Beijing had mysteriously canceled the February Warsaw ambassadorial talks that it had requested after the Soviet invasion of Czechoslovakia, the prospects for a Chinese-American rapprochement were encouraging, particularly in light of the armed clashes that flared up along the Sino-Soviet frontier beginning in March 1969.[43]

What all this meant, of course, was that for the time being Washington was putting aside its relation with Moscow. Though the Russians seemed eager to talk and even to compromise in a number of areas (regarding SALT, economic relations, and the Middle East, for example), Nixon and Kissinger were intentionally being nonresponsive.[44] The reasons were clear. First, by dangling attractive possibilities before the Russians and then withholding them, they hoped to achieve the maximum leverage on the Soviet government (to them, the ultimately responsible party in Vietnam) to work for peace. Second, they realized that their bargaining position on other issues would be stronger if the Vietnam conflict was settled and American social divisions overcome before the two countries sat down to negotiate. Third, they wanted to buttress the American position vis-à-vis Moscow by achieving a prior understanding with China and by regaining the military advantage with MIRV and an ABM system. Fourth, they needed time to form a clearer picture of what they were prepared to offer the Soviets regarding such matters as SALT.

In the meantime, the administration proceeded with its efforts to bolster the South Vietnamese government and army and to begin extracting its own troops from the continuing conflict in Southeast Asia. As early as March 1969, Nixon borrowed the term *Vietnamization* from Secretary of Defense Melvin Laird to describe the buildup of South Vietnamese military forces that had been initiated at Washington's request to "de-Americanize" the war.[45] The word itself would not be in common usage until June, but the process was alluded to by the president on several occasions before then, and it was implicit in his television address of May 14, in which for the first time he openly spelled out his proposals for the simultaneous withdrawal of American and North Vietnamese armies and for internationally supervised elections.[46]

Three weeks later, acting ostensibly in response to increasing strength in Saigon, Nixon met with President Nguyen Van Thieu of South Vietnam on Midway Island and won his agreement to an immediate, public, and unilateral withdrawal of 25,000 American combat troops from the war zone, the first of a series of withdrawals that would stretch out over four years.[47] Then in July, on the first leg of a trip around the world, the president utilized a stopover on Guam to fit Vietnamization into a larger and more general framework, announcing what in future months would become known as the Nixon Doctrine. The United States, Nixon declared, would no longer assume the primary responsibility for the defense of its allies around the world. America would honor its commitments and provide a nuclear shield, but from now on Washington would expect the nation directly threatened to generate the essential manpower for its own defense.[48]

Nevertheless, policies for the future did not accomplish peace in the present. Though Nixon believed that he was buying time from (that is, undermining support for) the peace movement at home with such policies as Vietnamization, troop withdrawal, and the Nixon Doctrine, Kissinger worried that the United States was also losing valuable international leverage and that the unilateral withdrawal of forces would become irreversible.[49] As the summer wore on, both men became more and more disappointed with Hanoi's lack of response to their May offer and with the silence of the Soviet leadership and its tendency to inch closer to the North Vietnamese as its relations with the Chinese deteriorated.[50] In frustration, Nixon and Kissinger began to seriously consider the advisability of employing increased violence against the North Vietnamese as a means of compelling them to be more forthcoming.[51]

During these same months (the spring and summer of 1969) the president was also vigorously engaged in trying to shore up what, in his view, was a badly weakened American strategic position. Though in one of his first presidential statements, Nixon had espoused "sufficiency" rather than "superiority" as the proper criterion for judging the nation's military posture (thereby sending an encouraging signal to Moscow), the president was by no means ready to stop competing with the Soviet Union in weaponry whenever he had the means to continue.[52] This was particularly evident with regard to two strategic systems that, as noted earlier, were at the point of deployment when Nixon became president: the ABM and the MIRV. In choosing to support versions of each weapon, he demonstrated not only his anxiety about America's place in the military balance of power but also his strong belief that "bargaining chips" were needed for arms control negotiations.

Of course, the MIRV had been looked upon in the Johnson years primarily as a way of countering the Russian ABM, and Secretary McNamara had used its potential existence as an argument against deploying a "thick" American ABM coverage to balance out the Soviet system.[53] Unfortunately, however, as the U.S.S.R. strengthened its ABM network and passed the United States in numbers of land-based offensive missiles (1,200 to 1,054 by the end of 1969), the MIRV became steadily more attractive to American military planners as a means of keeping the United States ahead in overall strategic power. It was apparent that, given the MIRV and a substantial ABM as well, American forces would once again be much stronger than the Russian, at least until the Soviet Union acquired the technology to "MIRV" the large missiles in its own arsenal.[54]

Moscow's recognition of this fact was undoubtedly one of the considerations driving it to take up arms control diplomacy.

Nonetheless, the Johnson (Sentinel) ABM was not a substantial system nor was it designed to fend off the Russians (oddly enough, it provided an anti-Chinese message at a time when Nixon was eager to woo Beijing), and for this reason the incoming Nixon administration felt compelled to reevaluate the situation and to develop a new approach. In March 1969, following an intensive review, Nixon decided to expand the Sentinel program (now called Safeguard), modifying it to protect the nation's capacity to retaliate after a Russian nuclear attack.[55] This set the stage for a gigantic political battle in the Senate, where the mood had changed substantially from the days in which that body had urged McNamara to deploy an ABM and where a large minority, mainly Democrats, now saw such a program as needlessly provocative in the face of Soviet overtures to negotiate.[56] Nixon and Kissinger, however, unlike some in the administration, were not ones to forgo taking an advantage, especially when they persuaded themselves that Russia might go on building offensive missiles indefinitely. By pressing the Senate hard (to the point of Secretary Laird's exaggerating the threat from the Russian SS-9), they obtained authorization of the first funds for Safeguard by the narrowest of margins (one vote) on August 6.[57]

In the interim, a somewhat quieter struggle was being waged over the MIRV. A maverick Republican, Senator Edward Brooke of Massachusetts, had urged the new president as early as April to end testing of the MIRV (testing begun in August 1968 and scheduled to resume in May 1969) in order to avoid triggering a new round in the arms race. Put off by Nixon, Brooke subsequently took his campaign to Congress and on June 17, together with forty other senators, introduced a resolution calling for an American MIRV moratorium.[58] The point, of course, was that, once the United States successfully completed its testing, the Soviet Union could do no less than follow suit, hence the attempt to preclude testing.

But Nixon and Kissinger argued that things had gone too far to try to reverse course now. The administration therefore proceeded to test the MIRV and then, in June 1970, to deploy it, acting despite the Senate's having voted 72 to 6 on April 9, 1970, to ask the United States and the Soviet Union to stop testing and deploying such weapons while SALT was going on.[59] During this period the president came under intense pressure from the Joint Chiefs of Staff and Melvin Laird to reject all constraints on the MIRV, their contention being that there was no means of verifying Soviet compliance with any ban.[60] In response to this, and probably as a result of the closeness of the ABM vote and the doubts raised about that system by scientists who testified against it, Nixon and Kissinger apparently concluded that, in the context of arms control, the ABM was expendable but the MIRV was not. Though in April 1970 they instructed the American SALT delegation to offer the Russians a MIRV ban coupled with on-site inspection, it is clear from the record that the president and his adviser were only covering their political flanks and had actually designed this proposal to be unacceptable to Moscow.[61]

In any event, the peace movement and the proponents of arms control in the United States did not accept the policies of the government passively, and their protests had a crucial impact on its thinking. During the first few months of the new administration, there was a noticeable falling off of antiwar activity, but by summer dissatisfaction with the rate of troop withdrawal mounted to the point that massive protest demonstrations were being planned for Washington in October and November 1969.[62] Moreover, Congress was now as hostile to military activism as at any time since its investigations of the munitions makers in the 1930s. In both the House and Senate new political coalitions were being formed to oppose the ABM and the MIRV and to resist and reduce the military budget as a whole.[63] As Henry Kissinger recalls it, "the pervasive anti-military atmosphere" created "a cloud of uncertainty over defense planning and our long-term security."[64]

But war protesters on the streets and antimilitarism in Congress were not the only things giving Nixon and Kissinger headaches. The president and his national security adviser were also concerned about the growing independence of America's European allies and, in particular, about the developing tendency of the West Germans to work toward an understanding with the Russians. At the beginning of his presidency Nixon had traveled to Europe and achieved some success in ending Washington's long-standing differences with Paris and Bonn, although at that point de Gaulle was within a few weeks of resigning his country's presidency and the Bundesrepublik was on the verge of a bitterly contested electoral campaign.[65] By autumn 1969, the situation was becoming unsettled again, since the new French leader, Georges Pompidou, was not easily predictable and Willy Brandt, elected West German chancellor in September, was making clear his intention to pursue an unusually active and accommodating *Ostpolitik*.

Indeed, in Brandt's inaugural address of October 28, the chancellor offered to negotiate renunciation-of-force treaties with Eastern European states, *including the German Democratic Republic,* and within a month he had signed the nuclear nonproliferation treaty (much to Moscow's delight) and agreed to hold talks with the Soviets about exchanging pledges of nonviolence.[66] Moreover, in early October, even before Brandt's government was formally installed, he sent his confidante, Egon Bahr, to Washington to inform the Americans of the course he planned to follow—

leaving, as Kissinger remarks, "little doubt that the policy itself was not subject to discussion."[67] One result was that Kissinger became anxious and hostile, and though Nixon was less fearful than Kissinger of Brandt's initiatives, there can be little doubt that his first reaction was also one of suspicion. Neither the president nor Kissinger wanted to lose control or be preempted in dealing with the Russians. By December 1969, therefore, they persuaded the country's NATO allies (including the West Germans) to create explicit linkages among the Soviet-German negotiation, the Berlin issue, and the possible European security conference. These linkages would, they thought, enhance the bargaining position of West Germany but also "set limits beyond which it could not go without an allied consensus."[68]

Meanwhile, the combined impact of developments—the failure of Washington to induce Moscow to pressure North Vietnam, the return to life of the American peace movement, the increasing interest of West Germany in reaching out to Eastern Europe, and the continuing buildup of Soviet missile strength—made it impossible for the administration to continue putting off the beginning of the strategic arms limitation talks. As early as May, despite the fact that not all of Kissinger's national security study memoranda on arms control were complete, Secretary of State Rogers, Director of the Arms Control and Disarmament Agency Gerard Smith, and others in the administration (and outside it) began to press actively for a commitment to an opening date. In June Nixon authorized Rogers to suggest to the Soviet ambassador that SALT get under way on July 31, but this time it was the Soviets' turn to delay.[69] Concerned about the implications of Nixon's ABM and MIRV policies, stung by the announcement that the president would visit Romania in August, and involved in stepped-up efforts to coerce the Red Chinese into border talks, Moscow allowed the American proposal to lie on the table for several weeks. It was not until October 20, the very day that formal Sino-Soviet consultations began in Beijing, that Dobrynin indicated to Kissinger and Nixon that his government was ready to initiate SALT.[70]

Kissinger, ostensibly disappointed at the three-month wait, was in actuality delighted, for it allowed him time to study the issues further and to centralize authority for SALT preparations in a new NSC group, the Verification Panel, formed, with him as chairman, in July.[71] Still, by autumn even Kissinger was eager for SALT negotiations, convinced that, under his guidance, they would provide an opportunity to stimulate Russian cooperation and to reduce pressure on the administration both at home and abroad.[72] That Nixon and he were prepared to proceed slowly could be seen from the instructions issued to the SALT delegation for the preliminary meeting: to conduct discussions and exchange views with the Soviet delegates, not to present proposals.[73]

The first session of SALT took place in Helsinki, Finland, from November 17 to December 22, 1969, and was significant primarily because it demonstrated that both sides were serious about arms control. From the beginning both Gerard Smith, the head of the American delegation, and Vladimir Semyonov, the Soviet chairman, made it clear that they saw grave danger in an unrestricted arms race and mutual annihilation in any war between their two countries.[74] According to Raymond Garthoff, the executive officer of the American team, "the most notable feature of the Soviet position was a strong endorsement of mutual deterrence and . . . readiness to bolster [it] through strategic arms limitations." Moreover, in a reversal of earlier policy, the Soviets emphasized their desire to limit, or even ban, ABM deployment.[75]

With this in mind, the Nixon administration, during the three months before SALT reconvened in Vienna, Austria, in April 1970, undertook extensive exercises designed to work out its negotiating position. As late as March, however, according to Kissinger, "there was no consensus; there was [only] a babble of discordant voices." In desperation, and "since the President had left the ordering of options on SALT to me," he writes, "I issued a directive asking the agencies to reduce the chaos to four options."[76] When this was done, four alternatives were presented by their proponents to (in Kissinger's words) a "President bored to distraction [by all the detail]" at the National Security Council meeting of April 8.

Option A, preferred by the Department of Defense and the Joint Chiefs, would have limited ICBMs and SLBMs to the current U.S. total (1,710) and frozen the number of bombers on both sides (527 American, 195 Soviet). In other words, it would have required a sizable reduction in the Soviet missile force while leaving the American ABM and MIRV programs untouched. Option B, ultimately Kissinger's preference, offered the same offensive limits as option A but either restricted the ABM systems of both sides to the capital cities (called national command authorities, or NCAs) or else banned them altogether. Option C, the most radical proposal and the favorite of the Arms Control and Disarmament Agency and the Department of State, included the same limitations as option B but added a ban on MIRVs. Option D, endorsed by the Department of Defense but not by the Joint Chiefs, proposed major reductions in ICBMs and SLBMs to a level of 1,000. It also banned the ABM or limited the system to national command authorities (NCAs), but it did not regulate the MIRV.[77]

As Kissinger recalls the situation, "I knew that my recommendation would carry an unusual weight [because] Nixon simply would not learn the technical details well enough to choose meaningfully."[78] So, "[swayed by] bureaucratic and political considerations" to a much greater degree than he normally allowed for, Kissinger recommended to the president that options C and D be selected as opening positions. "This would respond to Congressional and bureaucratic supporters of MIRV and ABM bans," he notes; "it would give us the positive public posture of having favored comprehensive limitations, [and] if the Soviets rejected [the proposals], as I firmly expected, we could then put forward Option B from a much stronger domestic and bureaucratic position."[79]

Nixon accepted Kissinger's recommendation but not before the two men further reduced the attractiveness of option C by attaching to the MIRV ban a requirement for on-site inspection not even requested by the Central Intelligence Agency, the primary monitoring authority.[80] Option D was already loaded with features that would make it unacceptable to the Russians: it omitted from limitation, for example, American forces in Europe capable of striking the Soviet Union (the so-called forward-based systems), while it singled out for reduction an area of particular Soviet strength, land-based missile forces and, especially, large MIRVable missiles like the SS-9.[81] The result in Vienna, as Nixon and Kissinger foresaw, was a quick rejection of both options by the Soviet delegation, though Semyonov at the same time surprised the Americans by accepting their proposal for an NCA-level limitation on ABM deployment.[82]

In any case, the way was now cleared for the introduction of a new American initiative along the lines of option B, and this was presented in Vienna on August 4, 1970. Stipulating a ceiling of 1,710 on ICBM and SLBM launchers and a sublimit of 250 on large ICBMs (but no limit on MIRVs), the proposal went on to offer an ABM ban as an alternative to the NCA-level limit on ABMs that the Soviets had already accepted. As Kissinger later confessed, there was an ulterior motive. "[An ABM ban] was certain to be rejected, especially when linked to an offensive freeze, and would enable us to move from there to insisting that the existing [Safeguard] sites be continued."[83] In other words, Kissinger was still fighting to preserve at least a minimal nationwide ABM defense and the MIRV while achieving the limits on the Russian building program (and restrictions on their MIRVing capacity) that the Department of Defense was demanding. He viewed himself as "trying to preserve the sinews of our defense and to catch up [with the Soviet Union] numerically in the face of the stormy dissent produced by Vietnam."[84] But in reality he was striving to maintain an American military dominance that was slipping rapidly toward parity. It is not surprising that the negotiations remained deadlocked for the remainder of the year.

None of this could help but be influenced by what was transpiring with regard to the Vietnam War. Neither Vietnamization nor unilateral reductions in force nor pressure on the Soviet Union had been successful in obtaining North Vietnam's agreement to mutual withdrawal from the South, and during the summer of 1969 Nixon and Kissinger became increasingly frustrated and even desperate regarding the situation. Their immediate, if private, reaction was to think in terms of forcing North Vietnam to its knees with a "savage, decisive [military] blow", but, though plans for such an operation (code named Duck Hook) were actually discussed, and though threats of escalation were secretly conveyed to Hanoi, Nixon's experience with the Washington antiwar moratorium in mid-October led him to realize that any recourse to extreme violence would have a catastrophic effect on public opinion.[85]

With this in mind, Nixon decided to address an appeal on November 3 to "the great silent majority" of his fellow citizens, vowing to continue on the dual track of Vietnamization and negotiations until "peace with honor" had been achieved and asking for patience with his efforts to preserve America's "free world leadership."[86] The response to the speech was more positive than even Nixon had dared hope. It succeeded in its immediate purpose, which was to buy the administration time and put its critics on the defensive.[87] By the end of the winter, as the White House stepped up its surveillance of suspected radicals, replaced the military draft with a more acceptable lottery system, and announced the withdrawal of 50,000 more troops from Vietnam, the antiwar movement was dividing against itself and losing much of its momentum.[88]

The trouble was that Nixon could not leave well enough alone. In his desire to strengthen the Vietnamization process, achieve a foreign policy success (to counteract several domestic setbacks), and demonstrate his ability to act forcefully, he succumbed in future months to the temptation to go on the military offensive in regions bordering South Vietnam, with disastrous results. Thus in February 1970 his authorization of bombing raids by B-52s on North Vietnamese troops in northern Laos was quickly discovered and led to serious protests in the Senate and a questionable attempt on the part of the administration to justify this action as an aspect of Vietnamization.[89] Even worse, at the end of April, six weeks after the neutralist regime of Prince Sihanouk in Cambodia had been overthrown by the reactionary General Lon Nol, Nixon's decision to send South Vietnamese and American troops into the Communist "sanctuaries" of neutral Cambodia produced an explosively negative reaction on the part of the American public.

University campuses across the country erupted, as students and faculty, astonished and suspicious at what they saw as an unjustified expansion of the war, marched, picketed, and protested. The killing of students at

Kent State University and an angry antiwar demonstration in Washington the following week raised the level of outrage and emotion to unprecedented heights.[90] In Congress Senators John Sherman Cooper (R-Ky.) and Frank Church (D-Idaho) introduced an amendment to a sales bill that prohibited American military activities in Cambodia after June 30, the date that Nixon quickly announced for the withdrawal of forces from that country. The Senate's approval of the Cooper-Church stipulation by a vote of 58 to 37 at the end of June was an indication of how impatient the country was becoming with the conflict in Southeast Asia.[91]

For the Nixon administration, the second half of 1970 was a time of frustrations and troubles. Under the shock of the Cambodian affair, the president now accepted Kissinger's suggestion that in the Paris negotiations a proposal for a "cease-fire in place" be substituted for the previous American demand for mutual withdrawal. Yet when Kissinger offered this major concession to the North Vietnamese in secret meetings in September, the representatives of Hanoi were unimpressed.[92] Equally disappointing was that Nixon's campaign to achieve reconciliation and leverage with Communist China appeared to have come to a grinding halt. Despite ambassadorial meetings in Warsaw during early 1970, and despite the administration's continued signaling of its interest in better relations, Beijing displayed a clearly pro-Soviet tilt in its foreign policy throughout the year and especially after Nixon's Cambodian incursion. Not until the none-too-public triumph of Jou Enlai's "moderate" faction at the Communist Party's Central Committee plenum of September 1970 were the alignments created for a Chinese opening to the United States, and it was December before Nixon and Kissinger became aware of new Chinese overtures.[93]

Progress in dealing with the Russians was also elusive. In the spring of 1970, tortured by Vietnam and deeply concerned about the autumn congressional elections, Nixon dreamed of silencing his antiwar critics by arranging an early summit meeting with Brezhnev and Kosygin. Indeed, according to Kissinger, the president's desire for a summit in the post-Cambodian period "reached a point of near obsession," Nixon being so eager that he would have accepted an "ABM only" agreement in order to see the Russian leaders before November.[94] Significantly for the future, however, Brezhnev was cautious enough about Nixon (or perhaps focused enough on Bonn and Beijing) to insist upon prior commitment not only to an ABM treaty but also to a European security conference and to a protocol on "accidental war" that the Americans believed (wrongly, it turned out) amounted to a de facto military alliance against China.[95]

So no summit occurred, and during September Nixon showed his

SEEKING AMERICA'S ESCAPE FROM VIETNAM • 89

irritation with the Russians, his hierarchical perspective, and his penchant for campaigning as an anti-Communist by the way he allowed such issues as hostilities between Syria and Jordan and crew stops by Soviet submarines in Cienfuegos (Cuba) to be magnified into ostensible crises involving the superpowers.[96] During these same months, between May and August 1970, the West German and Soviet governments were proceeding with the negotiations that culminated in an unprecedented understanding between them on the renunciation of force. As Willy Brandt journeyed to Moscow in August to sign this treaty and to engage in extended talks with Brezhnev, it must have seemed to the American president as if the German chancellor had stolen his summit conference.[97]

Back in February 1970 Richard Nixon had been the first president ever to submit an annual foreign policy report to the Congress. This volume, entitled *A New Strategy for Peace,* had been almost four months in preparation and was intended to highlight the ideas and achievements of the new American "realism." Contending that, because of declining Communist unity and the resurgence of America's allies, "the postwar period in international relations has ended," the president made clear his intent to develop "a new approach to foreign policy to match a new era." This approach was based, he asserted, on three principles: partnership with allies, strength at home, and a willingness to negotiate. Since the ideological "isms" had lost their vitality, according to Nixon, it was now possible to "regard our Communist adversaries first and foremost as nations pursuing their own interests." We are willing "to negotiate our points of difference in a fair and business-like manner," he insisted. "No nation need be our permanent enemy."[98]

But the reality of Nixon's first year in office was more complex than the plan. In the first place, despite the ostensible strategy of negotiation (and manipulation) without regard to ideology, Nixon and Kissinger were still too deeply wedded to conservative notions of East-West polarity, political hierarchy, and American primacy to forgo the attempt to hold Soviet Communism responsible for most of the world's instability and turmoil. Thus they attempted to ameliorate such trauma, and in particular the conflict in Vietnam, by bringing a none-too-subtle pressure on Moscow in addition to dealing directly with the areas involved. The trouble, of course, especially after the spring of 1969, was that none of the Communist powers—not Russia or North Vietnam or even China—was eager enough to negotiate with the capitalist superpower that it would run the risk within the Communist world of appearing to help Washington win a war it was well on the way to losing. In fact, the Soviet Union, sorely troubled by its competition with China, was moving during these months to take advantage of the chance to practice what Kissinger called "selective détente," improving its relations with West Germany rather than with the United States.[99]

Nevertheless, certain things were occurring within the major powers and beneath the diplomatic surface that would make 1971 and 1972 more eventful than the preceding years for bargaining and agreement. In the United States the resistance of a war-weary public and Congress to military appropriations and commitments was worrying the president greatly, while overseas the readiness of the Brandt government to negotiate with the Russians was troubling him as well. These anxieties, combined with frustration at the lack of progress on other fronts, drove Nixon to the point of near despair in the weeks immediately following Republican losses in the congressional elections of November 1970, a period that the president later described as the blackest of his entire first term.[100]

As fate would have it, however, and as we shall see, it was not only Richard Nixon who was in a serious dilemma. In Russia—and in China, too—trends were growing that would soon compel the leaders of these countries to seek new arrangements of power and relationship.

5

FINDING AMERICA'S WAY
TO DÉTENTE

If the significant factors of Soviet-American relations were somewhat mixed in their impact during most of 1970, in December of that year an increasing number of developments began to push both Moscow and Washington in the direction of greater collaboration. Of paramount importance was the decision by China's leaders to convey to the Americans a genuine interest in better relations, a decision that gave the Russians serious cause for alarm and opened up the possibility to Nixon of possessing a substantial new leverage vis-à-vis the Soviet Union. Almost simultaneously, rioting broke out in Poland in response to shortages of consumer goods, producing a confrontation that was bound to increase Soviet anxiety and eagerness to improve East bloc economic performance. Meanwhile, the success of West Germany's *Ostpolitik* and its tie to the continuing four-power negotiations over Berlin meant that Washington and Moscow came under growing pressure from Western Europe to solve the political riddle of the former German capital and clear away one of the continuing sore points of the Cold War.

Other factors also became conducive to the enlargement of superpower détente. The growing noncompetitiveness of the American economy, particularly as it manifested itself in a weakening dollar and an adverse balance of trade, rendered the prospect of a large and technology-starved Russian market enticing to Washington. A renewed congressional assault upon the administration's defense budget, an outgrowth of a reviving antiwar movement, encouraged both Nixon and Kissinger to think in terms of achieving an arms accord with Moscow while they still had assets with which to bargain. Finally, their frustrated efforts to negotiate a conclusion to the Vietnam War led them not only into ill-advised ventures like the South Vietnamese invasion of Laos (February 1971) but also into substantial political concessions to the enemy in Hanoi. Yet nothing they offered seemed enough to bring the North Vietnamese to an agreement, and as American military withdrawals continued, there seemed less and less chance that the United States would be able to bring the war to a quick end. With the election of 1972 rapidly approaching, and the president falling in the opinion polls, Nixon and Kissinger were driven to obscure their lack of success in Vietnam with a peace policy on other fronts.

In explaining why there was suddenly so much progress in Soviet-American relations, Kissinger suggests that by the end of 1970 America had finally moved into an advantageous situation:

> We were, in fact, in the strongest position since Nixon had come to office. We had [the crises of] Cienfuegos and Jordan behind us; we had demonstrated our determination to resist pressures; Moscow had experienced the brittleness of its East European dominion. And we had a safety valve [in that] we [had] received the first direct communication from the Chinese leadership proposing high level talks.[1]

Yet as understandable as it is for statesmen to justify their actions as part of a design or a response to opportunity, the fact is that Nixon and Kissinger were also very much propelled by need in their efforts to establish an understanding with Moscow. In truth, there was an element of near panic in the way they sought out and achieved an arrangement with the Russians that they could later use to their advantage at home and in Vietnam. Indicative of this deep anxiety were the remarks Kissinger made to Admiral Elmo Zumwalt, chief of naval operations, in a private encounter on an afternoon in December 1970:

> K feels that the U.S. has passed its historic high point like so many other civilizations. He believes U.S. is on downhill and cannot be roused by political challenge. He states that his job is to persuade the Russians to give us the best deal we can get, recognizing that the historical forces favor them. He says that he realizes that in the light of history he will be recognized as one of those who negotiated terms favorable to the Soviets, but that the American people have only themselves to blame because they lack the stamina to stay the course. . . . K said "You don't get re-elected to the Presidency on a platform that admits you got behind. You talk instead about the great partnership for peace achieved in your term."[2]

In short, American leaders had some sense of operating from strength, but they also believed that they were in a position of peculiar vulnerability and weakness. The fascinating thing is that the same can be said about their opponents in the Kremlin.

Nixon, and later Kissinger, had worked hard to make clear to the government of Communist China that they were attracted by the possibility of developing a new and more cooperative relation with that country. Even after the Chinese broke off the Warsaw talks in February 1969, the new administration continued to signal its interest by means of messages delivered through intermediaries, a reduction of trade and travel restrictions (July 21), and after rumors of a Soviet attack on China began circulating, a speech by the undersecretary of state expressing concern about the escalation of the Sino-Soviet quarrel (September 5).[3] Subsequently, the Chinese responded to an American overture and met with American representatives in Warsaw in January and February 1970—only to end these sessions in the wake of the Cambodian invasion.[4] Nixon and Kissinger, however, were not to be discouraged and continued to offer "gestures [to China] that could not be rejected and did not need to be acknowledged."[5] On August 26, 1970, for example, the American government unveiled a further reduction in trade restrictions, and in October Nixon not only referred publicly for the first time to the "People's Republic of China" but also sent a confidential message to Beijing underlining his flexibility on the issue of Taiwan.[6]

By contrast, it was only with great difficulty that Mao and Jou were able to reorient Chinese foreign policy so as to create a genuinely triangular situation. It was not until the plenum of the Communist Party's Central Committee in the late summer of 1970 that they and their moderate allies were able to overcome the resistance of the military faction and institute a decisive change.[7] And not until December 9 were the Chinese leaders able to unmistakably convey to the Americans that they were receptive to the idea of high-level negotiations.[8]

Nixon and Kissinger were, of course, immensely pleased and relieved to finally receive this invitation, but from their perspective the Sino-American relation remained extremely complex. Just as in May 1970 the Cambodian intervention had set back efforts to improve Washington's connection with Beijing, so in February 1971 the invasion of Laos by the South Vietnamese army and its American support groups slowed the move toward rapprochement with China. Still, Nixon's unwillingness to redeem the failure in Laos with further intervention seems to have reassured the Chinese leadership, and on April 6, Jou En-lai stunned the world by inviting the American table tennis team (then in Japan) to visit China.[9] The White House quickly reciprocated by announcing a substantial dismantling of its twenty-year trade embargo,[10] and on April 27, Jou informed the anxiously waiting Nixon and Kissinger of his government's readiness to receive in China a "special envoy, *or* the Secretary of State, *or* even the

President of the United States himself."[11] Further negotiations, carried on in complete secrecy, and on the American side even in the face of unhelpful public statements by unsuspecting colleagues, resulted in an agreement that Kissinger would fly to Beijing from Pakistan on July 9 to begin arranging a presidential visit.[12]

Thus by mid-1971 a significant change was occurring in the structure of major power relations. Driven by its fear of and hostility toward the Soviet Union and by its realization that the United States no longer constituted a pressing threat, China was inching its way back into a position of genuine strategic freedom. Confronted with this development, Nixon and Kissinger were wise enough (and needy enough) to stimulate, assist, and relate to the process in every way they could. Indeed, they were willing to pay a high price for the prospective advantages that it gave them in dealing with domestic critics and with the Vietnamese and the Russians. In his July meeting with the Chinese, Kissinger went so far as to promise an early withdrawal of American troops from Taiwan and to give the Chinese classified intelligence about the disposition of Soviet forces in Siberia. He also agreed to inform Beijing in detail "of any understanding affecting Chinese interests that we might consider with the Soviets."[13] This extraordinary pledge was honored by Kissinger throughout the summer and fall and during his second trip to China in October, which Nixon and he scheduled knowing full well that it would occur during the opening session of the United Nations and would assist the Chinese Communist government in finally gaining admission to that organization.[14]

As important as China was, however, it was not the only "socialist" country that was creating problems for the Russians and opportunities for the Americans during 1971. The previous December, after Willy Brandt's interest in normalizing relations with Warsaw had resulted in West German recognition of Poland's post-Potsdam boundaries, the regime of Wladislav Gomulka attempted to use this foreign policy success as a cover for the introduction of price increases designed to ease the economy's chronic food shortages. It was a serious miscalculation, since severe riots, led by the workers themselves, broke out in several Polish cities and within two weeks necessitated the replacement of the veteran Gomulka by Edward Gierek as party secretary. The new Polish leadership acted quickly to suppress the disturbances by rescinding price increases and promising improved distribution of supplies, but given the region's obvious economic weakness, tension in Eastern Europe continued at substantial levels.[15] Meanwhile, the lesson of the food riots was not lost on Russian planners, who stepped up their efforts both to assist the Polish economy and to produce more grain and meat for their own internal market.[16]

What the Polish unrest suggested to Washington, however, according to the memoirs of both Kissinger and NSC staff member William Hyland, was that the Soviet Union could not continue to pursue détente in Europe without the collaboration of the United States. "[With] détente with Bonn at least temporarily slowed down," Kissinger wrote to Nixon on December 20, "the Soviet leaders, if they choose to maintain some prospect of détente, may be inclined to show some improvement in their relations with us."[17] In any case, Nixon and Kissinger persuaded themselves to go on the offensive in the days that followed.

Exactly what form this initiative took is still not completely clear; some students of the period conclude that the president actually offered Brezhnev assistance in modernizing the Russian economy in return for concessions on an array of issues.[18] But we know from Kissinger's memoirs that on December 22 and again, more directly, on January 9, 1971, he proposed to Soviet Ambassador Dobrynin that they utilize their private "channel" to solve "some of the outstanding issues," specifically, the matters of Berlin and SALT. Kissinger says he told the ambassador that the United States wanted just two things from the Soviet Union concerning Berlin: (1) improved access to the city, and (2) a Soviet guarantee of the new arrangements. On SALT, he writes, "I told Dobrynin we would accept the Soviet proposal to negotiate an ABM treaty provided the Soviets undertook to begin negotiations immediately on offensive limitations; the two negotiations would conclude simultaneously."[19]

What Kissinger does not explain clearly is that, in his eagerness to push forward, he was making a significant concession with regard to arms control: he was indicating a willingness to abandon the tight link, which the administration had previously demanded, between a treaty on defensive weapons and one on offensive weapons. He was opening the door to combining an ABM treaty with an interim agreement on offensive weapons that would require no more than a freeze on construction of new ICBMs while negotiations on a permanent treaty continued.[20]

The truth is that, as much as Americans and Russians may reminisce about negotiating from strength, both were under increasing pressure to compromise their differences. Willy Brandt in particular was growing more and more insistent about moving forward, for he was eager to supplement the West German–Soviet treaty of the previous August with a successful four-power agreement on Berlin and thus clear the way for the treaty's early ratification.[21] Indeed, a six-week recess in the quadripartite talks after December 10 touched off a minor crisis in German-American relations. Brandt's response was to write personal letters to Nixon, Pompidou, and Heath in which he asked that the Berlin negotiations be put into "continuous conference"; he also hinted that his government saw no reason why discussions with East Germany or ratification of the German-

Polish treaty of December should have to wait for an agreement about Berlin.[22] In January 1971 Brandt backed down on both these threats, but not before they had caused Nixon and Kissinger considerable concern.[23] As Kissinger recalls in his memoirs, "a prolonged stalement [over Berlin] offering no hope of solution could damage US-German relations severely. We could become the whipping boy, accused by Brandt of blocking his policies. . . . If there were another Berlin crisis, the onus could fall on us."[24]

When Dobrynin informed Kissinger on January 23 that the Soviet leadership was pleased he was willing to "engage" himself in the Berlin talks (i.e., to circumvent regular channels), Kissinger was quick to notify the West Germans (through Egon Bahr, Brandt's confidante) that "we were prepared to accept the Chancellor's suggestions to speed up the Berlin negotiations."[25] At the end of the month, Bahr visited the United States, and soon thereafter, with the collaboration of Kenneth Rush, the American ambassador to West Germany, Kissinger's secret "channel" to Bonn became "operational."[26] It continued to function throughout the spring and summer as the formal negotiations moved toward resolution. In late April, after Bahr flew to Washington once again to urge the Americans to use the Soviet demand for a consulate in West Berlin as a bargaining point, Kissinger and Dobrynin decided to enlarge their channel with private talks in Bonn among Bahr, Rush, and Valentin Falin, the Soviet ambassador to West Germany.[27] Two weeks later, the Stalinist Walter Ulbricht, a long-time critic of Brandt's *Ostpolitik,* was forced out as party boss in East Germany. It seemed clear that major changes were about to occur with regard to Berlin.[28]

Other major pressures on Nixon and Kissinger, in addition to that from Germany, derived from Congress and the domestic political situation. "We were again about to face the now annual ritualistic assault by Congress on our defense budget," Kissinger writes concerning the winter of 1970–71, adding sarcastically that the legislature seemed driven by a "myth assiduously fostered by various peace groups: that only if the Congress emasculated our military establishment would our government behave responsibly and end the war in Vietnam." Yet Kissinger admits that that very congressional impatience was a factor in causing him to expedite the negotiations on arms control. "If we failed [to achieve a deal with the Russians]," he writes, "Congressional pressures might cause us to lose any leverage on the Soviet strategic buildup."[29]

The Ninety-second Congress and the American public were very critical of the apparent lack of progress in arms control and in ending the war in Vietnam. On January 17, 1971, the *New York Times,* eager for an identifiable success, condemned the president's insistence on linking offensive and defensive weapons; on February 3, Senator Frank Church (D-Idaho) called for "an ABM-only agreement as a first step" toward later agreements; and in March this suggestion was endorsed by Senators Hubert Humphrey (D-Minn.), Harold Hughes (D-Iowa), and George McGovern (D-S.Dak.). Meanwhile, serious efforts were being made to cut military appropriations. Senator Edmund Muskie of Maine, the Democratic presidential front-runner in the polls, proposed that the United States abandon both Poseidon and Minuteman III missiles and agree to a mutual suspension of ABM deployment, and Senator William Proxmire (D-Wis.) campaigned vigorously against funding for the B-1 bomber and other aircraft.[30] Senator Mike Mansfield (D-Mont.) revived his perennial resolution to withdraw half of the 300,000 American troops from Europe and saw it garner thirty-six votes in the Senate on May 19.[31] In the summer, Congress cut more than $3 billion from the president's $73 billion defense request and substantially reduced the budget for weapons from that of the previous year.[32]

This widespread dissatisfaction was compounded by the administration's decision to sponsor an incursion by South Vietnamese forces into Laos during February in an attempt to cut the Ho Chi Minh trail.[33] Though the response of the antiwar movement to this unexpected attack was nowhere near as emotional as its reaction to the Cambodian invasion, there were impressive demonstrations during February and April.[34] Congress, also, was extremely disturbed, particularly after the Laotian operation collapsed into a demoralizing withdrawal. During February and March no fewer than five resolutions were introduced aimed at restricting the president's war-making authority, prohibiting expenditures for combat, and fixing a date for American withdrawal from Vietnam. Between April 1 and July 1 there were seventeen House or Senate votes on resolutions of this nature.[35]

Overall, the political prospects of the president were bleak. The Gallup poll reported in early spring that Nixon's popularity had sunk to the lowest level of any president since Harry Truman. The Harris poll showed him running barely even with, and even behind, Senator Muskie.[36] Nixon speaks of the winter of 1970–71 as the "lowest point of my first term," but he was not the only one who had a sense of impending disaster. As Jeb Magruder of the Committee for the Reelection of the President remembered it two years afterward, "All of us who were later in the campaign were still on the White House staff [in January 1971], and there was a considerable degree of concern that the President would have a very difficult time being re-elected. . . . We felt it was going to be a very difficult race."[37] It was in this situation, then, that Nixon came face to face with his most significant foreign policy decisions—decisions regarding China, Russia, SALT, and Vietnam.

One further pressure on the president must not be overlooked, although it remained somewhat in the background until the summer of 1971: that of the economy. We have observed that the United States was suffering economically both from creeping noncompetitiveness and from the aftereffects of the Vietnam War inflation. At the beginning of 1971 a number of unhappy trends came together: inflation was more than 5.5 percent (despite vigorous efforts to dampen it); unemployment was at 6 percent; balance-of-payment deficits were the most severe in U.S. history; and speculation against the dollar had become almost constant.[38] Nixon, not unconcerned, responded to the situation in three ways: first, by appointing one of the strongest personalities he could find (also a Democrat and an ardent nationalist)—John Connally of Texas—to be secretary of the treasury; second, by creating a new economic coordinating agency within the administration, the Council on International Economic Policy, chaired by Peter Peterson, a well-known banker; and third, by casting about for a new "game plan" (his phrase) that would at one and the same time stimulate the economy, control inflation, and improve the balance of trade.[39] The final result, of course, was the Camp David "summit" of August 1971, where Nixon and his advisers decided upon a package of surprising innovations, including tax credits for business, controls on prices and wages, an import surcharge, and the closure of the "gold window" (i.e., suspension of the dollar's convertibility into gold).[40]

While all of this was going on, more voices continued to be raised on behalf of liberalizing trade with the Communist world. Secretary of Commerce Stans was bolder than ever, predicting to the press a worsening of America's trade position during 1971 and calling for expanded commerce with Russia and its European allies. Stans contended that the United States, which now accounted for only 4 percent of East-West trade, could do much better. "This is a market where American goods are needed and wanted, and one that we are ideally suited to satisfy."[41] In April 1971, Peter Peterson submitted a 132-page report to the president entitled "The United States in a Changing World Economy," which asked pointedly, "Are we advocating our own economic interests as forcefully as we should?"[42] Three months later, Peterson wrote to Nixon privately, "You know, I'm sure, that [pressure from] the U.S. business community and the Hill is growing daily to liberalize East-West trade, and our second successive month of trade deficit is being used as another reason [to do this]." He added that he nevertheless understood "the primacy of demonstrated progress on the other negotiations."[43]

Nixon and Kissinger felt the economic pressure intensely, but it was only one of many reasons to make arrangements with the Russians, and they never gave way completely on their demand that they should get something for American trade. "We sat on a scheme to sell . . . machinery for a Soviet civilian truck plant on the Kama River for two years in the face of massive pressures from our economic agencies and the Congress," Kissinger admits, not approving it until "after the Soviets had agreed to the May 20 compromise on SALT." Similarly, he says, a number of commercial projects related to the Kama River plant were held up in Washington "until there was a breakthrough on Berlin."[44]

What Kissinger does not mention is that there were more transactions going on than these. Nixon, for example, found it mutually advantageous to promise the Soviets a lifting of the American grain embargo as part of the SALT "bargain" in May. With the U.S. corn supply near an all-time record and its balance of trade never more anemic, it must have seemed time to bring this factor into play.[45] The arrangement was kept secret at the time, partly to make the agreement regarding SALT appear fairer but also because the administration needed the permission of the maritime unions to ship grain in Soviet bottoms, and it believed it could more easily gain this without the glare of publicity.[46] Thus, it simply included a reduction of legal restrictions on grain shipments in a general relaxation of controls covering the export of nonstrategic items to the Communist world, announced on June 10 and presented to the public primarily in terms of American relations with China.[47]

The key negotiation of these months—and as it turned out, the one in which the major concessions were made—was that involving arms control. The reader will recall that, in January 1971, following an autumn of deadlock on SALT (due largely to instructions from Washington that required the American delegation to stand firm) as well as important developments regarding China, Poland, and Germany, Kissinger worked out an arrangement with Dobrynin that these negotiations would be conducted through their own private channel as well as by the national delegations in Vienna and Helsinki.

These back-channel negotiations (the existence of which would not be known to the American SALT delegation until May)[48] were to be difficult and controversial—and are to this day somewhat clouded in mystery. The issues included (1) whether or not an ABM treaty would be "tied" to an agreement on offensive weaponry, (2) what level of completeness a "ban" on ABMs would entail, and (3) what degree of comprehensiveness and reduction would be achieved in an understanding on offensive arms. Pressure on the American side (not to speak of the Russian) mounted as the talks went on. Originally, this derived primarily from the need to head off the proponents of "first, an ABM-ban" approach and from the related necessity of doing something about the unsatisfactory political situation. But as time passed such pressure was supplemented by the concerns of the Department of Defense, where analysts worried that limitations on Safeguard (as defined by the NCA proposal of the previous April) would leave Minuteman vulnerable to a Soviet first strike.[49] In February the Russians increased American anxiety by ending the moratorium on silo construction established at the start of SALT and by beginning to add new silos in SS-9 and SS-11 complexes at the rate of more than a dozen a month.[50]

As Kissinger and Dobrynin struggled in secret throughout winter and spring, both had multiple objectives. Nixon and Kissinger had been trying for almost a year to disengage themselves from their own ABM-NCA proposal (offered originally when Nixon was desperate for a summit conference in 1970). In doing this, they were driven first by the realization that such a proposal could not be made truly symmetrical (since Congress would not pay to build an ABM around Washington) and later by concern about its adequacy in protecting Minuteman.[51] (It is in this light that one can understand their perplexing proposals of August 1970 [zero ABMs] and April 1971 [four ABM sites for the United States to protect ICBMs and one for the Soviet Union to defend Moscow].)[52] Dobrynin and his government, on the other hand, were attempting to avoid having to pay for an ABM ban with a weapons freeze by putting off negotiations on offensive arms until after an ABM treaty was signed or, failing that, restricting any freeze to specified weapons.[53] Kissinger, of course, hoped to exclude from the discussions what the Russians called forward-based systems (aircraft deployed by the United States in Continental Europe and on carriers in the Mediterranean and the northwest Pacific).[54] Dobrynin wished to avoid any mention of SLBMs, which the Russians were building at a rapid rate (though their force did not yet equal that of the Americans), and of weapon modernization, since the Soviet Union was unwilling to accept constraints on its right to MIRV.[55]

In the end, a deal was struck that involved concessions on the part of the Soviet Union but that cost the United States substantially more. As Kissinger tells it, on March 15 Dobrynin abandoned the Soviet demand that ABM be confined to the capitals (NCA) but remained insistent that an agreement on ABM precede discussions on offensive weapons. On April 23 the Soviets conceded the point that offensive limits could be discussed (and a freeze on deployment established) before an ABM treaty was completed but made this dependent on the United States accepting an NCA arrangement. Finally, on May 15, the Soviet ambassador accepted the "simultaneity of [offensive/defensive] negotiation" and abandoned his insistence on the NCA system, thus clearing the path for an agreement between the two countries.[56]

However, there is more to the story than Kissinger tells us. In the process, he paid for what he got from the Russians in a number of significant ways: (1) by allowing the weapons freeze to be tentatively defined without reference to SLBMs, (2) by accepting language that permitted the Soviets to continue modernizing and replacing missiles without restraint, and (3) by secretly promising the Soviet Union access to the American corn and grain market. Furthermore, in return for the exclusion of FBS from the strategic balance (and negotiations), the Americans implied that they would accept unequal ratios of missiles between the two countries in the final interim agreement on offensive weaponry.[57]

On May 20, 1971, Nixon and Brezhnev simultaneously and proudly announced that a procedural "breakthrough" had been achieved in SALT, a development that pointed to the desirability of a summit meeting the following year.[58] At the time, this breakthrough was received with great enthusiasm,[59] but in retrospect it does not seem as exhilarating. It did provide a valuable lift to American morale at a difficult point, and it did in all likelihood provide the key to the Soviet-American summit that would usher in détente. Nevertheless, it was negotiated from weakness as well as strength, and as a result, Kissinger would have to spend much of the next year secretly attempting to recapture part of what he had given away to get it. Moreover, in another sense the breakthrough obscured what was a largely lost opportunity. In terms of the arms race, an ABM ban was a genuine accomplishment, but with regard to offensive weapons, the probability now was that over the long haul the Soviet Union would be limited only a little and the United States not at all.[60]

Contributing to the situation that made these agreements possible, of course, were the political developments occurring within the Soviet Union. We shall examine the causes and consequences of internal Soviet change later, but it suffices at this point to note that March and April 1971 were the months of the Twenty-fourth Communist Party Congress, the congress at which Leonid Brezhnev established his leadership of the Politburo in foreign affairs and enunciated his "peace program," with its attendant opening to the West. Having attacked Kosygin's stewardship of the sluggish Russian economy and openly identified himself with the Soviet response to Brandt's *Ostpolitik*, Brezhnev had put himself in a position where he could plausibly argue that American capital and technology were the answers to the economic problems plaguing the U.S.S.R. When the threat of a Chinese-American rapprochement was added to the equation, his case for reaching out to the United States became truly persuasive. In any event, possessed of increased power and faced with the concessions

Nixon and Kissinger were willing to offer, Brezhnev moved quickly. In the space of one month (May 1971) he not only arranged to displace Walter Ulbricht as leader of East Germany and to endorse the breakthrough in SALT but also announced his willingness to sign a treaty outlawing biological weapons and to talk about reducing conventional forces in Europe (mutual and balanced force reductions, or MBFR).[61]

Yet where Brezhnev's new flexibility became most apparent was in the continuing negotiations regarding Berlin. The first hint of this came on May 25, when the Soviet ambassador, in the twentieth round of the four-power talks, indicated the readiness of his government to draft a common text of an agreement on Berlin in lieu of the separate Allied and Russian drafts of February 5 and March 26. Then, on June 7, moving sharply toward the Western position, the ambassador agreed both to abandon his refusal to guarantee West German access to Berlin and to accept the continuation of Bonn's "official presence" in the former capital.[62] In mid-June, Brezhnev himself, speaking in Berlin, emphasized that the Soviet Union was prepared "to make efforts to bring this matter to a successful conclusion."[63] In June and July the ambassadors met more and more frequently and narrowed their differences substantially.

The motivations of the principal actors are not as easy to track as their actions, however. Nixon in his memoirs, for example, strongly implies that real progress on the Berlin settlement did not occur until after the July 15 announcement that he would go to China.[64] Similarly, Kissinger asserts that "after the announcement of the President's trip to Peking, the unsettled issues on Berlin were resolved in one week to our satisfaction."[65] But both contentions tend to exaggerate Nixon's and Kissinger's (if not China's) roles in this, as does Kissinger's claim that he and Dobrynin, through their secret channel, arrived at answers to a number of deadlocks regarding Berlin.[66]

Kenneth Rush is probably closer to the truth when he asserts that China was not an appreciable factor in the bargaining and that perhaps Kissinger's discussions with Dobrynin on Berlin were "never important."[67] The sequence of events indicates that Brezhnev wanted a Berlin agreement primarily because he wanted the Soviet-West German treaty of August 1970 ratified. Deteriorating Soviet ties with China made friendship with Bonn more attractive, especially after a gratuitous intervention by Beijing in Balkan affairs during the summer of 1971, but one should not underestimate Moscow's desire for trade and for "normalizing" European affairs in its push for accommodation.[68]

So was a solution in Berlin the key to unraveling the East-West conundrum? Nixon seems to have felt that it was and said so on several occasions. On the margin of a briefing book in March 1971 he noted, "progress on Berlin can be the breakthrough to progress on normalization of East-West relations generally."[69] Subsequently, in his press conference of October 12, 1971, he asserted: "We have had an agreement coming out of the SALT talks with regard to the hot line and accidental war and, of course, most important of all—and I think this is the item that, for both us and for them, led us to conclude that now was the time for a summit meeting—we have had an agreement on Berlin."[70] Still later, in his memoirs, Nixon put it this way: "Before 1971 it was common to consider Berlin and the Middle East as the greatest stumbling blocks in US–USSR relations. By removing at least one of these obstacles we were able to clear the way for a summit meeting."[71]

Nevertheless, with due regard for Nixon's acumen in reading the images and realities of the Cold War, it seems more accurate to consider the Berlin settlement a symptom rather than a cause of the change occurring in major power relations. The strategic bargain of May, the West German concessions of the previous August, the prospect of trade and technology for faltering economies, and the need to distract the American electorate from the unending war—these factors were more basic than the Berlin agreement in moving the participants toward a new relation. Indeed, though Moscow had made the holding of a Soviet-American summit conditional on a Berlin settlement since April 1971, it is instructive that the Kremlin's invitation to the summit was actually extended on August 10, a month before the final Berlin agreement (and a week before the American concession regarding a Soviet consulate in West Berlin).[72] One could argue, certainly, that there had been very significant progress by that point in the Berlin negotiations (Nixon himself said this on August 4), but if Berlin was so central, why did the Russians not wait to invite the president until after the agreement was complete?[73]

In any case, by the autumn of 1971 the administration could take some pleasure in its achievements. Not only had a breakthrough to China occurred and two international summits been arranged for an election year, but East and West had compromised long-standing differences on Berlin, and Soviet-American agreements on weapons and trade seemed to be taking shape. Moreover, Nixon and Kissinger fortified the trend, offering consolation to Moscow for the American rapprochement with China by signing two understandings negotiated in SALT that Washington originally intended to save for the Moscow summit.[74] The first of these was an agreement designed to upgrade the hot line by switching to satellite communications; the second was an agreement on measures to reduce the risk of "accidental war" in cases of technical malfunction.[75] The hot line understanding had been ready to sign since May, the accidental war protocol since August, and in each case the Soviets were eager to render the agreement effective as soon as possible. The formal signing of both took place in Washington on September 30, 1971, the occasion of Foreign Minister Gromyko's annual trip to the United States.[76] Two weeks later President Nixon announced to the public that he would be visiting the U.S.S.R. the following spring, after he returned from China.[77]

Another important way in which Nixon and Kissinger pacified the Russians (while also helping the economy) was to approve long-pending Soviet-American commercial transactions and to send Secretary of Commerce Maurice Stans on an exploratory visit to Moscow. Two weeks before Stans set out, on November 5, administration officials revealed that they had reached an understanding with the maritime unions that would allow the Soviet Union to purchase $136 million in American grain for use as livestock feed.[78] Then, immediately before Stan's departure, the Commerce Department announced that it had approved the leasing of $528 million worth of equipment for the construction of the Kama River project.[79] Stans's stay in the U.S.S.R. was itself quite successful and featured extended talks with Premier Kosygin and other officials about the prospects for increased trade.[80] Later, in December, Soviet Agricultural Minister Vladimir Matskevich was also hosted royally when he visited the United States at the invitation of the American Department of Agriculture.[81] During these same weeks Secretary of the Treasury John Connally was meeting with Allied finance ministers in Rome and bludgeoning them into agreements that effectively devalued the dollar.[82] Russian purchases and a cheaper dollar would work together to improve the badly weakened American balance of trade.

The one real setback to Soviet-American relations during the winter grew out of events in a surprisingly distant area: the Indian subcontinent. Long-smouldering ethnic and political tension in Pakistan had given rise to brutal repression by Yahya Kahn in East Pakistan, to a massive flight of Bengalis (largely Hindu) from that area into India, and finally, in December, to war between India and Pakistan.[83] Further complicating the matter from the perspective of Washington was the long-standing dislike that Nixon felt toward Indira Gandhi, the Indian prime minister, and the fact that, in Kissinger's words, Pakistan "was our crucial link to Peking; and Pakistan was one of China's closest allies."[84] Indeed, the evidence indicates that the determining consideration for Nixon throughout this entire episode was his desire to preserve the forthcoming Chinese-American summit.

Nixon and Kissinger persuaded themselves, largely on the basis of secret and highly suspect intelligence, that Gandhi's government was waging and prolonging the war not only to assist East Pakistan (Bangladesh) in obtaining a decent (and probably independent) status but also in order to attack and dismember West Pakistan itself.[85] Moreover, completely apart from the issue of Pakistan's usefulness as a message carrier to and from China, Nixon and Kissinger saw these events hierarchically, that is, as part of a struggle among the superpowers. Thus, if the United States were unable to prevent India and its "ally," the Soviet Union, from humiliating (and injuring) Pakistan and its "ally," China, the result would be doubly negative. The balance of power would be weakened, and the United States would lose credibility with China, perhaps even to the point of forfeiting the scheduled summit. It was to avoid these eventualities that the president insisted on maintaining a "tilt" toward Pakistan, despite explicit opposition from his own officials in the field, area specialists in Washington, and the secretary of state—none of whom were as impressed as he was with Pakistan's moral position or with India's threat to Pakistan.[86]

The confrontations with Moscow developed suddenly in December 1971. The Soviets had urged restraint on Mrs. Gandhi ever since (and even before) she signed a treaty of friendship with them the previous August, but this did not prevent Kissinger from calling in Dobrynin's deputy on December 5 and demanding that the U.S.S.R. stop encouraging India. Subsequently, the same official was handed a letter written by Nixon to Brezhnev urging the Soviet leader, "in the spirit" of the forthcoming summit, to persuade the Indians to moderate their demands (the implication being that the demands involved the dismemberment of Pakistan).[87]

What is more, on December 10, after the Indian ambassador refused to give assurances that India would not attack West Pakistan, the president dispatched an American naval force from the Pacific toward the Bay of Bengal.[88] Two days later, according to Nixon's and Kissinger's memoirs, the two men decided in a meeting at the White House that if China entered the war and the Soviet Union threatened China, "we would not stand idly by."[89] Whether this threat was actually conveyed to the Russians is still not completely clear, although Kissinger did make a point of telling a group of journalists on December 14 that, if the Soviet Union did not restrain India, the president might have to reconsider his plans for attending a summit.[90] Neither is it clear to what extent those threats that were transmitted to Moscow were taken seriously. On December 15, after Gandhi offered Pakistan an unconditional cease-fire, Nixon and Kissinger were quick to conclude that India had responded to Soviet pressure, and the Soviet Union to U.S. pressure; but Gandhi herself later openly expressed amazement at the Americans' beliefs.[91]

What is clear, aside from the impressive hierarchical quality of Nixon's and Kissinger's thinking, is that they were willing to run risks with the Soviet summit in order to be sure they could count on a meeting with the Chinese leadership. This order of priorities would show up again the following April, when they were confronted (after the Chinese summit) with the need to do something about a serious military challenge from Moscow's "client" in Hanoi.

An interesting side effect of the events of this winter (1971–72) was an increase in tension between Nixon and Kissinger. A number of factors were involved, including the anxiety of the president at the possibility of losing the opening to China and his irritation at the opposition within his own government. "I've been catching unshirted hell every half-hour from the President, who says we're not tough enough [on India]," Kissinger is reported to have told the administration's crisis management team, the Washington Special Action Group, on December 3.[92] Ten days later, the rift deepened considerably when classified documents revealing the administration's tilt toward Pakistan reached the press and Nixon quickly concluded (as he had on earlier occasions) that the "liberals" on Kissinger's staff must be "leaking" information to reporters.[93]

An added factor in Nixon's displeasure was the celebrity status that Kissinger had acquired as a result of his two trips to China. Nixon had long complained to his staff about Kissinger's penchant for giving "backgrounders" to the press, but he was particularly infuriated when (as happened twice in December) Kissinger was quoted extensively by name.[94] In January 1972 he told H. R. Haldeman and Alexander Haig that he "wanted to take a very hard line with Kissinger," even to the point of replacing him if necessary.[95] Yet, for all his anger and jealousy, Nixon was much too dependent on Kissinger to fire him.

The Vietnam War, of course, remained the main problem for the administration and one of the paramount factors in maintaining the momentum toward Soviet-American détente. (Nixon was willing to gamble with the Russian summit, if necessary, to head off a severe loss of face, but he was still persuaded that the route to peace in Southeast Asia lay largely through Moscow.) Neither public nor private negotiations with the Vietnamese had produced much agreement during 1970, despite (or perhaps because of) the fact that the United States continued to withdraw its troops from the war zone at a substantial rate. The administration's position, as outlined by Nixon in his speech of October 7, 1970, was that peace could be achieved only through a cease-fire in place, linked with mutual (American and North Vietnamese) withdrawal from South Vietnam, the release of American prisoners of war, and an Indochina peace conference. The North Vietnamese position required unconditional American withdrawal combined with the removal of President Nguyen Van Thieu.[96]

A significant reduction in American demands occurred at the end of May 1971, however, immediately following the administration's understandings with China regarding Kissinger's first visit and with the Soviet

Union regarding SALT. It was almost as if Nixon and Kissinger were attempting to test the potency of their new connections, although they must also have been concerned that the number of American troops in South Vietnam had already declined from 540,000 to 270,000 and was scheduled to be cut another 100,000 by December (the beginning of the presidential election year).[97] In any event, Nixon now chose to make an important concession, fully of a piece with, and not unrelated to, the concessions that had just been made to the Soviet Union on SALT. In a secret proposal in Paris on May 31, not revealed to the public for almost eight months (and even then incompletely), Washington offered to accept a deadline for the withdrawal of all American forces from Vietnam in return for a cease-fire and the release of American POWs. In other words, Kissinger was no longer making mutual withdrawal a major issue in the negotiations and was even hinting at a more explicit American concession if Hanoi dropped its insistence on removal of the Thieu regime.[98] Obviously, the American leaders were going some distance to make a bargain possible.

Even so, when North Vietnam responded on June 26 with a nine-point plan that would have required the United States to support free elections in South Vietnam during the fall, Nixon and Kissinger refused to take the final step in abandoning Thieu. Apparently, they continued to hope that his government could put down the insurgency, and their own desperation diminished with their diplomatic successes of the summer. They now developed variations of their May 31 proposal, on August 16 offering to withdraw all American troops nine months after the completion of a peace treaty and on October 11, eight days after Thieu was reelected in "uncontested" balloting, suggesting that a multiparty electoral commission hold a new presidential election six months after a final agreement was signed.[99]

Nixon and Kissinger seemed content to build a record of secret negotiations that they could reveal to the American public at a politically advantageous moment. Hanoi, on the other hand, felt compelled to undertake preparations for another major military offensive.[100] Finally, in December, after three months in which the secret Paris sessions were repeatedly canceled by the North Vietnamese, the Americans carried out bombing raids over North Vietnam, warning both Moscow and Beijing that "an offensive would evoke the most serious retaliation."[101] On January 25, 1972, alarmed at the continued North Vietnamese buildup and silence (as well as slippage in his reviving popularity), Nixon "went public" with his October peace proposal (freshly presented and now stipulating *mutual* withdrawal of forces) and the fact that Kissinger had been holding private meetings with Hanoi's representatives since August 1969. The domestic political impact was immediate. By early February the president had recaptured the lead in the polls that he had established during the previous summer and autumn.[102]

A few days later, Nixon, Kissinger, Rogers, their immediate staffs, and over 150 representatives of the television and press embarked for China on what the president described as his "historic mission for peace."[103] The phrase was apt, of course, to the extent that the trip was intended to mend a long-damaged relation, but the venture was also designed to bolster the two nations and to create leverage against their enemies. Nixon and Kissinger were euphoric at being able to bring the Chinese into a new and more favorable international balance of power. It had been their dream, and especially Nixon's, to be able to play the "China card" against the Vietnamese, the Russians, and (as a result) even the Democrats at home. Mao and Jou had analogous aspirations. They saw the American connection as a way to reduce the Soviet danger, constrain Japan, and not least important, weaken the Nationalists on Taiwan.

Both sides to the bargain got much of what they wanted from it, but both paid substantially for the advantages gained. In terms of American politics, Nixon's pilgrimage to China, with its comprehensive television coverage and dramatic encounters, was an almost unqualified success. None of the Democratic candidates, in the weeks following the summit, could mount a serious challenge to his popularity in the polls.[104] Moreover, the president's hand was undoubtedly strengthened vis-à-vis Hanoi and Moscow. Even before February, Mao and Jou had begun to urge the North Vietnamese to compromise with the Americans,[105] while Soviet leaders displayed increasing nervousness about Chinese and American intentions.[106] On the other hand, there was also a down side for the Americans. As much as they tried to obscure the fact in the summit's final (Shanghai) communiqué, Nixon and Kissinger found it necessary to virtually abandon the alliance with Taiwan and to commit themselves to the removal of American troops from that island.[107] Such a change, despite Beijing's promises of good behavior, was bound to make conservatives in the United States unhappy.

From the Chinese point of view, the obvious advantage of a rapprochement with the Americans lay in its impact on the Soviet Union and Japan; the other advantages as well as the disadvantages were more subtle. The crucial object, clearly, at a time when the superpowers were edging toward greater cooperation, was to ensure that they would not collaborate against China. (This is why Kissinger's willingness to share military intelligence and to brief the Chinese leadership on Soviet-American negotiations was impressive.) This objective the Chinese-American reconciliation accomplished, just as it understandably strengthened Washington's resolve to maintain its nuclear umbrella over Japan (despite Japanese "shock" at Nixon's overture to China).[108] Beyond this, the new détente took the United States out of the Chinese civil war and also promised China a relaxation in American trade restrictions and greater access to Western capital and technology. Even so, the cost of such gains was high: China's long-standing identification with, and reputation as a champion of, Third World revolutions was inevitably weakened when Beijing treated with the leading capitalist nation and muted its support of the North Vietnamese Communists.[109]

The immediate result, however, was that Hanoi's leaders disregarded Mao's direct advice and embarked upon a vast military offensive in South Vietnam. On March 30, 1972, three North Vietnamese divisions crossed the demilitarized zone and began an aggressive advance down the coast. Within a week a second front was opened northwest of Saigon. And within three weeks a third operation was initiated in the Central Highlands. In the north the North Vietnamese attacked the provincial capital of Quang Tri, which fell on May 2. In the south they laid siege to An Loc, near Saigon, and seized control of the delta region as the South Vietnamese sent their reserve units north to protect important cities in the Highlands.[110]

The military onslaught was highly traumatic to Washington, altering American policy and seriously straining relations within the government. Nixon, experiencing visions of what the Tet offensive had done to his predecessor, took the North Vietnamese attack personally and found himself increasingly angry not only at the Russians, whom he held ultimately responsible, but also at Melvin Laird and Henry Kissinger, whom he suspected of faintheartedness.[111]

> Henry, with all his many virtues, does seem too often to be concerned about preparing the way for negotiations with the Soviets. However, when he faces the facts, he realizes that no negotiation in Moscow is possible unless we come out all right in Vietnam. . . . Both Haldeman and Henry seem to have an idea—which I think is mistaken—that even if we fail in Vietnam we can survive politically.[112]

In the president's view the proper response to the situation was twofold: to bomb the North Vietnamese as never before and to press the Russians as vigorously as possible to use their influence in Hanoi to bring the offensive to a halt. These weeks therefore were witness to an unprecedented and savage air war. At Nixon's direction more than 700 B-52 raids were flown over North Vietnam during April, while the number of comparable missions carried out in the South often reached 75 a day. This was in addition to the more than 500 sorties flown daily by American and South Vietnamese aircraft in conjunction with battlefield operations.[113] While this was going on, the president made it very clear to Dobrynin and others that he held Moscow accountable (and punishable) for supplying the sinews of war that supported the Vietnamese attack.[114]

Kissinger minimizes the extent to which he disagreed with Nixon about the wisdom of the president's actions, but the fact is that his and Nixon's attitudes were diverging with regard to the necessity for violence (too much of which, Kissinger feared, might alienate the Soviets) and also with regard to specific dealings with the Russians and the North Vietnamese.[115] This became clear after April 20, when Kissinger journeyed to Moscow on a secret mission to negotiate with Brezhnev about a number of items that needed to be settled before the summit could occur. Nixon flirted with the idea of not letting him go at all but relented after insisting that Vietnam be the first subject on the agenda and that Kissinger break off the talks if the Soviets did not produce immediate progress toward a settlement of that war.[116] Once in the Soviet capital, however, Kissinger proceeded to make significant concessions on several fronts—concessions of which we are still not certain Nixon was fully apprised.[117] Kissinger was taking considerable risks to try to end the war, or at least to prevent it from torpedoing the summit.

In his talks with the Russian leader regarding Vietnam, Kissinger for the first time made explicit to the Communist side what had been implicit in the secret proposal of May 31, 1971—namely, that the United States would not insist on the North Vietnamese withdrawing their military forces from South Vietnam in a final negotiated settlement. He did this indirectly by demanding the withdrawal of only the three divisions that had crossed the demilitarized zone in late March to attack Quang Tri, though even this requirement, he has admitted, was a throwaway, later to be quietly dropped.[118] Moreover, Kissinger hinted that those North Vietnamese troops that did remain in the South could consider the area they occupied the territory of the Provisional Revolutionary Government.[119] In short, Kissinger was making an all-out effort to persuade the Soviets of American reasonableness even as he emphasized to them that a continuing North Vietnamese offensive would quickly lead to devastating American air attacks. Brezhnev seemed to understand this, encouraging Kissinger considerably by agreeing to convey his newest proposals to Hanoi.[120]

At this point, the president's representative, despite Nixon's instructions, was ready to turn to other matters, specifically SALT. Kissinger would like us to believe that Brezhnev now offered a reasonable compromise on the remaining ABM issues and "major concessions" regarding the interim agreement on offensive weapons.[121] The truth, however, is much more intricate, since Brezhnev was actually adopting suggestions that Kissinger himself had made earlier (almost certainly unbeknownst to Nixon) via Dobrynin.

With regard to SLBMs, for example, Kissinger had long since resolved to finesse the issue (and to silence those in the Pentagon and the SALT delegation who had criticized him for not including SLBMs in the "breakthrough" understanding of May 1971) by proposing an arrangement the Russians simply could not refuse. Thus in March he indicated to Dobrynin ("thinking out loud," he says) that a limit of 950 SLBMs (and 62 submarines) would be acceptable in a SALT agreement even though this number was at the upper end of what the CIA estimated the Soviets could conceivably build within the next five years.[122] Small wonder, then, that Kissinger was ready to accept this proposal when Brezhnev offered it, particularly when the latter also endorsed Melvin Laird's idea (passed on to Dobrynin by Kissinger) that Russia could "trade in" older SLBMs and ICBMs in order to stay under 950.[123]

Brezhnev did accede to a five-year term for the offensive freeze, as the Americans had been demanding, but his "new plan" to resolve the ABM dispute by permitting each side to protect its capital and one site was hardly a concession. This had been the position of the Russian SALT delegation for some time, and the American delegation in Helsinki had requested, and received, permission to agree to it before Kissinger reached Moscow.[124]

There were other areas as well in which Kissinger was extremely accommodating, obviously with the intention of stimulating Russian interest in the forthcoming summit. He made it clear that he had no serious difficulties with the Soviet revision of his earlier draft of the Declaration of Basic Principles to be issued at the summit, a declaration the Russians had suggested and to which they attached considerable significance. Indeed, working from the Soviet version, he and his assistant, Helmut Sonnenfeldt, were able, without consulting Washington, to produce a statement that Gromyko and Kissinger agreed upon before the Americans left Moscow.[125] Meanwhile, with regard to trade and economic relations in general, Kissinger appears to have made important oral commitments to Brezhnev. Official White House policy was to defer economic programs until there was political progress, but the Russians were pressing hard for assurances that satisfactory economic arrangements could be achieved, if not at the summit, then within a few weeks.

In subsequent years Kissinger attempted to minimize both his awareness of Russian eagerness (particularly with regard to grain) and his involvement in the economic negotiations, but the evidence indicates that he was deeply involved and may even have promised Brezhnev financial credits with which to make grain purchases.[126] A columnist with access to Kissinger disclosed in May 1972 that, in reporting to the president three weeks before, Kissinger told Nixon of his "perfect astonishment" at the vast importance Soviet leaders placed on concluding a comprehensive trade agreement. Not only was this one of their highest priorities, he concluded, but so also was an arrangement guaranteeing access to American grain.[127]

The president, after some vacillation, was able to convince himself that his adviser had actually obtained significant concessions from Brezhnev in Moscow. At least Kissinger had not made the concession that Nixon apparently was least willing to grant, namely, a promise to call off the American bombing of North Vietnam.[128] And in fact, for a moment in late April it looked as if the Russians might vigorously press Hanoi to be cooperative.[129] In this hope, and as a sweetener for the newly scheduled secret session in Paris on May 2, Nixon quickly announced on television that he was ordering the withdrawal of yet another 20,000 men from Vietnam within sixty days.[130]

Unfortunately, Kissinger's meeting with Le Duc Tho in early May turned out to be surprisingly unproductive, driving the president back to his earlier plans to cripple North Vietnam and its continuing offensive by means of air strikes.[131] At this point, Kissinger, fearing an extremely negative Soviet reaction, tried to convince Nixon to cancel or postpone the summit, but the president could not bring himself to do this. Kissinger could only hold his breath as Nixon, encouraged by John Connally and Alexander Haig (Kissinger's less-than-loyal deputy), ordered an intensive bombing north of the seventeenth parallel as well as the mining of North Vietnamese harbors. Connally was convinced that the Russians wanted the upcoming summit so badly, primarily because of their eagerness for American grain and Western trade, that nothing could compel them to call it off. Kissinger was not so sure, suspecting that the United States needed the summit as much as the Soviet Union and concerned that the bombing and mining of a Soviet ally would be too humiliating for Moscow to accept.[132]

As it turned out, Connally and Nixon were right: as painful as the situation was, Brezhnev simply had too much invested in the success of the summit to give it up. Evidence of this appeared very quickly, despite the uproar of criticism concerning the president's actions that erupted in Congress and the nation's press.[133] On May 10, in delivering a protest regarding the damage done by American bombers to Soviet ships in Haiphong harbor, Dobrynin also expressed the hope that the president would personally receive Soviet Minister of Trade Nikolai Patolichev, who was currently in Washington. The next day, after presenting a more comprehensive complaint from Brezhnev concerning the blockade and bombing, Dobrynin declared his readiness to resume discussions with Kissinger regarding preparations for the president's visit to Russia.[134]

Thus the Moscow summit, only the fifth meeting of Soviet and American leaders since World War II, would take place as scheduled. Nixon had gambled and won. Faced with an apparent choice between building accord with the Soviet Union and avoiding defeat in Vietnam, he had opted for the latter, hoping against hope that it would not jeopardize the creation of a politically useful understanding between the superpowers. That it did not was due in no small measure to his and especially Kissinger's willingness to offer the other side much of what it needed and wanted.

On May 22 the president and his party arrived in the Soviet capital for what was to be a busy week. The opening plenary session on the 23d—involving Nixon, Kissinger, Rogers, and Ambassador Jacob Beam, on the American side, and Brezhnev, Kosygin, Podgorny, Gromyko, and Dobrynin, on the Russian side—was essentially a general discussion and an assignment of subject responsibilities. The agreed procedure was to reserve the big items—SALT and Vietnam—for the meetings of Nixon, Kissinger, Brezhnev, Kosygin, and on occasion, Podgorny. Gromyko and Rogers were assigned to deal with European security issues; Kissinger and Gromyko were asked to serve as a backup on SALT and "give some thought to general principles that should govern relations" (this subterfuge was necessary because Rogers was still unaware of the Kissinger-Brezhnev negotiations in April). When economic matters were discussed, Kosygin, Gromyko, and Trade Minister Patolichev represented the Soviet side, while Rogers and Peter Flanigan, the White House coordinator on foreign economic policy, negotiated for the United States.[135]

Because both sides recognized that major agreements would not quickly be accomplished, it was decided to exploit the attention of the world press during the first few days by staging the signing of recent understandings on a number of technical subjects. "These accords were not politically significant," according to Kissinger, who remarked that many of them had "lain dormant" in the bureaucracies for years, but in his view they did "demonstrate that the United States and the Soviet Union . . . had common interests in a variety of fields."[136] Four protocols featured commitments regarding medical research, environmental cooperation, scientific-technological collaboration, and a joint program for orbital missions in space. Soviet and American representatives also endorsed rules designed to avoid accidents between their navies at sea.[137]

While this was occurring, the principal conferees plunged with some energy into the resolution of the remaining issues with regard to SALT. Fortunately, what remained to be worked out was only marginal to the essence of the agreements. Unfortunately, however, the negotiations at the summit were seriously hampered by the complexity of the matters in dispute and by Nixon's earlier decision to leave the American SALT delegation in Helsinki (and thus largely inaccessible), a decision that Kissinger in retrospect regretted and attributed to his own and Nixon's desire to maintain "control."[138] The result was a good deal of confusion and several unsatisfactory compromises that Kissinger later tried to portray as more advantageous to the United States than they actually were.[139]

There were essentially three areas of disagreement regarding SALT, all of which derived in some way from Kissinger's negotiations in the secret channel. First, there was the question of which Soviet submarines would be counted as contributing to 740 operational SLBMs, the baseline at which the Russians would have to begin trading in old missiles if they wished to expand their force to 950. The Soviets accepted the figure of 740 but insisted on excluding the approximately 90 SLBMs on older H-class nuclear and G-class diesel submarines, vessels they claimed were of limited utility. The Pentagon and Gerard Smith in Helsinki opposed such an exclusion because it would enable Moscow to build a greater number of more modern submarines.

The second and third matters of disagreement had to do with the efforts of the Nixon administration (now attempting to be less permissive than Kissinger had been in the spring of 1971) to place limits on the modernization of the Russian ICBM force. One dispute grew out of Kissinger's attempt to develop a rule that changes in the size of existing missile silos could not exceed 15 percent. Strangely enough, the Soviets were willing to accept a more stringent stipulation than this with regard to the diameter of silos—though not with regard to their depth, since they knew that their successor missiles were longer but not wider than existing weapons. But they had not made this clear to the Americans in Moscow, who believed that the alternative to their suggested rule was no constraint at all. The other disagreement regarding modernization was related to the first and derived from the failure of the two sides to agree upon a definition of light and heavy missiles. The problem went back to the fact that, from the American point of view, the replacements for the "light" SS-11 (the larger and potentially MIRVable SS-17 and SS-19) would increase the number of heavy ICBM launchers beyond the 305 stipulated in the overall freeze.[140]

Kissinger and Nixon's resolution of these points was, if not brilliant, at least not disastrous. After considerable wrangling by cable with both Smith and the Pentagon, Kissinger was able to persuade the president (if not Smith, who remembered well Kissinger's April dealings) to accept a Russian "compromise" that excluded only the sixty G-class submarines from "baseline" calculations as long as the Soviets did not put "modern" missiles on these boats without counting them.[141] Regarding changes in silo size, Kissinger and Nixon rejected the advice of the American SALT delegation (which preferred the text of the Russian proposal) and opted for a ban on "significant" increases in dimension—*significant* being defined as more than 15 percent. They did not realize, apparently, that when the Russians construed the measurement in depth as well as width, which they did, such limits actually allowed a volumetric increase of 32 percent.[142] Concerning missile definition, they contented themselves in the end with a unilateral statement stipulating that the United States regarded any missile larger than the SS-11 as a heavy missile.[143] Having accomplished these "solutions," the Americans were prepared to endorse the entire SALT accord; the signing ceremonies for both the ABM Treaty and the Interim (five-year) Agreement on Offensive Weapons took place in the Kremlin on May 26.[144] The president and his party were delighted at having negotiated the first arms control agreement of our era—largely forgetting, it would seem, the substantial price they had paid for it in inflated limits and domestic commitments.

If SALT was the centerpiece of the summit for the Americans, it only shared that role with the Declaration of Basic Principles for the Russians. Though this agreement on U.S.-Soviet relations, signed on May 27, was not accorded much attention during the conference (due to its prior negotiation and the peculiar way in which the Americans required that it "surface"), Soviet leaders were quick to emphasize that they took the document with utmost seriousness.[145] Indeed, Brezhnev in his first (private) meeting with Nixon told the president that he considered the declaration "even more important" than the SALT agreement.[146] Unlike Nixon and Kissinger, who largely neglect this understanding in their memoirs and referred to it at the time almost slightingly as a "road map" and the symbol of "an aspiration and an attitude," Soviet commentators have consistently attributed great international significance to the Declaration of Basic Principles.[147]

The explanation for this puzzling contrast in attitudes toward what has been called "a charter for détente" is both ironic and revealing.[148] We can perhaps understand Nixon's and Kissinger's disregard for the declaration (despite the continuing power of liberal idealism in American history), knowing what we do about the inclinations of the president and his adviser toward classic conservative beliefs and their emphasis on human frailty, the need for hierarchy, and the centrality of power. But why would a set of principles be so important to the tough-minded elite of the Soviet Union? The answer apparently lies in Nixon and Kissinger's willingness to include the old Communist concept of "peaceful coexistence" among the principles and in what that willingness implied about American recognition of Soviet equality.[149] The principles became, in effect, the long-sought American acknowledgment that the "correlation of forces" had shifted to the point of making Soviet parity inevitable. In a similar way, American willingness to attend a European "security" conference designed largely to ratify existing borders (a concession at the summit that was hardly noticed) was seen as a recognition of Soviet permanence, well worth the cost of having to participate in future talks on the reduction of conventional forces (MBFR).[150]

The major hidden question of the summit, of course, was what to do about Vietnam. Nixon opened the discussion of that subject early in the conference by emphasizing that, unless Hanoi developed a more cooperative negotiating stance, he would have no choice but to continue the bombing and mining of the North. Brezhnev, Kosygin, and Podgorny responded with extensive criticism of American policy, the thrust of Brezhnev's remarks being that it was a mistake to destroy North Vietnam when Hanoi was eager to negotiate and had a "reasonable" political program.[151]

It was left to Kissinger to indicate in a subsequent session with Gromyko that the administration had not yet exhausted the store of concessions it was willing to make to preserve the image, if not the reality, of success in Southeast Asia. After explicitly abandoning an earlier stipulation that the bombing could not end until all American prisoners of war were released, Kissinger announced that the United States was prepared to see an electoral commission in South Vietnam that included elements from the Vietcong and the neutralists as well as the Saigon regime. The Americans were edging closer and closer to Hanoi's position, revealing such flexibility that it is not surprising that Brezhnev later asked Nixon if it would be useful for a high Soviet official (Podgorny was mentioned) to go to Vietnam "in the interest of peace." Nixon was pleased to assent. Kissinger was encouraged too, though in his memoirs he is less than candid about the meaning of the Soviet offer.[152]

Another aspect of the summit that was largely hidden from public notice was the economic. Here again there is a rather misleading treatment of the subject in the participants' memoirs and their postconference statements, a treatment that suggests that Nixon and Kissinger were using economic factors as leverage on the Soviets (and to "civilize" them) and did not even expect to achieve a trade arrangement at the summit.[153] The records show, however, that the American leaders were every bit as eager for an understanding as their opposites and had been planning at least since March to have an interlocking package of economic agreements ready for signature in Moscow.[154] In fact, as late as May 23 Flanigan still hoped to finalize a long-term grain sale to the Soviets at the summit and to announce it before leaving Russia.[155] (At Moscow, Nixon not only offered Brezhnev a three-year grain deal with $750 million in credit—essentially the same terms the U.S.S.R. agreed to in July—but also vigorously pressed the Soviet leader to accept it.)[156]

In any event, the original intention was to have, in addition to the grain sale, a "balanced" assortment of economic understandings for approval, involving a settlement of Soviet lend-lease debts to the United States, the extension of most-favored-nation (MFN) status to the Soviet Union, the establishment of commercial facilities in each other's country, and the creation of a joint U.S.-U.S.S.R. trade commission.[157] What blocked final agreement on this package apparently came down to three things: (1) Soviet refusal to pay market-level interest (6 percent) on the loan granted for the purchase of American grain (they offered 2 percent), (2) Soviet refusal to pay the high (union) shipping rates on the 50 percent of mutual trade that would be carried in American ships, and (3) continuing disagreement as to the sum the Russians would pay in settling their lend-lease debt to the United States. (The United States had asked for $800 million on an $11 billion debt; the Soviets were offering $300 million.)[158] The result was that the summit ended with only one important economic agreement: a protocol establishing a Joint Commercial Commission charged with working out new credit and trade arrangements as well as a lend-lease settlement.[159]

In the weeks and months immediately following the Moscow conference, the Soviet and American governments maintained the momentum of cooperation on many different fronts. At the beginning of July, a Soviet deputy minister of agriculture visited Washington and accepted terms for the purchase of wheat that were close to those Nixon had offered in May.[160] Later that month Secretary of Commerce Peterson went to Moscow for the first meeting of the Joint Commercial Commission and achieved enough success at negotiating outstanding economic issues that a draft agreement was drawn up. In September Kissinger returned to Moscow to review the general situation and worked out a compromise on the lend-lease debt with Brezhnev, accepting a figure of $722 million.[161] This cleared the way for Minister Patolichev's appearance in Washington in October for the signing of a maritime accord (ratifying shipping allocations and opening up Soviet and American ports), a lend-lease agreement, and a three-year trade pact that included a promise to ask Congress for MFN treatment for Soviet imports.[162] In the meantime, the two countries entered into a miscellany of noneconomic understandings, including agreements on the sharing of anticancer drugs (June), the pursuit of joint scientific research (July), the exchange of technological processes (August), and the selection of projects for environmental cooperation (September).[163]

To be sure, there were clouds on the horizon. The Soviets decided to buy a surprisingly large quantity of American grain in July and August, and these purchases, combined with the Department of Agriculture's slowness in withdrawing export subsidies to grain companies, resulted in higher bread prices in the United States and strong feelings of resentment against the Russians on the part of the American public.[164] A new Soviet exit tax on Jewish emigration, announced in August with no explanation, provoked considerable outrage in Congress and led in October to the first of the congressional efforts that would ultimately tie the issue to the granting of MFN status.[165] In employing an exit tax, the Soviets were apparently attempting to strengthen their relations with the Arabs after the decision by Premier Anwar Sadat in July to expel Soviet military advisers from Egypt.[166] In any case, since Sadat's action reflected deep Arab dissatisfaction with Soviet passivity, it seemed obvious that Moscow would reassess its willingness to play a cautious role in the Middle East.[167]

Meanwhile, though Russian and Chinese influence certainly contributed to North Vietnam's decision to reopen negotiations with the Americans in July 1972, the war in Asia dragged on until after Nixon's reelection and was settled only after a bloody military climax and on the basis of a fragile compromise.[168] A vivid reminder of the lingering suspicion on both sides of the East-West divide was an article in *Izvestiya* on September 4, 1972, charging that the efforts by the American Department of Defense to secure funds for new weapons systems like the Trident submarine and B-1 bomber were in violation of the "spirit" of the U.S.-Soviet arms agreements.[169]

Nevertheless, when President Nixon left Moscow at the end of his first summit conference on May 30, 1972, he could justifiably feel that his policies were helping to alter international relations and to launch a major détente with both the Russians and the Chinese. Nixon's hand had been forced by his inability to end the Vietnam War to his own satisfaction and by the erosion of the Cold War consensus and American economic power, but he had responded to this situation with creativity, working to reduce the power of his nation's adversaries in order to redress the decline in American capacities. In the process, he benefited politically, but the world at large benefited as well, not only from a substantial growth of trust and cooperation but, in particular, from the easing of the German problem, the achievement of certain controls on weaponry, the strengthening of economic interdependence, and the development of plans for further international collaboration. Though the agreement was so conservative as to contain the seeds of its own undoing, it was also a meaningful point of transition on the way to a more relaxed and less deadly world.

6

BREZHNEV AND SQUARING
THE CIRCLE

Having traced the development of superpower détente from the point of view of the American actors, I turn now to discuss these events with the focus on Moscow. In the process I attempt to throw additional light on Soviet motives and objectives and to clarify how these differed from U.S. motives and objectives. I also endeavor to show how it happened that Leonid Brezhnev came to rely on improved relations with the United States to establish his own preeminence within the Moscow leadership and to solve the dilemmas the Soviet Union faced both at home and abroad with regard to commitments and resources.

The men who displaced Nikita Khrushchev in November 1964 had in common a commitment to predictability, caution, and orthodoxy in Soviet and international affairs. What this meant specifically and immediately in terms of foreign policy was the abandonment, or substantial downplaying, of Khrushchev's "flirtations" with the United States and (potentially) West Germany and a renewal of efforts to put the Communist world back together, that is, to reconcile the U.S.S.R. with China and to fortify its ties with East Germany—and with Eastern Europe in general. The assumption or belief was that Khrushchev and his rash policies were the foremost problems in Eastern bloc relations. With more "normal" leaders and attitudes in the Kremlin, it would become obvious how crucial it was for the Communist nations to stand together behind the Soviet Union in its dealings with the capitalist powers.

Thus the first few months after the change in leadership witnessed a number of important shifts, despite the fact that the new regime's foreign policy remained relatively subdued. The conference of Communist parties scheduled by Khrushchev for December (and presumably called to isolate the Chinese) was transformed into a "consultation" and put off until spring, while overtures were made to Beijing for an end to open polemics. Khrushchev's planned visit to Bonn was quickly dropped. In lieu of it, in early 1965, Soviet and East German authorities carried out a series of harassments of Western land and air traffic to and from Berlin, ostensibly in response to use of the city by West German parliamentary bodies. Simultaneously the Soviets hardened their line with regard to American encouragement of German "revanchism" and particularly with reference to Lyndon Johnson's increasing intervention in Vietnam. They combined this with a number of gestures indicating support for de Gaulle's independent attitudes and for closer Soviet-French relations.[1]

Even more critical decisions were being made in military and domestic affairs. The collective leadership wasted little time in assuring the armed forces that, unlike Khrushchev, it was sympathetic to the growth of almost all services, especially those involved in projecting Soviet military power at some physical distance. In succeeding years, military allocations rose steadily as notions of minimum deterrence were abandoned, strategic missile forces were radically enlarged, an ABM system was installed around Moscow, and naval and conventional units were expanded.[2] Meanwhile, the March 1965 plenum, following Brezhnev's lead, approved a five-year plan for agriculture that promised an investment of 71 billion rubles (more than the total spent in the previous twenty years), together with greater incentives to peasants and the reduction of state quotas on collective farms.[3] In the autumn of 1965 Premier Alexei Kosygin announced what contemporaries called the Kosygin reforms—measures designed to transform the economy by giving more authority to centralized ministries in Moscow while providing for greater initiative and freedom at the factory management level.[4]

Significantly, all of this occurred in the midst of an increasingly conservative, quasi-Stalinist mood within the leadership, which lent support to the military buildup and surfaced in a campaign during the autumn of 1965 to crush dissent. This conservatism, identified in the Politburo especially with Mikhail Suslov, Alexander Shelepin, and Pyotr Shelest, would ultimately play a role in stifling the Kosygin reforms, as well.[5]

Following the conclusion of the Twenty-third Party Congress in the spring of 1966 (a Congress remembered primarily for its return to Stalinist nomenclature and its surprising increases in the projected allocations for consumer goods), the Brezhnev-Kosygin regime was finally ready to move aggressively on behalf of its foreign policy aims. This became apparent in its efforts to improve relations with all the nations of Western Europe except West Germany; in its attempt to weaken European-American ties by criticizing Washington's intervention in Vietnam; and in its use of the Bucharest conference (July 1966) to push the Warsaw Pact states toward organizational reform and to offer both East and West proposals for the settlement of issues. The Soviet Union was prepared to reap the reward for having become a "normal" and "stable" state at a time when both the United States, with its Asian war, and China, with its Cultural Revolution, had descended to the depths of barbarism.[6]

The new Soviet policy line was perhaps the most completely spelled out in the Kremlin's rejection of the West German "peace note" of March 1966 and in the declaration on "peace and security in Europe" of the Bucharest conference. The rebuff to Bonn occurred on the occasion of the Erhard government's decision to pursue a "policy of reconciliation" with its Eastern European neighbors by offering to renounce the use of force in settling international disputes. Since the offer did not acknowledge the existence of the German Democratic Republic, it was obviously unpalatable to East Berlin, and the Soviet Union quickly denounced it as merely a continuation of West Germany's "aggressive and revenge-seeking policy."

Later, in its longer response of May, Moscow went on to stipulate as a condition for improving Soviet–West German relations both the calling of a European conference on questions of security and the prior settlement of virtually all outstanding political problems. This position was formally reiterated at the gathering of Warsaw Pact countries in Bucharest in July, a meeting at which the Soviet Union was clearly trying to bind itself more closely to its Eastern European allies and to shepherd them toward a new post-NATO European order based on the permanent division of Germany.[7] In the meantime, encouraged by de Gaulle's decision to withdraw French forces from NATO, the Soviets continued their efforts to develop stronger bilateral ties with Paris, building a relationship that achieved conspicuous success on the occasion of the French president's state visit to the U.S.S.R. in June 1966.[8] At the same time, Moscow turned a cold shoulder toward the repeated overtures of President Johnson (the best known being that of October 1966) aimed at stimulating the "building of bridges" between the United States and the U.S.S.R.[9]

In 1967 the Soviet diplomatic offensive against NATO reached new intensity. Governmental leaders, appealing for an end to alliances and more technical cooperation, engaged in an unprecedented series of visits to the capitals of Western Europe during the winter, Premier Kosygin traveling to Paris, Ankara, and London and President Nikolai Podgorny visiting Vienna and Rome.[10] Simultaneously, Moscow responded harshly to the latest conciliatory gesture from Bonn, the expressed willingness of the Grand Coalition (Kiesinger-Brandt) government in December 1966 to abandon the Hallstein Doctrine and to establish diplomatic relations with the nations of Eastern Europe.

The fact that Romania broke ranks in January and formally recognized the West German regime was especially infuriating to the Kremlin, which reacted by denouncing "militarism, revanchism, and neo-Nazism" in the Bundesrepublik and by organizing and renewing bilateral defense treaties between the countries of the Warsaw Pact. Behind the scenes, however, there was a second and perhaps ultimately more significant response on the part of Moscow: during the summer and fall of 1967, it quietly initiated conversations with Bonn, designed, apparently, to see to what extent the West Germans were altering their traditional positions on such issues as Berlin, nuclear proliferation, and recognition of East Germany. Then, in December 1967, after a number of discussions regarding a renunciation-of-force agreement, Soviet representatives made it clear that such an understanding would require maximum concessions by Bonn, including the loosening of the federal republic's ties with Berlin.[11] The Soviet attitude seemed to be that West Germany could serve as either a bogeyman or a lackey but as nothing in between. Still, the two sides had begun to talk, and in this lay the seeds of future change.

The Soviet effort to use the Vietnam conflict to bring about an American retreat from Europe did not prevent the Kremlin leadership from negotiating with the United States when it thought this was essential. Thus an agreement not to place weapons of mass destruction in outer space was worked out by the superpowers in the latter part of 1966 and signed in January 1967.[12] Similarly, an understanding was achieved with regard to a nuclear nonproliferation treaty in December 1966, although an additional year was required before this was submitted to other potential signatories.[13] Most notably, on the occasion of Kosygin's visit to the United Nations in June 1967 after the disastrous Six-Day (Arab-Israeli) War, the premier was not averse to meeting with President Johnson at Glassboro, New Jersey, in an attempt to bolster the fortunes of his demoralized Arab allies. This of course provided an opportunity for Johnson and Secretary of Defense Robert McNamara to urge upon their guests the wisdom of acceding to their January proposal for talks on eliminating strategic weapons. But Kosygin and his advisers were not ready for this, probably in large measure because the Soviet program to build an ICBM force as large as, or larger than, that of the Americans was still in its early stages.[14]

As it happened, the Six-Day War was only the first of three successive international crises impacting on the U.S.S.R. during 1967, 1968, and 1969—crises that had the effect of reinforcing, among other things, pressure for the expansion and enhancement of the Soviet military establishment. Following the Israeli triumph, for example, the Soviet Union's prestige in the Middle East was so shaken that Moscow saw no alternative but to involve itself in rebuilding and assisting shattered Arab armies. It also sought to win influence in the area by leaving in the eastern Mediterranean the augmented naval force it had sent there during the Six-Day War. In subsequent months the Kremlin chose to expand its naval activity as far as the western Mediterranean and Indian Ocean and, in addition, to intervene militarily in the civil war in Yemen.[15]

Another effect of the new tension was to strengthen the hand of those conservatives in the Politburo who had been campaigning for a return to orthodox values and limitations on domestic dissent. Governmental policy regarding freedom of speech had been somewhat erratic during 1965–67, going from relaxed to harsh to somewhat relaxed again.[16] Beginning in mid-1967, however, as neo-Stalinists like Suslov and Shelest took the offensive, there was a systematic turn toward a more restrictive line. During the following January, the dissident poet Alexander Ginsburg was tried and convicted, and in March 1968 Brezhnev himself issued a call for "iron discipline" within the ranks.[17] By that time, the leadership's anxiety about nonconformity at home had begun to merge with concern about the spillover of reform ideas generated by developments in Czechoslovakia. The result was a tightening of ideological controls and "a noticeable deterioration of the psychological and political climate within the country."[18] This in turn contributed to the context in which Soviet leaders would subsequently make their decisions to intervene with force in Czechoslovakia and to pursue an increasingly hostile policy toward Mao's China.

Throughout these first years of the new regime, Leonid Brezhnev, as party leader, continued to walk a tightrope as he struggled to develop his own agenda and to increase his authority within the oligarchy. A man of conservative tendencies but ameliorative personality, Brezhnev had clearly not thought much about issues of "big" policy before he became first secretary. Burdened at first by the orthodoxies of his trusted and long-time aides (men like Sergei Trapeznikov), he only gradually came to enlarge the circle of his advisers to include more moderate individuals like Andrei Alexandrov and G. E. Tsukanov and representatives of the scientific-intellectual elite like Nikolai Inozemtsev and Georgi Arbatov. Arbatov, in his memoirs, recalls that at this stage Brezhnev

> showed a lively interest in many things and eagerly listened to his interlocutors. . . . Interestingly enough, he was usually more receptive to ideas in the areas he did not consider himself an expert on, like foreign policy to a certain extent, culture, [or] even ideology and Marxist-Communist theory. On the other hand, he was convinced he was an expert on agriculture, practical economics in general, and military affairs. He also considered himself a shrewd judge of people, cadres, and party work.[19]

As this learning process progressed, Brezhnev moved to strengthen his position within the party structure and in relation to governmental leaders. The first step necessarily was to capture the strategic heights of the party secretariat, but even before this was accomplished in 1966 Brezhnev and other members of the Presidium acted to reduce the power of Alexander Shelepin, the youngest, most clearly ambitious, and most intimidating individual within the ruling group. Shelepin's demotion occurred in several stages, the first at the end of 1965 and the most obvious in mid-1967, when his friend Vladimir Semichastny was replaced by Yuri Andropov as head of the KGB and when Shelepin himself was removed from the secretariat.[20] Meanwhile, Brezhnev succeeded in weakening another potential rival in December 1965, when Podgorny was "promoted" to the presidency of the Supreme Soviet and dropped from the secretariat.[21] This left only Premier Kosygin as a potential threat to Brezhnev's leading role, although Kosygin's intellectual style and bland personality seemed to preclude that he could ever aspire to be the "number-one" man. Still, the general secretary always treaded warily in dealing with the Politburo for fear that, if he appeared too dominant, Suslov or others might attempt to mobilize the collectivity against him.[22]

A subtle indicator of the shifting balance of power between Brezhnev and Kosygin was their continuing struggle regarding allocation of resources, administrative reform, and popular participation in the government. Thus, although there was no Brezhnev-Kosygin debate about the decisions of 1965 that gave defense and agriculture resource priority, there was a recurring difference between them about the extent to which light industry should be cut back to the advantage of rural investment. Indeed, having established the ratios in favor of agriculture at the beginning of the Eighth Five-Year Plan in 1966, Brezhnev was forced to accept a downward revision in the farming allocation during the next year and succeeded in reversing this reduction only in 1968.[23] In the interim, Brezhnev and Kosygin clashed repeatedly over the wisdom of administrative changes implicit in the 1965 (Kosygin) economic reforms. Kosygin's speeches of 1965–68 were full of references to decentralist methods and managerial autonomy; Brezhnev's by contrast stressed administrative centralization and party intervention. Both emphasized the importance of the "scientific technical revolution," but only Kosygin argued that the Soviet Union should obtain and utilize foreign technology. As the conservative tide grew stronger, Brezhnev became increasingly the defender of the privileged role of party officials, in contrast to Kosygin, who continued to dwell upon the importance of governmental responsiveness to societal demands.[24]

The Czechoslovak crisis in the summer of 1968 was in many ways a transition point in Brezhnev's relationship with Kosygin as well as in his career in general. Since Khrushchev's time, foreign affairs had generally been left in the hands of the premier (Kosygin) and his foreign minister

(Andrei Gromyko), but with the Czech problem and later the Chinese crisis, this began to change, in large part because, as socialist countries, they naturally fell within the concerns of the party leader (Brezhnev). At any rate, after Brezhnev's rather traumatic brush with responsibility in foreign matters during 1968 and 1969, he was not willing, or felt he could not afford, to allow relations with the major Western powers to remain outside his purview. He must also have been aware that both West Germany and the United States were becoming much less predictable in matters of foreign policy and in the process were creating both serious dangers and unprecedented opportunities for the Soviet Union.

Brezhnev's difficulties with Czechoslovakia began in December 1967, when he traveled to Prague in an apparent attempt to "save" the fifteen-year-old regime of Antonin Novotny; it ended by clearing the way for a new party secretary, who rapidly developed destabilizing tendencies.[25] Alexander Dubček was not an unknown quantity to Brezhnev, but there can be little doubt that the Dubček government's liberalizing reforms of the following winter and spring caught the Soviet leader by surprise and left him vulnerable in his relationships with his own colleagues. By summer, the issue had become personal enough to Brezhnev for him to confide to an adviser that if "revisionist" tendencies were to gain an upper hand in Prague, he would be forced to resign as general secretary, for "it would look as if I lost Czechoslovakia."[26]

Dubček himself attempted to slow the process of change, but neither cautious language nor affirmations of loyalty to the Warsaw Pact could reduce either the liberalizing momentum or Soviet concern. As the Prague Spring blossomed, Moscow fretted—the Soviet military was having nightmares about a possible fissure among its "northern" allies, while party elders worried that Czechoslovakia was opening the gates to subversive ideas. In March, Brezhnev spoke out strongly for orthodoxy, but subsequently he and the Politburo vacillated over how best to exercise leverage. The first political and economic arm-twisting by the Soviets came in April, following the issuance of the Czech regime's reformist "action program." In June came threats of Soviet military intervention, though Politburo conservatives were themselves badly divided about such action (Shelest demanding it, and Suslov having serious reservations), while Brezhnev was indecisive. Finally, in July Moscow mounted an intensifying war of nerves against the Dubček government, culminating in the conference of the two countries' Politburos at Cierna, Czechoslovakia, and its deceptively hopeful truce on August 1.[27]

When the Soviet leadership, frustrated by lack of success, chose to invade Czechoslovakia on August 20–21, 1968, the consequences were far-reaching. On the one hand, of course, despite their inability to find enough "orthodox" Communists in Prague to replace the Dubček regime immediately, the Soviets achieved a greater measure of outward conformity and political discipline in both Eastern Europe and the Soviet Union as a result of the intervention.[28] On the other hand, however, as Brezhnev and others had feared, the effect on the outside world would cast the Soviet Union in the role of ogre, resuscitate NATO, and put new strength into American–Western European ties. The invasion also had a chilling impact on Soviet-American relations, compelling the Johnson administration to postpone SALT—which Moscow only the previous week had finally agreed to undertake with Washington.[29]

In the long run, perhaps the most significant consequence of the Kremlin's resort to force was that it alienated and disturbed the Soviet Union's own allies. The Brezhnev Doctrine, claiming for the U.S.S.R. the right to intervene in the affairs of any socialist nation to preserve orthodoxy, understandably left the rulers of such Communist countries as Yugoslavia and China fearful for their independence. In fact, the invasion and doctrine so unnerved the world Communist movement, and particularly the Communist parties of Western Europe, that the Soviet Union found it expedient to put off until the following summer the international party conclave scheduled for November.[30] In using violence to bolster the old order, Russia had created a situation in which, more than ever before, it needed new friends and new support systems.

Worse was yet to come, from Moscow's point of view. The Soviet-Chinese relation, which had been deteriorating for more than a decade, now entered upon a genuine crisis. Concerned by the excesses of the Cultural Revolution (1965–68) and by Beijing's hostility to its every move, the Soviet leadership began in early 1966 to shift military forces to its Far East provinces and to equip them with considerable weaponry. Though the process developed slowly at first, between 1967 and 1969 the Soviets more than doubled the number of divisions on the Chinese border, creating an army of more than 300,000 combat troops.[31]

Beijing largely ignored this buildup for many months, but events in Czechoslovakia during the summer of 1968 prompted a complete change of course. Beginning in September 1968 with a formal protest regarding alleged Soviet intrusions into China's air space, the Chinese government unleashed a denunciation of Moscow's "social imperialism" and "collusion" with capitalist powers. It supplemented this by attempting to solidify its relations with Albania and Romania, to patch up its ties with France, Yugoslavia, and North Vietnam, and amazingly enough, to reconvene the Warsaw ambassadorial talks with the United States. Then on March 2, 1969, just two weeks after a meeting with the Americans had been canceled as a result of leftist opposition in Beijing, Chinese forces ambushed a Soviet unit at Chenpao Island in the Ussuri River on the Soviet-Manchurian border. Mao Zedong was determined to demonstrate that he would not be intimidated by what the Soviets had done in Prague.[32]

Faced with the danger that the Chinese might begin to send military patrols into some 9,000 square miles of disputed borderlands, Brezhnev and Kosygin embarked on a two-pronged effort, first, to compel Beijing, by use of superior power, to respect the existing boundaries of the Soviet Union and, second, to lead Beijing, through a gradual increase in military and diplomatic pressure, to begin negotiations for a general settlement. As a result, the summer of 1969 witnessed a variety of Soviet moves, including offers to undertake consultations, a continued reinforcement of the Red Army on the Asian frontier, and a series of barely disguised public threats of conventional or nuclear attack. Ominous editorials, articles by important generals, speeches by party leaders, discussions of a possible "surgical strike" against Chinese nuclear facilities—all contributed to a growing tension.[33]

In the end, China capitulated, taking advantage of Premier Kosygin's September visit to Beijing (after his return from Ho Chi Minh's funeral) to initiate discussions that led to an October agreement on undertaking negotiations. Nevertheless, cessation of aggressive patrolling and a reduction in abusive language did not mean that the situation was returning to one of cooperation. The ensuing talks remained stalemated, and in the interim the Chinese hastened to perfect their modest nuclear deterrent, to strengthen their influence in neighboring states, and to revive their connections with Washington.[34] This time Beijing was frightened enough of a Soviet attack that discussions with the Americans in Warsaw could actually occur. In Moscow, meanwhile, it became clear that the need for an expanded military presence in the Far East would not soon be reduced. For the third time in three years the military had demonstrated its centrality in Soviet foreign policy.

There were new players and new factors that made themselves known, however, in the course of 1969, among them, American and West German. Richard Nixon assumed the U.S. presidency in January of that year, and Soviet leaders began a long process of feeling out the new administration. Believing as they did that the "correlation of forces" between the superpowers was shifting to their advantage, the men in the Kremlin were understandably divided—the more fearful wanting to exploit the United States' relative weakness by promoting the erosion of American influence, the more hopeful hoping to use the opportunity to achieve a genuine collaboration with the United States (and thus solve some of their own immediate problems). Soviet observers were also curious and puzzled as to who was winning the inevitable battle for power within American society and politics—the "reasonable" forces or the "adventurous" ones. There were a number of encouraging indications—Nixon's reference to an "era of negotiations" in his inaugural speech, for example, and his willingness to accept "sufficiency" in nuclear arms. On the other hand, the new president's decision to support a revised ABM system was disappointing, as was the administration's delay in agreeing to begin SALT.[35]

Nevertheless, the Soviet government initiated and clung for several months to a conciliatory line in its relations with Nixon. In February Ambassador Anatoly Dobrynin emphasized to Washington Moscow's willingness to negotiate on a number of issues immediately and simultaneously, singling out in particular arms control and the Middle East.[36] In June, addressing the world conference of Communist Parties, Brezhnev reaffirmed an intention to pursue peaceful coexistence with all capitalist states.[37] A month later, Foreign Minister Gromyko spoke out for closer Soviet-American relations, responding specifically to Nixon's call for negotiations.[38]

Only in the latter part of 1969 did the Soviet leadership face the fact that the fit was not good in terms of the cooperation each side desired. Nixon and Kissinger, above all else, wanted help in escaping Vietnam and in resolving the Berlin dilemma; they did not want to press ahead with arms control negotiations or commercial talks unless there had been progress on those fronts or until they had established better relations with China. The Soviets, on the other hand, were interested primarily in arms control, although they were also ready to bargain with the Americans over such matters as the Middle East, a European security conference, and trade. Soviet unhappiness with American priorities, and especially with Nixon's decision to visit Romania in August, became evident when Moscow waited as long to respond to the American offer to begin SALT (four months) as Washington had delayed in making the proposal (until June).[39] In October and again in December Dobrynin complained with some vehemence to Nixon and Kissinger about "the slow progress of US-Soviet relations in general."[40] From Kissinger's point of view, the Russians were "stonewalling." From Moscow's perspective, the Americans were linking the entire Soviet-American relationship to Vietnam.[41]

SALT provided the Soviets with grounds for both encouragement and discouragement. The businesslike approach of the American delegation to the initial (November) SALT meeting was impressive enough that the Politburo sought and secured an endorsement of the negotiations from the Central Committee plenum in December 1969. Yet during the spring, and despite clear progress in the April sessions, the Soviets became increasingly nervous about American strategic policy. Charges of bad faith became common after the March disclosure that the United States would begin to equip Minuteman missiles with MIRV. Secretary of Defense Melvin Laird, in particular, was viewed as attempting to revive the "myth" of a Soviet threat in order to justify new weapons programs.[42]

In the meantime, the Soviet leadership, responding to electoral changes in West Germany, was inaugurating a massive and potentially crucial reassessment of the U.S.S.R.'s relations with that country. There had been indications as early as the previous March of a reduction in Soviet hostility toward Bonn, possibly motivated by a desire to lower tension in the West after the outbreak of fighting on the Chinese border.[43] (The March 1969 Budapest Declaration by the Warsaw Pact was so much less extreme than previous pronouncements on West Germany that some observers see Budapest as the birthplace of Brezhnev's *Westpolitik*.)[44] These hints became more obvious in the summer, when the Kiesinger government proposed the resumption of "non-use of force" negotiations and Moscow quickly agreed to this without demanding recognition of East Germany.[45] In September, Gromyko, meeting with Foreign Minister Willy Brandt in New York, made it clear that the Soviet Union was interested in improving relations with the Bundesrepublik, if only Bonn's policy "developed a more realistic shape."[46]

Actually, Gromyko was one of the more skeptical members of the Soviet elite with regard to the wisdom of drawing closer to the West Germans. Cautious and status conscious, the Soviet foreign minister's natural inclination was to strive for better ties with the more powerful opponent (the United States) and to retain West Germany as a demon with which to frighten and discipline the Eastern Europeans. As Egon Bahr later noted, "in dealing with Gromyko, one always had to remember that in his list of priorities, first came the US, second the US, and third the US."[47] Even after Brandt's electoral victory in September 1969 and his announcement of a new and more active *Ostpolitik*, Gromyko still dragged his feet. Georgi Arbatov remembers that, when Bahr first came to Moscow in January (as Brandt's representative), "I was asked to entertain him while we got Gromyko on board."[48]

It was Brezhnev and his more moderate advisers like Yuri Andropov who were the first to realize that détente could be built with West Germany as well as with France or the United States.[49] This is not to say that the Kremlin was without hope that a détente with Western Europe would weaken American influence there, but it is to suggest that the Soviets were not primarily interested in practicing what Henry Kissinger calls "selective détente" (playing one détente relationship off against another).[50] Note for example, that Moscow's response to Brandt's November endorsement of a European security conference and a nonproliferation treaty (two major Soviet aims) was to announce that it had dropped its opposition to *Ameri-*

can participation in the security conference.[51] Note also, with reference to Brezhnev's role and motivations, that, at the very moment of his notable attack on Kosygin's economic policies at the December 1969 plenum, his confidante, Alexandrov, was establishing a secret "back channel" to Egon Bahr to assist in ameliorating Soviet–West German relations.[52] It is no accident that on February 1, 1970, West Germany and the U.S.S.R. signed the largest East-West business deal ever concluded up to that time.[53] Thirteen days later Bahr achieved his first hints of a breakthrough in the negotiations with the Russians on a renunciation-of-force treaty.[54]

The bargaining was hard but the general direction was now clear. That Brezhnev was committed to a new West German relationship can be inferred not only from his call in April for "a new approach" to modernize and strengthen the Russian economy but also from the constant efforts by the Soviet negotiators to broaden the draft treaty to include a "formalized state of peace."[55] Neither the Politburo's April rebuff of Brezhnev's plans to replace Kosygin as premier nor Bonn's insistence that the new treaty remain "narrow" could derail the negotiations.[56] The essential drafting was completed by May 22, and after the West Germans obtained further narrowing in July (as well as made clear that a Berlin agreement among the Allies would have to accompany the treaty), the renunciation-of-force agreement was signed on August 12, 1970.[57] At the special invitation of the Russians, Willy Brandt flew from Bonn to Moscow for the ceremony and for an extended conversation with Brezhnev, who, he recalls, had clearly now "reached the stage at which [he] had resolved—and been empowered—to take personal charge of important aspects of Soviet policy toward the West." Moreover, adds Brandt, "the first thing to emerge from our discussions was his interest in economic matters."[58]

There was good reason for such an interest on Brezhnev's part. A loss of momentum in the Soviet economy, first evident in 1968, had become painfully obvious to the leadership during 1969. The U.S.S.R.'s industrial growth rate had fallen off to 7 percent that year, the lowest rate since 1928. Labor productivity had dropped to the lowest point since the Khrushchev period, and agricultural output was 3 percent less than the 1968 figure. One result of these trends was a governmental decision to scale down virtually all economic goals for 1970, presumably because they now seemed far beyond reach.[59] Another effect was to generate an intense struggle within the Soviet oligarchy over the economic priorities of the Ninth (1971–75) Five-Year Plan, the outlines of which had been expected as early as 1968 but were not actually published until 1971.[60] A third, and extraordinarily significant, consequence was that Brezhnev opted to use the troubled state of the economy as an excuse to thrust himself forward as a critic of Kosygin and of the reforms with which the latter was identified.

Brezhnev's offensive against the decentralizers at the December plenum was couched in terms of old-fashioned orthodoxy and party (not governmental) responsibility, but it included something new as well. His remarks, though not published, were shortly reflected in a press campaign on behalf of greater labor discipline, tougher measures against absenteeism, and more party activism in industrial enterprises.[61] Yet, in seizing the initiative against Kosygin, Brezhnev was not averse to shifting his ground somewhat, building a comprehensive program that, in addition to previous emphases on agriculture and heavy industry, incorporated certain approaches that Kosygin had championed. Thus, as quickly became evident, Brezhnev looked with new favor on material incentives as a means, along with exhortation and coercion, of increasing industrial productivity. He also placed new stress on the need to accelerate Soviet technological progress.[62] It was in this connection, for example, that in March 1970 *Pravda* published the letter to party and government leaders from Andrei Sakharov and other scientists bemoaning the fact that Russia had fallen so far behind the West in computer technology.[63]

As noted above, Brezhnev's efforts to assume a paramount governmental role soon produced a countervailing response by the collective leadership (the so-called minicrisis of April–July 1970), but the struggle in the Kremlin did not seem to alter Brezhnev's course significantly. In fact, when Kosygin, after a compromise achieved at two July plenums, was called upon to continue as head of government, the premier seems to have fallen in behind Brezhnev politically and to have reinforced the new line.[64] The next month, during Willy Brandt's visit, both Kosygin and Brezhnev were explicit with the chancellor about Soviet interest in "developing . . . economic links with the Federal Republic, both by treaty and by cooperation between individual concerns."[65] Brezhnev, in effect, had forged a new governmental consensus around an agreement to play down and supplement economic reforms with other, more traditional measures. Clearly now the dominant leader, he was weaving a programmatic synthesis designed to solve the immediate crisis and to mollify conservatives at home by using Western Europe to enlarge Soviet resources without challenging the existing system.

Progress in Soviet-American relations did not come as easily as rapprochement with the West Germans. The most obvious reason, of course, was the Soviet Union's unwillingness or inability to assist the United States by putting pressure on Moscow's North Vietnamese allies to compromise with South Vietnam to end the Asian war. Indeed, after Nixon sent American troops into Cambodia in May 1970, Moscow felt compelled to protest in Washington against what it understandably interpreted as an unnecessary widening of the Vietnam conflict.[66]

Meanwhile, a further impediment to Soviet-American cooperation developed as a result of the Politburo's March 1970 decision to dispatch 300 surface-to-air missiles and several thousand combat personnel to Egypt to protect Nasser and his country from Israeli air raids. The Nixon administration insisted on seeing these forces as a presence that "threatened Israel and would be useful later in collusion with Nasser against any moderate Arab government."[67] Nasser only compounded American concern when, after an Egyptian-Israeli ceasefire in August, he moved his air defenses forward into the Suez area in direct violation of the armistice agreement.[68]

During the summer and fall of 1970, suspicion and resentment continued to plague the Moscow-Washington relationship. Nixon, buffeted by criticism following the Cambodian invasion and eager to discomfort his enemies before the midterm elections, pressed hard for a Soviet-American summit in 1970—only to conclude by September that the Kremlin wanted too high a price for it, "paid in advance."[69] Nixon and Kissinger, however, grossly misread the international situation—not once but several times—leaving the Soviets irritated and severely confused. The national security adviser, for example, apparently advised the president in July that one of the Soviet prices for a summit was "collusion against China," completely misconstruing evidence that Moscow's offer to sign an ABM treaty plus an "accidental war" agreement was an attempt to overcome U.S. reluctance to accept an ABM treaty by itself.[70] Similarly, in September Kissinger badly misinterpreted both the Jordanian-Syrian conflict and the Cienfuegos naval base incident, treating them as Soviet-American confrontations when in fact they were regional and relatively unimportant incidents.

For Kissinger, eager to demonstrate his hard-line credentials to the president, this was an "autumn of crises" involving probes and challenges aimed at the United States.[71] For Moscow, this was a season of perplexity, a period of wondering whether the American leadership would agree to an ABM treaty at all, or a workable Berlin settlement, or a European security conference. Soviet puzzlement was such that Dobrynin told Kissinger in mid-October 1970, on the occasion of the Soviet foreign minister's visit to Nixon in the White House, that "Gromyko had come [to Washington] to find out whether we [i.e., the president and Kissinger] had made a decision to adopt a *hard* line."[72] That very month, while Nixon played up to conservative American voters by offering the North Vietnamese an unacceptable cease-fire and by having his secretary of defense complain openly of the Russian "arms buildup," the Soviets (1) backed down on the Cienfuegos matter, (2) signaled their interest in arms control by openly dismantling eighteen of their most recent ICBM silo starts, and

(3) displayed a new seriousness in the four-power talks regarding Berlin.[73] It is not hard to see why they found the Americans frustrating.

Nevertheless, the year 1971 ushered in a more positive stage in relations, as Washington and Moscow responded to new pressures and new opportunities. For Nixon and Kissinger, the overture from China in December (1970) and reports of food riots in Poland before Christmas created a feeling of relative strength they had not previously experienced.[74] They were now eager for progress on Berlin and SALT, especially given Willy Brandt's recently expressed impatience, Congress's call for an arms treaty limited to defensive weaponry, and the fact that the reconvened Congress would soon renew its attack on the ABM.[75] On the Soviet side, the Polish crisis produced an even greater effect, alerting the men in the Kremlin to the danger of ignoring the morale of the Russian working class, prompting them to further revise the pending five-year plan and strengthening their determination to protect the German treaty by achieving a breakthrough on Berlin.[76]

As a consequence, when Kissinger approached Dobrynin with the idea of activating their "back channel" in January to deal with major issues, Moscow proved extremely agreeable. Dobrynin was authorized to proceed and as early as January 23 was able to tell Kissinger, with regard to the Soviet position on SALT, that there was "a good possibility . . . of combining a defensive treaty with an offensive freeze."[77] Within a week he was back to make an unprecedented offer concerning Berlin, namely that "each of the Four [occupying] Powers . . . [should] have the right to call violations [of access arrangements] to the attention of the others."[78] (The Kremlin, obviously, was wrestling with the problem of how to reconcile its need to meet the access demands of the Western powers with its wish to achieve sovereignty for East Germany.) On February 10 Dobrynin explicitly confirmed his agreement with Kissinger to "link offensive and defensive limitations" in SALT.[79] Then, for several weeks, he hedged on this as things ground to a halt in Moscow in preparation for the party congress in March and April.

As it turned out, the Twenty-fourth Party Congress was the forum where Brezhnev chose to offer—and proclaim—the fully integrated version of his revised domestic and foreign policies. As such, the meeting became an important milestone on the general secretary's road to a summit meeting with Richard Nixon. It also became a significant way point on Brezhnev's personal path to the leading position in the Soviet oligarchy.

Speaking at length in the opening week of the congress, Brezhnev presented himself as the leader who best knew how to fit all the policy pieces together. Explaining and justifying the newly released five-year plan, he noted that for the first time in Soviet history the consumer goods sector would grow more rapidly than heavy industry. The industrial sector, he promised, would not be forgotten (and, in fact, would be used in part to produce for the consumer), nor would agriculture (which would continue to be assigned capital at unprecedented rates), nor would the military. Nonetheless, despite such commitments, Brezhnev left little doubt that it was his intention to usher in a new consumer era. Not only would there be more products to buy, there would also be higher wages and more social benefits.

How would all this be accomplished in a period when the labor force was increasing only slightly? The answer, according to Brezhnev, was a more rapid growth in labor productivity, an acceleration to be achieved through rationalization of planning and through new forms of organization, specifically the "production association" (a combination of enterprises in related activities). Brezhnev was giving the Kosygin reforms his personal, more conservative slant; new productivity would derive not from market economics but from a "scientific technical revolution" dependent in large measure on the importation of foreign capital, goods, and expertise. In Brezhnev's words, "the improvement of the system of foreign relations is an important reserve for increasing the economic efficiency of the national economy."[80]

Logically, then, despite "the [Nixon] administration [having lately] taken a more rigid stance on a number of international issues," Brezhnev emphasized that he gave the highest priority to the strengthening of Soviet-American relations and to the achievement of peaceful coexistence *with the entire capitalist world.* The Soviet Union would continue to oppose Western imperialism wherever it encountered it, but it would do so in the context of a six-point "peace program" that called for (1) a political settlement in Southeast Asia and the Middle East, (2) the convening of a security conference in Europe, (3) agreements on control of nuclear arms, (4) reductions in spending on conventional weapons, (5) the completion of decolonization in the Third World, and (6) the "deepening of relations of mutually advantageous cooperation in every sphere." In Brezhnev's view, growing Soviet strength, international détente, and an advancing world socialism were all mutually reinforcing.[81]

An indication of Brezhnev's improving political position was his success in enlarging the number of his allies and supporters on the new Central Committee and Politburo. Of the 241 full members of the Central Committee, Brezhnev's "clients" now numbered at least thirty, a twofold increase, and many more could be viewed as friends. Moreover, of the four men added to the Politburo at this time, two (Vladimir Shcherbitsky and D. A. Kunayev) were Brezhnev loyalists, while a third (Fyador Kulakov) was a dependable associate.[82] On the other hand, that Brezhnev's control was still incomplete could be seen from his inability to rid the Politburo of either Gennady Voronov or Pyotr Shelest, his severest conservative critics (this would require another two years).[83] The limitations of his power were also evident in the fact that Brezhnev's foreign policy recommendations were not always endorsed by other speakers at the congress. Indeed, his "peace program" would not be formally adopted by the party leadership until the November plenum.[84]

Revealing as well, both of Brezhnev's beliefs and of his political situation, was his willingness to compensate for his *Westpolitik* by intensifying the struggle against dissident groups within the U.S.S.R. Proposing to extend party control to research institutes, educational establishments, and cultural and medical organizations, the Soviet leader made it clear that diversity and pluralism could not be allowed to flourish. "We are living in conditions of an unabating ideological war," he declared as he called on "workers on the propaganda and mass agitation front to administer a timely, resolute, and effective rebuff to . . . ideological attacks." Détente in international relations did not mean relaxation of internal discipline. On the contrary, it required increased vigilance.[85]

In the weeks following the party congress, Brezhnev, fortified by new political strength and clarity of purpose, embarked on an impressive array of diplomatic initiatives. At Tbilisi, Georgia, on May 14, just before the U.S. Senate was due to vote on the Mansfield resolution to reduce American forces in Europe, he reiterated for the second time in two months his readiness to accept NATO's proposal for talks with the Warsaw Pact on mutual and balanced force reductions (MBFR). (In so doing, he consciously contributed to the defeat of the resolution, probably out of his concern at the consequences of a sudden and massive American withdrawal.) Admittedly, he linked an agreement on talks to Western acceptance of his own repeated appeals for an international conference on European security and cooperation, but in the process he took a big step toward ensuring that both negotiations would ultimately take place.[86]

Meanwhile, Brezhnev also pressed hard to achieve progress with SALT. Indeed, Dobrynin, upon his return to Washington from the party congress in April, was instructed to accede to the basic American demand (with which, after all, the Soviets had been flirting for several months), namely, that an interim freeze on strategic offensive weapons could be negotiated simultaneously with an ABM agreement.[87] Though there was still to be considerable wrangling over the Soviet attempt to obtain American endorsement of an ABM regime limited to national capitals (the American proposal of the previous year, which Kissinger now regretted making), by May 15 Dobrynin had dropped this issue and cleared the way for the May 20 announcement of an intergovernmental understanding on future objectives.[88] What is more, though the final agreement made clear that, under any negotiated arrangement, modernization and replacement of offensive weapons would be allowed to continue (the loophole Kissinger had *not* fought to close), following the May 20 accord the Soviet government reinstituted its earlier self-imposed freeze on the construction of additional ICBM silos. This positive Soviet "action" was hard for the White House to ignore.[89]

Other "positive" developments occurred rapidly with regard to Soviet policy on Berlin. Despite Brezhnev's plea at the Twenty-fourth Congress for a speedy agreement concerning that city, four-power negotiations languished throughout the spring of 1971, primarily as a result of foot-dragging by Walter Ulbricht, the seventy-seven-year-old East German party leader, who held out for formal Western recognition of East Germany as a sine qua non. Then, on May 3, under obvious Soviet pressure, Ulbricht was forced to step down as first secretary, and the logjam was quickly broken.[90] On May 18 his successor, Erich Honecker, was in Moscow to voice "general approval" of the Brezhnev peace program.[91] In mid-June Brezhnev himself spoke at the Eighth East German Party Congress and emphasized that the Soviet Union was prepared to make the effort necessary to bring the quadripartite talks "to a successful conclusion."[92]

By early July progress in the Berlin "back channel" (the secret avenue of negotiations organized by Rush, Bahr, and Valentin Falin, the Soviet ambassador to Germany, which met for the first time on May 10, one week after Ulbricht's fall) was so rapid that Kissinger directed Rush to delay the conclusion of the Berlin agreement until after July 15, when the national security adviser's visit to China would be announced.[93] According to Kissinger, "the last contentious issue" was settled in the back channel on July 24.[94] When the formal agreement was signed on September 3, it was clear that, aside from gaining certain concessions, the Soviet Union had yielded much: at least some West German presence in West Berlin was permitted; the city's consular and economic ties with West Germany were recognized; and although the Western allies were forced to accept de facto East German control of East Berlin, the Soviet Union now guaranteed Western (including West German) access to the city.[95]

Brezhnev's central role in all this was underlined by his personal invitation to Chancellor Brandt, conveyed in early September, to visit him in the Crimea. Hosting Brandt there at midmonth, without protocol or delegations, Brezhnev demonstrated clearly to the West German both that he, Brezhnev, was now the "dominant member of the Soviet leadership" and that he was immensely interested in the status of relations between Bonn and Moscow. Would the treaty of 1970 be ratified? And when? What was holding it up? When Brandt explained that "technical supplements" would have to be negotiated first, Brezhnev showed his impatience (and practiced some reverse linkage) by insisting that the Berlin protocol could not come into effect before the German treaty did. As was the case during their talks the year before, economic problems were very important to Brezhnev. "He recommended 'high yield' technological cooperation," notes Brandt, "among other things, in the construction of nuclear reactors."[96]

Pressed by Brandt to discuss the China factor, Brezhnev revealed only slight evidence of the anxiety attributed to the Soviet leadership by contemporary and later observers (Kissinger included) regarding the Sino-American reconciliation. Insisting that he was "not suspicious of Nixon's forthcoming visit to China," the general secretary went on to describe the Chinese as "hard to fathom" and predicted that "Nixon would have a hard time of it" in Beijing. Though he accused Mao of pursuing a "nationalistic and chauvinistic policy" and complained of China's "anti-Soviet activities" in the Third World, Brezhnev professed to see "no immediate military threat" from that quarter.

To be sure, what the Soviet leader said on this occasion was probably somewhat less than candid. (Why did he make no mention of his reactions to the declining fortunes of Lin Biao, for example?) But even assuming that he was seriously worried about Chinese hostility, it seems hardly necessary to credit American triangular diplomacy for all the thrust behind Brezhnev's *Westpolitik*. As he told Brandt, "the Soviet Union was ready to normalize relations with the United States, expand trade 'without discrimination' and initiate substantial exchanges 'including space technology.' "[97] This readiness to cooperate with America, in combination with a similar openness toward West Germany, had characterized Brezhnev's policy since early in the previous year. Moreover, now that the Berlin problem was largely settled, a Brezhnev summit with the U.S. president seemed almost inescapable. The proposal for a summit that Dobrynin conveyed to Nixon on August 10 (the acceptance of which was made public during Gromyko's trip to Washington in September) may have come a little earlier because of the China consideration (since the Soviets wanted Nixon to visit Moscow before Beijing), but it would have arrived all the same.[98]

As the autumn progressed, Brezhnev and his foreign policy acquired increasing recognition and momentum. A significant hint of changing attitudes came on August 5, when Nixon for the first time communicated directly with the general secretary (and not through Premier Kosygin), dispatching a letter in which he reviewed the international situation.[99] Shortly thereafter, in order to "balance off the US move to China," Washington acceded to a long-standing Soviet request and agreed to sign, before the summit, the understandings achieved in the SALT negotiations on avoiding accidental war and improving hot line communications.[100] (The signing was accomplished on the occasion of Gromyko's visit to the United States and constitutes the first tangible evidence that SALT could produce agreements.)

Meanwhile, in the weeks following the May 20 SALT bargain, and throughout the summer and fall, the president encouraged American businesses to enter into a variety of commercial arrangements with the Soviet government. The result, as we saw in chapter 5, was millions of dollars worth of contracts for American machinery and grain.[101] With such agreements as well as Nixon's acceptance of the summit invitation in his pocket, it is hardly surprising that Brezhnev's state visit to France in October would be described effusively in the Soviet media as occupying the "center of international attention."[102] Nor is it surprising that at the November plenum of the Central Committee Brezhnev finally pushed through a full endorsement of his "peace program," from this time on to be identified as "the foreign policy program of the XXIV Congress."[103] As early as September 1971 Politburo member Suslov (now prominent as champion of the drive for ideological discipline) had praised Brezhnev's foreign policy as an "outstanding contribution to Marxist-Leninist theory."[104] During the last two weeks of 1971, virtually the entire leadership group— including the secretaries of the Central Committee—toured the country urging support for the new foreign policy line.[105]

Yet, even with this support, Brezhnev could not dictate every decision. In fact, there is considerable evidence that the same Central Committee plenum that placed its imprimatur on the general secretary's foreign policy once again denied him the premiership to which he so obviously aspired. There were many indications in the months before the plenum not only that Premier Kosygin's political position was deteriorating (Podgorny, not Kosygin, went to Egypt to meet Sadat, for example, and he and Brezhnev met with Eastern European leaders in September) but also that Brezhnev was jockeying to have himself appointed head of government. Nevertheless, though Brezhnev played a central role in the discussions of the November plenum, it seems clear that Suslov, Podgorny, and others combined on that occasion to preserve the formal separation of party and government established after the fall of Khrushchev.[106]

Another setback for Brezhnev during late autumn lay in the diplomatic realm. Here, the problem derived from the fact that Nixon and Kissinger consistently misinterpreted Soviet motives as the United States and the U.S.S.R. attempted to relate to the developing crisis in Indian-Pakistani relations. This had been the case since the previous August, shortly after the announcement of Kissinger's visit to Beijing, when the

Soviet Union and India entered into a Treaty of Peace, Friendship, and Cooperation. Fearful that India would be encouraged to attack and even dismember Pakistan (newly vulnerable because of unrest in East Pakistan), Nixon and Kissinger were quick to conclude that "the Soviet Union had seized a strategic opportunity . . . to demonstrate Chinese impotence and humiliate a friend of both China and the United States."[107] As a result, when war broke out in December 1971, the president and his adviser attempted to limit Indian objectives (particularly with regard to West Pakistan) by applying pressure directly on the Soviet government, using the hot line, establishing deadlines, threatening to cancel the summit, and sending the U.S. Navy into the Indian Ocean.[108] They did this in spite of impressive evidence that the Soviet leadership did not favor war and was itself attempting to bring about a cease-fire and reassure Washington that Delhi had no aims beyond the independence of East Pakistan. (Indira Gandhi's government also gave assurances to this effect at least four days before an armistice was achieved on December 17.)[109]

In the end, of course, the Soviets had considerable reason to be pleased, their Indian ally having defeated and politically divided its arch rival in the face of extreme American and Chinese hostility. Yet at the same time, Brezhnev and his colleagues obviously felt pushed around by Nixon and Kissinger. More than three years later, during a discussion of Soviet intervention in Angola, Georgi Arbatov recalls that Andrei Alexandrov said to Brezhnev, "Remember, Leonid Ilyich, how the Americans behaved during the conflict between India and Pakistan?" According to Arbatov, Brezhnev reacted very emotionally, said something quite nasty about U.S. policy, and suddenly lost interest in the matter at hand.[110]

In any case, the first weeks of 1972, as Nixon prepared for and went on his much-heralded February visit to China, must have been a time of some unease for Brezhnev and his Politburo. The official attitude, as reflected in the general secretary's trade union address of March 20 (and Brezhnev's earlier remarks to Brandt), was that it was "quite natural" for Washington and Beijing to want to establish relations. But a hint of Brezhnev's deeper feelings is indicated by his public assertion that "one must not overlook certain statements by the parties to the Beijing talks which give us grounds to believe that the dialogue went beyond the framework of bilateral relations. . . . How else is one to understand . . . the statement made during the banquet in Shanghai that 'today our two peoples [i.e., American and Chinese] hold the future of the whole world in their hands'?"[111] Also revealing is the fact that, for about a month before Nixon's departure for China and throughout his visit, Moscow's press and radio waged an unusually vigorous campaign to undermine China's international prestige and to show that Chinese foreign policy was chauvinist and expansionist.[112] Ironically, by March 20 Brezhnev apparently decided to adopt a less belligerent line. "Chinese official representatives tell us that relations between the USSR and the People's Republic of China should be based on the principles of peaceful coexistence," he noted. "Well, if Beijing does not find it possible to go further in its relations with a socialist state, we are prepared to conduct Soviet-Chinese relations on this basis today."[113]

Within a few days, however, the strain of coping with China's opening to America was compounded as a consequence of North Vietnam's powerful invasion across the demilitarized zone. Nixon and Kissinger, of course, had been trying for many months to coax Hanoi into accepting the Thieu government in the South (and had "gone public" on January 25, 1972, for domestic political reasons, with the fact that Kissinger had been meeting secretly with the North Vietnamese for two and a half years). Furthermore, warned by U.S. generals as early as January of the likelihood of an enemy spring offensive, Nixon and Kissinger had repeatedly intimated to Moscow and Beijing that the United States would respond strongly if confronted with a military attack in Vietnam.[114] Hanoi, on the other hand, driven by the realization that Chinese and Soviet pressure might soon compel it to accept a truce, was not about to forfeit the chance for one last all-out effort to overthrow the Saigon regime. The attack across the DMZ on March 31 was only the first of a series of coordinated offensives that continued for several weeks and that appeared a number of times on the verge of unraveling and destroying the South Vietnamese army.[115] Thus Moscow was caught between its own need and desire for summit with the Americans and the needs and demands of its socialist ally on the far side of China.

As the intensity of Washington's defensive response in Vietnam mounted, the discomfort in the Kremlin grew as well. Unwilling to be driven from office by a North Vietnamese victory, Nixon (now largely without American land forces in Asia) stepped up the bombing of South and North Vietnam to an unprecedented extent.[116] In addition, after Hanoi's representatives turned down the revised American peace proposal in negotiations with Kissinger on May 2, the president arranged for the mining of Haiphong and other harbors even though he knew that the cost for this might well be the summit with Brezhnev. In the face of such dramatic violence, Soviet hard-liners became increasingly vocal.[117] Only after a prolonged and heated meeting of the Politburo on May 10 were Brezhnev, Kosygin, and Podgorny able to turn back the demands of Shelest and other conservatives for the cancellation of the summit. (Following this, they moved to protect their victory by depriving Shelest of his party chairmanship in Ukraine.)[118] The Soviet navy commander, Admiral Sergei

Gorshkov, suggested sending in minesweepers to clear the North Vietnamese ports, but this idea too was rebuffed.[119]

Brezhnev, obviously, decided that the war in Southeast Asia would not distract him from implementing the foreign policy he had previously defined. Indeed, his determination to stay the course despite provocative American actions is testimony to the power of his conviction that the Soviet Union required both a reduction in the costs of the continuing arms race and an infusion of the new technology that only the West could provide. His policy synthesis—which promised economic cooperation with Europe and America, less expensive military competition, more food and consumer goods, recognition as a superpower, domestic orthodoxy, and the ultimate triumph of socialism—continued to seem coherent and persuasive. Moreover, the pieces of the combination interlocked to such a degree that it did not seem possible to dispense with one of them without pulling down the entire structure.

The German treaty, for example, currently being debated in the Bundestag, could hardly be assured of ratification if the summit meeting with the Americans was called off.[120] Nor could the trade pact initialed by the Soviets and the West Germans on April 7, 1972, be expected to survive without the ratification of the renunciation-of-force treaty.[121] The American agreements hung together as well. Matters of trade were dependent on a SALT treaty, a security conference on an MBFR agreement, and so forth.[122] Finally, of significance was the fact that Brezhnev had apparently concluded (possibly as a result of Kissinger's April concession allowing North Vietnam to maintain its troops in the South after a negotiated settlement) that there was no reason why the war in that country had to be prolonged.[123] When Hanoi refused to halt its spring offensive, the Soviet leader is reported to have remarked in disappointment to the French ambassador: "I wish our Vietnamese comrades were as wise at the negotiating table as they are brave on the battlefield."[124]

Behind the scenes, agenda building and preparations for the Soviet-American summit had been under way for several months. As early as the previous September, in conveying the formal invitation to Nixon, Gromyko had suggested, for example, that trade must be an item for discussion (and Dobrynin had followed up by arranging for an exchange of visits by the cabinet officers responsible for commerce).[125] Subsequently, in January Brezhnev wrote the president and proposed a more extended list of summit topics, including SALT, the Middle East, European security, removal of obstacles to trade and economic cooperation, and expanding exchanges in science and technology. The Soviets also broached the idea of working out a Declaration of Basic Principles to govern relations between the two countries.[126]

The response in Washington was not terribly thoughtful or systematic. Since, as Kissinger put it, American "interest in the subjects listed in Brezhnev's January letter was not uniform," some of these topics were largely ignored (e.g., the Middle East and the European security conference). Others were kept substantially in the "back channel" (e.g., SALT and the Declaration of Basic Principles). Still others were relegated to the appropriate cabinet departments (e.g., economic relations and cultural and scientific contacts).[127] Meanwhile, Soviet leaders pressed hard for Kissinger to come to Russia for secret, presummit talks, in part because he had honored China with such a visit, but also, especially after the North Vietnamese offensive, because they saw this as a way of committing Nixon to the summit.[128]

When the president decided to send Kissinger to Moscow in April (enticed by Brezhnev's expressed willingness to discuss Vietnam), the Soviet leader took advantage of his chance to attack the major pending issues. Sensing Kissinger's eagerness to save the summit (particularly after the American offered the aforementioned concession on Vietnam), Brezhnev proposed a variety of attractive compromises and arrangements. With regard to the continuing dispute over ABMs, for instance, he suggested that each side be permitted to protect its capital and one ABM site, a formula that Kissinger found less than perfect but acceptable.[129] On SLBMs the general secretary obliged Kissinger by putting forward as his own the generous (to the U.S.S.R.) proposition that Kissinger had advanced to Dobrynin the previous March; he also agreed that the interim freeze on offensive weapons last for five years, as the Americans desired, rather than for three years, which was the most the Soviet SALT delegation at Helsinki had offered.[130] Finally, the Soviet leader proved to be accommodating in accepting Kissinger's revisions of Gromyko's changes in the original American draft of the Declaration of Basic Principles, clearly appreciative of the fact that Kissinger was willing to endorse the key concept of Brezhnev's "peace program," namely, that there was no acceptable alternative to "peaceful coexistence."[131] In parting, Brezhnev emphasized again how important trade was to both countries. As noted earlier, there is evidence that Kissinger responded with considerable encouragement.[132]

Three weeks later, following the unexpectedly mild Soviet protest regarding Nixon's bombing and mining of North Vietnam, the president arrived in Moscow for the long-awaited summit. The negotiations that followed (May 22–29, 1972), occurring despite the continuing struggle in Southeast Asia, would be a particularly triumphant moment for the Soviet leader. Staged for display more than negotiation, the conference demonstrated to the world not only that superpower cooperation was possible but also that the Soviet Union had obtained from the United States new respect, respite, and resources.

In truth, Brezhnev, loyally supported by Kosygin, Suslov, and Podgorny, was able to win American agreement to virtually his entire program. The Declaration of Basic Principles provided both an explicit endorsement of peaceful coexistence and an implicit, eagerly desired recognition of Soviet equality as a great power.[133] The ABM agreement relieved the Soviet Union of its foremost concern with regard to the continuing arms race.[134] The freeze on offensive strategic weapons was written in such a way as to minimize constraints on the modernization (and MIRVing) of Soviet missiles while putting a stop to mindless increases in existing weaponry.[135] (Nixon and Kissinger achieved very little at the summit with their efforts to restrict replacement of "light" with "heavy" missiles, to limit increases in size of missile silos, or to include older Soviet submarines within already generous upper limits on submarine launchers.)[136]

Though no agreements were signed at Moscow in the economic realm (aside from one establishing a joint U.S.–Soviet commission to resolve outstanding differences on economic issues), it was clearly understood that, as soon as questions of shipping arrangements and lend-lease debt were settled, a trade pact and financial credits would be within reach.[137] A separate bargain specified that discussions could begin on Brezhnev's much-desired European security conference in return for Soviet participation in MBFR talks.[138] Behind all of this, of course, was a hidden bonus for the Soviet Union: the summit, by the very fact that it was happening, tipped the balance in the West German Bundestag in favor of ratifying the Bonn-Moscow accords.[139]

This was not a zero-sum game, of course. The United States (and the West) also benefited, if in different ways, from Soviet promises to "exercise restraint" and avoid seeking "unilateral advantage" (in the Declaration of Basic Principles) as well as from an ABM treaty, a brief (though flawed) freeze on offensive weapons, and more intensive trade, not to mention an improved Berlin situation and the commitment to work for further force reductions. Still, when one considers that what Nixon and Kissinger originally wanted was help in ending the Vietnam War and a slowdown in Soviet missile building, it is clear that on balance they accomplished fewer of their objectives at the summit than did Brezhnev. Perhaps they realized, in the end, that he did not have as much power to end the war as they had hoped. Possibly they assumed that they could rectify their errors of omission and commission regarding weaponry during SALT II negotiations. Certainly they were pleased to achieve a "peace cover" for themselves in case Nixon had to go before the American electorate with the war in Asia still unsolved (or faced with having ended it in a brutal fashion).

Be that as it may, for Brezhnev, after the high point of the summit, the summer and fall of 1972 would be a period of only mixed success. On the plus side was the steady progress toward completion of arrangements to implement economic détente, climaxing in October with the signing of trade agreements stipulating a maritime accord, credit opportunities, settlement of the lend-lease debt, and a U.S. promise to seek most-favored-nation status for the Soviets.[140] How important this was to Brezhnev can be seen not only from his positive reaction at the time but from the way he behaved on trips to Bonn and Washington the following year, when he stressed to Germans how excited he was by giant cooperative deals and told Americans that he was eager for "large-scale trade worthy of the scale of our two big countries."[141]

The negative side of the latter half of 1972 for the Soviets included both foreign and domestic developments. First came the bombshell from Anwar Sadat in July, when (frustrated, he said, by Brezhnev's failure to do something for the Middle East at the Moscow summit) the Egyptian leader terminated the mission of the more than 15,000 Soviet military advisers in his country.[142] Then came the great American grain fiasco of the later summer (following unprecedented crop failures in the U.S.S.R.): Soviet representatives purchased over $1 billion worth of grain, which drove up the price of wheat (and bread) in the United States and generated substantial American ill will.[143] The agricultural setbacks in the Soviet Union were part of, and contributed to, a general economic slowdown in that country, manifested at the end of the year in growth rates that were even worse than those of 1969. At the plenum of the Central Committee in December Brezhnev was forced to begin a redefinition of his "peace program" of 1971, cutting back on his commitments to light industry and consumer goods in order to maintain agricultural and military-industrial investment.[144]

Nevertheless, the general secretary clung steadfastly to détente and to the idea that international trade would solve his domestic economic difficulties. As it happened, 1973 would be a better year, with a record harvest, implementation of commercial arrangements, and following the Yom Kippur War and the OPEC oil embargo, a fivefold increase in the price of oil and gold (with which the U.S.S.R. was well supplied). It was not until 1974 that the policy synthesis with which Brezhnev justified, and for which he required, détente began to come apart.[145]

EPILOGUE: FROM DÉTENTE TO THE GORBACHEV REVOLUTION

We have seen that similar dilemmas in the situations of both super-powers in the early 1970s made it possible and necessary for them to break through Cold War inertia to achieve a period of better relations. Though the leaders of each nation were confident that in the long run history was on their side, in the short term both ruling groups were facing shortages of the economic, political, and other resources they needed to maintain morale in their countries and to continue to compete successfully. Moreover, in a marvelous irony, it was for both of them the other superpower that held (or seemed to hold) the key to freeing up or creating these resources, the Soviet Union ostensibly possessing the power to help the United States extract itself from a damaging war, while America was thought to enjoy the skills and capital that would solve the Soviet problem of productivity. Thus an international bargain grew from the fit of need and capability. An added incentive was that even a modicum of cooperation could go a long way in reducing the nuclear risks that both powers confronted.

When we look closer, of course, we discover important differences in the desires and requirements of the Soviet Union and the United States during these years. If America had powerful economic reasons (not the least, an adverse balance of trade) to be interested in Soviet trade, it did not share the pressing need for technology and investment that drove the Soviet Union toward establishing commerce with the West. Similarly, though Washington was concerned about maintaining its alliances with states like France and West Germany (and therefore had to honor their movement toward détente), it was not experiencing the kind of challenge or danger that the Soviet Union faced in dealing with its estranged Chinese partner. On the other hand, while the U.S.S.R. was sorely troubled by ethnic tension, the alienation of the young, and other divisiveness, these tribulations paled by comparison with the social polarization and political agony the United States was undergoing as a result of the war in Southeast Asia. The crucial missing ingredient among the resources Nixon required for an assertive foreign policy was public support.

In any case, one must recognize the caution and conservatism in both Nixon's and Brezhnev's approaches to détente. Neither statesman ever contemplated the possibility of abandoning his country's role as a dominating power, for example, or of actually bringing the Cold War to an end. Neither had the slightest interest in altering his nation's internal order (e.g., with democratization or with a disciplining of their defense industries) as a means to reducing the pressures that make for international conflict. Nixon and Kissinger may have talked "sufficiency" and placed caps on existing strategic vehicles, but behind the scenes they were MIRVing in order to retain a lead in warheads and moving as fast as they could to persuade Congress to support the creation of new weapons like the Trident, the B-1 bomber, and the MX missile. Brezhnev took his commitments to his own military with equal seriousness. Persuaded as he was that the Soviet Union's acceptance by the United States as an equal was largely a function of its increasing ability to match and project military force at any distance, he continued to appropriate the sums needed to create an army and navy ready for any eventuality. SALT may have saved him money, but it did not alter his course.

There is a paradox here, however, that must be examined lest I seem to be accusing Nixon and Kissinger of being reckless (soft on Russia) and cautious (hard on Russia) at the same time. Its resolution, I think, lies in a recognition of the self-interestedness and opportunism as well as the realism involved. This is not just a question of normal bargaining. These men *were* reckless on occasion in specific negotiations (as when Kissinger conceded excessively high limits on Soviet SLBMs), because they often were as interested in achieving the appearance of success as achieving success itself. They knew that in order for Nixon to be reelected in 1972 they needed to have a "peace cover," especially if the war continued or if the only way they could end it was to bomb Vietnam back to the Stone Age. Thus they were eager for a SALT agreement and a summit—but for electoral as much as national reasons. They counted on a second term and new American weapons (as well as the China factor) to keep the United States ahead in the arms race and possibly to reinstitutionalize a favorable balance of power. As a result, they offered the Soviets an advantageous arrangement in the short term (that is, a relatively unconstraining treaty and enriching trade) but much less in the long term (a continuing Cold War, or if Moscow was ready, an opportunity to acquiesce in the status quo for the world at large).[1]

Brezhnev, though his weakness was not so much political as economic, could play the same game. He was willing to offer much (e.g., Berlin, even East German instability) to obtain new technology and investment for his country. What it meant to him was productivity growth, personal political success, and the chance to keep shifting the correlation of forces in favor of the Soviet Union.[2]

The denouement was both sobering and provocative. The bargains struck in May 1972 ushered in approximately two years of substantial collaboration (the era of high détente), characterized on each side by a certain exuberance as well as wariness. Brezhnev came to Washington in the summer of 1973 for a second summit, a meeting in which he and Nixon signed a formal agreement to consult each other on any situation that might lead to nuclear war. The following year, though sorely burdened by the Watergate scandal, the president returned to Moscow, this time to approve an extension of the interim freeze on offensive weapons and a reduction in the number of ABM deployment sites. Later in 1974, in December, Brezhnev and the new president, Gerald Ford, met in Vladivostok, where they were able to establish a framework for SALT II that put equal (but high) limits on each nation's launchers and bombers. In the interim, negotiations went forward regarding mutual and balanced force reductions in Europe and the Soviets' much desired European security conference, the latter discussions leading in the summer of 1975 to the signing of accords at Helsinki. These protocols were an East-West compromise in the best sense of the word, ratifying the political and territorial status quo in Eastern Europe while offering pledges of human and personal rights throughout the thirty-five signatory nations.[3]

Even with such progress as this, however, it was clear by 1974 that the spirit and momentum of détente were beginning to falter. On the Soviet side the first negative shock occurred in September 1973, when Salvador Allende's government was overthrown in Chile with the obvious connivance of the U.S. Central Intelligence Agency. Less than two months later the shoe was on the other foot, when Washington interpreted Moscow's threatened intervention on behalf of the cease-fire in the Yom Kippur War as a gross violation of détente. Strengthened by public dismay, Senator Henry Jackson (D-Wash.) stepped up his efforts to tie the lifting of Soviet restrictions on Jewish emigration to the passage of the administration's trade bill (which granted most-favored-nation status to the U.S.S.R.). When negotiations among Jackson, Kissinger, and the Soviet leadership during 1974 produced no lasting compromise, the Senate's approval of the Jackson-Vanik Amendment to the Trade Act in December prompted Moscow to reject the entire trade package with the United States. In April 1975 Soviet-American collaboration was further undermined by the victory of the Communist armies in South Vietnam. The end of the year brought added tension with the Soviet-Cuban intervention in Angola, the Senate's passage of the Clark Amendment to the Defense Appropriations Act (prohibiting American involvement), and White House protests to Moscow. By the early months of 1976 détente was in such ill repute with the public that President Ford asked his own secretary of state to avoid using the term during the upcoming political campaign.[4]

Richard Nixon, understandably, blames Watergate and the weakening of the American presidency for much of the deterioration of détente during this period, and there is probably some truth in this.[5] Certainly it is hard to imagine that the SALT II negotiations would have progressed so slowly or that the Jackson-Vanik Amendment would have become such an obstacle had the presidency been fully functioning. Yet, given the mood of the United States, not even a Nixon with "normal" powers could have saved South Vietnam from its enemies in 1975 or intervened to any real extent in Angola.

Moreover, neither party to détente had promised to stop "assisting" history or trying to head off what it considered to be unnatural developments in the Third World. SALT I (aside from the ABM Treaty) did not substantially limit the arms race, and Nixon not only knew this but had intentionally arranged that it work that way. The truth is that détente had been oversold to the American people from the very beginning (Kissinger, for example, in 1973 described as "a significant step toward the prevention of nuclear war" an agreement at the Washington summit he would characterize six years later as "a bland set of principles that had been systematically stripped of all implications harmful to our interests").[6] Small wonder that the public was confused and not a little disillusioned when the Soviets continued to behave as if they were competitors.

The 1970s was a turbulent decade, particularly in the Third World, and the resulting trauma was bound to put détente to a special test. The huge OPEC price increase of 1973–74 was even more painful and destabilizing for the poor countries than for the rich, and it left much of Africa and South Asia on the edge of chaos and desperation. The decolonization process had finally reached those nations that were least prepared to cope with it, impelling Angola and Mozambique, among others, into anarchic independence. The horn of Africa, southern Arabia, indeed the whole Middle East gave the appearance of being up for grabs. A major new factor, of course, was that, whereas in previous years it was the United States that had functioned as the world's policeman, now the Soviet Union (due to its enhanced air and naval capabilities) also possessed the power to project itself into other countries' business. To Moscow, this meant only that it could behave as the other superpower had always behaved. Viewed from other quarters, Soviet actions did not seem so benign.

In the meantime, the Jackson-Vanik and Stevenson amendments to the Trade Act of January 1975 struck Brezhnev at his most vulnerable point and, by forcing him to renounce what he had most wanted and promised, dealt détente a stunning blow.[7] Soviet-American trade, which had increased astonishingly in 1972 and more than doubled again in 1973, now fell by almost half. What is more, though the United States continued to sell agricultural products to Russia (especially after the renegotiated grain agreement of October 1975), by that date Soviet imports of machinery and equipment, financed by generous commercial credits, came almost entirely from Western Europe and Japan.[8] The mutual dependency that Kissinger had hoped to build was being aborted and transformed.

The revolution in the price of oil turned out to play a major part in this, a role that in later years led Georgi Arbatov to conclude that "the main victim of OPEC was the Soviet Union."[9] What allowed Brezhnev to dispense with American credit, trade, and technology in the period after 1974 was not only assistance from and commerce with countries like France, Japan, and West Germany but also the quadrupled return he received on the steadily increasing quantities of oil the Soviet Union produced and sold. Soviet oil production rose from 353 million metric tons in 1970 to 489 million in 1975 and 604 million in 1980—an output second only to Saudi Arabia's. By the 1970s the U.S.S.R. was exporting nearly one-quarter of its total oil production, with slightly less than half of its exports being shipped to the West. Profits from these sales paid the costs of Soviet military buildup and overseas involvement in the later 1970s, while the growth rate of the Soviet economy continued to decline.[10]

The availability of resources *plus* instability abroad *plus* the wrangling over cruise missiles and Backfire bombers that followed Vladivostok combined to put Brezhnev in a position where it was difficult for him to resist the demands of hard-liners to stand firm on military issues and to support national liberation movements.[11] Nor were Brezhnev's inclinations to reject such advice strengthened by his health, which never fully recovered from the stroke he suffered the day after the Vladivostok meeting.[12] As early as 1973–74 Brezhnev made peace with the Soviet defense industry (sacrificing a promised emphasis on consumer goods). At the Twenty-fifth Party Congress in February 1976 (in the wake of the terrible drought of 1975) he retreated from his 1971 commitments to light industry.[13]

Jimmy Carter came to the presidency in January 1977 seeking radical reductions in the arms buildup but also demanding internal changes in the U.S.S.R. that made it difficult for the Soviet leadership to do anything but hold fast to the Vladivostok accords as the basis for SALT negotiations. Meanwhile, the American public was becoming more irritable and less trusting as post-Vietnam isolationism faded, the Republican Right revived, and a series of Third World confrontations developed involving the superpowers or their proxies. Disillusionment grew as the struggle for power in Angola ended in 1977 with 20,000 Cubans occupying that country. It increased markedly as superpower clients realigned themselves in eastern Africa, Ethiopia obtained massive infusions of Cuban troops and Eastern bloc arms, and Soviet military advisers became involved in Yemen's civil war.

If there remained any doubt in American minds about Moscow's intentions, it vanished with the Iranian Revolution of November 1979 and the subsequent Soviet invasion of Afghanistan (a "defensive" action, according to Moscow). Indeed, the impact of the latter event was such as virtually to preclude the possibility that the United States would ratify the SALT II treaty, signed by Carter and Brezhnev in June 1979 after painful bargaining on both sides (including promises by Brezhnev to the Soviet military that its new SS-20 IRBMs could be deployed in Eastern Europe to counter opposing "forward-based systems"). As the decade ended, American aggravation at these setbacks merged with a more general rage at national helplessness regarding OPEC price hikes, rapid monetary inflation, and Iranian hostage-taking to produce the election of Ronald Reagan and an administration dedicated to anti-Communism and a strengthening of the military.[14]

Yet, strangely, the mid-1980s were to witness a kind of replay in Soviet-American relations of what had happened fifteen years before. On this occasion, it was the pressure of a struggling Soviet economy combined with the effects of the Afghanistan war and new military demands that produced the willingness in Moscow to reconsider long-accepted foreign policies. Reagan's pessimism about the "evil" Communist empire had led him in 1983 to seek the "perfect defense" (the strategic defense initiative) as a cover for his militarism (thus making strategic reductions impossible). But in 1987 Mikhail Gorbachev, a genuine reformer, was able to outflank the president by accepting an intentionally "unacceptable" offer that Reagan had made earlier, that is, by agreeing to remove existing SS-20s from Eastern Europe in return for a U.S. promise not to install cruise missiles and IRBMs in NATO Europe.

Reagan was hoisted with his own petard, and by this time he needed such an agreement as a way of helping to distract the American public from the shabby Iran-contra scandal. Gorbachev accompanied his shift with other radical changes designed to escape the arms race and de-demonize the Soviet Union: withdrawal from Afghanistan, large unilateral cuts in

Soviet forces, and a new emphasis on "defensive" defense and internal democratization. He was feeling his way toward 1989, the annus mirabilis in which Eastern Europe would transform itself and the Warsaw Pact would cease to exist.[15]

In later years, some observers argued that the Reagan administration deserved credit for ending the Cold War because it forced the Soviet Union to spend itself into instability. The sad truth, however, is that the fifty-year struggle had physically exhausted both leading contestants.[16] Only Gorbachev was wise enough to realize this and try to do something about it. Unfortunately, the Soviet leader did not have a clear picture of how the transition to a socialist-capitalist economy, limited government, and peace was to proceed, and his lack of clarity ultimately undid him as well as the Soviet Union. Today, one can only hope that the Soviet successor states will revive enough economically to reduce growing ethnic tension and political cynicism within their societies. One can also hope that the West will actively assist in rebuilding the region's economy, not so much by sharing its high technology (as Brezhnev may have wished) as by offering experience, a market, and, especially, investment.

In view of what has happened since 1972 in Soviet-American relations, some may see it as a good thing that the Nixon-Brezhnev détente did not survive, since (they may argue) at least in Moscow's case its success could hardly have done other than prop up a dying regime. To me, however, such an argument slides over too many historic connections and possibilities. Who is to say that, in the face of a perseveringly cooperative American foreign policy, the Soviet system could not have transformed itself into something less expansive and threatening? Would it not be better today to have that kind of integrated country than sixteen disunited successor states?

To my mind, there was both accomplishment and tragedy in détente. The new relation made an important, even indispensable, contribution to breaking down the logic and momentum of the Cold War. Though the leaders on both sides were not ready to give up national ambitions and illusions (not to speak of personal ambitions), they were, to an inspiring if limited extent, caught up in the process of building integrative institutions.

Yet, there was also an element of tragedy. Whether détente, given less conservative leadership, could have been enlarged upon and made into a safer, if slower, route to altering the participating societies is impossible to know. But the fact is that the attempt to enlarge it beyond a mere international balance was never really made by either side. The achievements and the mood were half-formed and were allowed to wither half-formed, with the result that another generation was unnecessarily subjected to the risks and costs of continuing Cold War. In this sense, then, the détente of the 1970s represents one of the truly great missed opportunities for re-forming international relations in recent history. Circumstances conspired for peace, but the leaders on both sides, as creative as they were, were simply not creative enough.

NOTES

Introduction

1. Richard M. Nixon, *The Real War* (New York, 1980), 5.

2. Henry A. Kissinger, "The Fall of Saigon, a Death of Consensus," *Los Angeles Times,* Apr. 28, 1985.

3. See, as evidence, "The War That Won't Go Away," *Newsweek,* Apr. 15, 1985, 32–71.

4. Opinion about foreign policy among leaders, however, is much more divided than before the Vietnam War. On this, see Ole R. Holsti and James N. Rosenau, *American Leadership in World Affairs: Vietnam and the Breakdown of Consensus* (Boston, 1984), chaps. 5–7.

5. Those who assume that "normal" attitudes are sufficient to break through accumulated layers of distrust in major power relations should consider that previous détentelike collaborations have frequently occurred in the wake of frightening events, for example, the rise of Japanese and German militarism in 1931–33, the Nazi attack on Russia in 1941, and the Cuban missile crisis in 1962.

6. See, for example, A. A. Gromyko and B. N. Ponomarev, *Soviet Foreign Policy, 1917–1980,* 2 vols. (Moscow, 1981), 456–78.

7. See, for example, A. Vakhrameyev, "Détente and the World Balance of Forces," *International Affairs* 25 (Jan. 1979): 78–86.

8. On the personalities and personal styles of Nixon and Brezhnev, here admittedly oversimplified, see Fawn Brodie, *Richard Nixon: The Shaping of His Character* (New York, 1981), chap. 34; James David Barber, *The Presidential Character: Predicting Performance in the White House,* 3d. ed. (Englewood Cliffs, N.J., 1985), chaps. 10–12; and George W. Breslauer, *Khrushchev and Brezhnev as Leaders: Building Authority in Soviet Politics* (London, 1982), chap. 16. See also chap. 6, n. 19, below.

9. Some writers employ the term *détente* as if it were a policy; others use it in reference to a condition, a period, or a process; still others attempt to construe a meaning empirically, from the indicators of détente (e.g., cooperation, economic and technical interactions, human rights and contacts, security and disarmament).

See Daniel Frei, ed., *Definitions and Measurement of Détente: East and West Perspectives* (Cambridge, Mass., 1981), chap. 6. For our purposes, Richard Stevenson's definition suffices: "the process of easing of tension between states whose interests are so radically divergent that reconciliation is inherently limited" (*The Rise and Fall of Détente: Relaxations of Tension in US-Soviet Relations, 1953–1984* [Houndmills, Eng., 1985], 11).

Perhaps the best discussion of the term is in Stevenson's book, 1–17, but Brian White, "The Concept of Détente," *Review of International Studies* 7 (1981): 165–71; and Michael B. Froman, *The Development of the Idea of Détente: Coming to Terms* (New York, 1991), 1–8, are also helpful. By far the soundest treatment of the differing Soviet and American perspectives is in Raymond L. Garthoff, *Détente and Confrontation: American-Soviet Relations from Nixon to Reagan*. 2d ed. (Washington, 1994), chap. 2.

For an attempt to measure the rise and fall of tension during the Cold War by means of a "détente index," see Paul F. Herman Jr., *Thinking about Peace: The Conceptualization and Conduct of US-Soviet Détente* (Lanham, Md., 1987), chap. 2. See also Mike Bowker and Phil Williams, *Superpower Détente: A Reappraisal* (London, 1988), which describes the Cold War as a mix of conflict and cooperation and sees détente as "minimal" between 1963 and 1968 and "maximal" during the Nixon years.

10. For more on this point of view, see Richard N. Rosecrance, *Action and Reaction in World Politics* (Boston, 1963). See also Stephen R. Rock, *Why Peace Breaks Out: Great Power Rapprochement in Historical Perspective* (Chapel Hill, N.C., 1989).

Chapter 1. The Developing Confrontation

1. Normal E. Saul, *Distant Friends: The United States and Russia, 1763–1867* (Lawrence, Kans., 1991), 6–51, 78–236, 312–401.

2. John Lewis Gaddis, *Russia, the Soviet Union, and the United States,* 3d ed. (New York, 1990), chap. 2.

3. Arno J. Mayer, *Wilson versus Lenin: Political Origins of the New Diplomacy* (Cleveland, Ohio, 1964), chaps. 1–4.

4. Richard Pipes, *The Russian Revolution* (New York, 1990), chaps. 10, 11.

5. Mayer, *Wilson versus Lenin,* chaps. 8, 9.

6. Betty M. Unterberger, *The United States, Revolutionary Russia, and the Rise of Czechoslovakia* (Chapel Hill, N.C., 1989), chaps. 13–19.

7. David W. McFadden, *Alternative Paths: Soviets and Americans, 1917–1920* (New York, 1993), chaps. 6–12.

8. Jon Jacobson, *When the Soviet Union Entered World Politics* (Berkeley, 1994), chap. 4. See also Stephen White, *The Origins of Détente: The Genoa Conference and Soviet-Western Relations, 1921–1922* (Cambridge, Eng., 1986), chaps. 5–7; and Dale Terrence Lahey, "Soviet Ideological Development of Coexistence: 1917–1927," *Canadian Slavonic Papers* 6 (1964): 80–94.

9. Joan Hoff Wilson, *Ideology and Economics: United States Relations with the Soviet Union, 1918–1933* (Columbia, Mo., 1974), 14–48; and Andrew J.

Williams, *Trading with the Bolsheviks: The Politics of East-West Trade, 1920–1939* (Manchester, Eng., 1992), 14–54, 151–63.

10. Jonathan Haslam, *Soviet Foreign Policy, 1930–1933: The Impact of the Depression* (London, 1983), chaps. 7–12; and Edward M. Bennett, *Recognition of Russia: An American Foreign Policy Dilemma* (Waltham, Mass., 1970), 139–87.

11. Jonathan Haslam, *The Soviet Union and the Struggle for Collective Security in Europe, 1933–1939* (London, 1984), chaps. 1–10; Thomas R. Maddux, *Years of Estrangement: American Relations with the Soviet Union, 1933–1941* (Gainesville, Fla., 1980), chaps. 3–7.

12. Robert Beitzell, *The Uneasy Alliance: America, Britain, Russia, 1941–1943* (New York, 1972), chaps. 2–4, 15–17.

13. Keith Sainsbury, *The Turning Point: Roosevelt, Stalin, Churchill, Chiang Kai-shek, 1943* (Oxford, Eng., 1985), chaps. 1–8.

14. Remi Nadeau, *Stalin, Churchill, and Roosevelt Divide Europe* (New York, 1990), 13–27.

15. William Taubman, *Stalin's American Policy: From Entente to Détente to Cold War* (New York, 1982), 74–75.

16. Victor Rothwell, *Britain and the Cold War, 1941–1947* (London, 1982), chap. 1.

17. John Lewis Gaddis, *The United States and the Origins of the Cold War, 1941–1947* (New York, 1972), 1–17.

18. Vojtech Mastny, *Russia's Road to the Cold War: Diplomacy, Warfare, and the Politics of Communism, 1941–1945* (New York, 1979), 207–12.

19. Lynn Etheridge Davis, *The Cold War Begins: Soviet-American Conflict over Eastern Europe* (Princeton, N.J., 1974), chaps. 4–8.

20. James L. Gormly, *From Potsdam to the Cold War: Big Three Diplomacy, 1945–1947* (Wilmington, Del., 1990), chaps. 1, 2.

21. Fraser J. Harbutt, *The Iron Curtain: Churchill, America, and the Origins of the Cold War* (New York, 1986), chaps. 6, 7.

22. Melvyn P. Leffler, *A Preponderance of Power: National Security, the Truman Administration, and the Cold War* (Stanford, Calif., 1992), 141–203.

23. Taubman, *Stalin's American Policy*, 166–82.

24. Leffler, *Preponderance of Power*, 203–86.

25. Adam B. Ulam, *Expansion and Coexistence: Soviet Foreign Policy, 1917–1973* (New York, 1974), 461–70.

26. David M. Oshinsky, *A Conspiracy So Immense: The World of Joe McCarthy* (New York, 1983), 72–157. On Communist motives in the Korean War, see Sergei N. Goncharov, John W. Lewis, and Xue Litai, *Uncertain Partners: Stalin, Mao, and the Korean War* (Stanford, Calif., 1994).

27. Vojtech Mastny, "Stalin and the Militarization of the Cold War," *International Security* 9 (Winter 1984–85): 109–29.

28. Leffler, *Preponderance of Power*, chaps. 10, 11.

29. John Lewis Gaddis, *Strategies of Containment: A Critical Appraisal of Postwar American National Security Policy* (New York, 1982), chaps. 5, 6. On Dulles, see Richard H. Immerman, ed., *John Foster Dulles and the Diplomacy of the Cold War* (Princeton, N.J., 1990).

30. James Richter, *Khrushchev's Double Bind: International Pressures and Domestic Coalition Politics* (Baltimore, 1994), chaps. 1, 2; and Breslauer, *Khrushchev and Brezhnev,* chaps. 2–4.

31. Richter, *Khrushchev's Double Bind,* chap. 3.

32. Stevenson, *Rise and Fall of Détente,* chap. 3.

33. Ulam, *Expansion and Coexistence,* 572–75.

34. Richter, *Khrushchev's Double Bind,* chap. 4.

35. Ibid., chap. 5; Breslauer, *Khrushchev and Brezhnev,* chaps. 5–7.

36. See Robert Schulzinger, "The Impact of Suez on United States Middle East Policy, 1957–1958," and Galia Golan, "The Soviet Union and the Suez Crisis," in Selwyn Ilan Troen and Moshe Shemesh, eds., *The Suez-Sinai Crisis, 1956: Retrospective and Reappraisal* (New York, 1990).

37. Robert Divine, *Eisenhower and the Cold War* (Oxford, Eng., 1981), 71–104.

38. Adam B. Ulam, *The Rivals: America and Russia since World War II* (New York, 1971), 270–81.

39. See Gordon Chang, *Friends and Enemies: The United States, China, and the Soviet Union, 1948–1972* (Stanford, Calif., 1990), chaps. 5, 6. See also Ronald Steel, *The End of Alliance: America and the Future of Europe* (New York, 1962), chaps. 1–5.

40. This was, in fact, a gigantic bluff, since he had chosen after the Sputnik achievement not to invest in a missile race. See Richter, *Khrushchev's Double Bind,* chap. 5.

41. On the test ban negotiations, see Robert A. Divine, *Blowing on the Wind: The Nuclear Test Ban Debate, 1954–1960* (New York, 1978), 206–323. On the U-2, see Michael R. Beschloss, *Mayday: Eisenhower, Khrushchev, and the U-2 Affair* (New York, 1986), chaps. 10, 11. Stevenson, *Rise and Fall of Détente,* views the Camp David sequence as a second instance of postwar détente (63–102), but it would seem that in this case the relaxation was even more negligible than three years before. See also Froman, *Development of the Idea of Détente,* 17–20.

42. Desmond Ball, *Politics and Force Levels: The Strategic Missile Program of the Kennedy Administration* (Berkeley, Calif., 1980), chaps. 2–5.

43. Gaddis, *Russia, the Soviet Union, and the United States,* 243. The most comprehensive treatment of the missile crisis is now Michael R. Beschloss, *The Crisis Years: Kennedy and Khrushchev, 1960–1963* (New York, 1991), chaps. 15–19. See also Nikita Khrushchev, *Khrushchev Remembers: The Glasnost Tapes* (Boston, 1990), 170–83.

44. Thomas W. Wolfe, *Soviet Power and Europe, 1945–1970* (Baltimore, 1970), 100–116.

45. Ronald J. Terchek, *The Making of the Test Ban Treaty* (The Hague, 1970), chap. 6.

46. Beschloss, *Crisis Years,* 561–678; and Ulam, *Expansion and Coexistence,* chaps. 20–23. On the Kennedy-Khrushchev "thaw," see Stevenson, *Rise and Fall of Détente,* chap. 5, and especially Bowker and Williams, *Superpower Détente,* 21–28.

47. Ulam, *Expansion and Coexistence,* 686–94.

Chapter 2. The Breakdown of Old Arrangements

1. Particularly helpful are Louis Harris, *The Anguish of Change* (New York, 1973), chaps. 11–15; and Edward Shils, "American Society and the War in Indochina," in Anthony Lake, ed., *The Vietnam Legacy: The War, American Society, and the Future of American Foreign Policy* (New York, 1976). See also Kenneth Heineman, "The Silent Majority Speaks: Antiwar Protest and Backlash, 1965–1972," *Peace and Change* 17 (Oct. 1992): 402–33.

2. Keith L. Nelson, ed., *The Impact of War on American Life: The Twentieth Century Experience* (New York, 1971), 1–7, 371–76.

3. For evidence of these interrelationships, see Louis I. Dubin, *Suicide: A Sociological and Statistical Study* (New York, 1963); Elwin H. Powell, *The Design of Discord: Studies of Anomie* (New York, 1970); and Donald T. Lunde, *Murder and Madness* (Stanford, Calif., 1976).

4. For a discussion of this schema, see Keith L. Nelson and Spencer C. Olin, Jr., *Why War? Ideology, Theory, and History* (Berkeley, Calif., 1979), 184–91. For the classic statement about cycles in U.S. foreign affairs, see Frank L. Klingberg, "The Historical Alternation of Moods in American Foreign Policy," *World Politics* 4 (Jan. 1952): 239–73.

5. William Watts and Lloyd A. Free, *State of the Nation III* (Lexington, Mass., 1978), 21.

6. Ben J. Wattenberg, *The Real America: A Surprising Examination of the State of the Union* (Garden City, N.Y., 1974), 198–200. Another manifestation of falling confidence during this period was the shift in perspectives on institutions. To the question, In which of these social institutions are you able to place a "great deal of trust"? the following answers were given (in percentages):

	1966	1971	Change
Medicine	72	61	−9
Banks and other financial institutions	67	36	−31
The military	62	27	−35
Educational institutions	61	37	−24
The scientific community	56	32	−24
Organized religion	55	27	−28
Major U.S. companies	55	27	−28
Mental health caregivers	51	35	−16
The Supreme Court	51	23	−28
Local retail stores	48	24	−24
Congress	42	19	−23
The executive branch	41	23	−18
The press	29	18	−11
Television	25	22	−3
Organized labor	22	14	−8
Advertising	21	13	−8

7. John E. Mueller, *War, Presidents, and Public Opinion* (New York, 1973), 54–55.

8. William L. Lunch and Peter W. Sperlich, "American Public Opinion and the War in Vietnam," *Western Political Quarterly* 32 (Mar. 1979): 21–44.

9. Ibid., 32–43.

10. Wattenberg, *The Real America,* 204.

11. Ibid., 204–5.

12. Holsti and Rosenau, *American Leadership,* chaps. 2–7.

13. Bruce M. Russett, "The Revolt of the Masses: Public Opinion on Military Expenditures," in John P. Lovell and Philip Kronenberg, eds., *New Civil Military Relations: The Agonies of Adjustment to Post-Vietnam Realities* (New Brunswick, N.J.: 1974).

14. Edward Laurance, "The Changing Role of Congress in Defense Policy-Making," *Journal of Conflict Resolution* 20 (June 1976): 213–53.

15. Francis O. Wilcox, *Congress, the Executive, and Foreign Policy* (New York, 1971), 31–32.

16. Alton Frye, *A Responsible Congress: The Politics of National Security* (New York, 1975), 15–30.

17. Robert Bernstein and William Anthony, "The ABM Issue in the Senate, 1968–1970," *American Political Science Review* 68 (Dec. 1974): 1198–1206.

18. John Lehman, *The Executive, Congress, and Foreign Policy: Studies of the Nixon Administration* (New York, 1974), 42.

19. Alan Platt, *The U.S. Senate and Strategic Arms Policy, 1969–1977* (Boulder, Colo., 1978), 42.

20. Paul Burstein and William Freudenberg, "Changing Public Policy: The Impact of Public Opinion, Antiwar Demonstrations, and War Costs on Senate Voting on Vietnam War Motions," *American Journal of Sociology* 84 (July 1978): 99–122.

21. Thomas F. Eagleton, *War and Presidential Power: A Chronicle of Congressional Surrender* (New York, 1974), 119–23.

22. Frye, *Responsible Congress,* 209–10.

23. Jacob K. Javits, "War Powers Reconsidered," *Foreign Affairs* 64 (Fall 1985): 130–40.

24. Thomas M. Franck and Edward Weisband, *Foreign Policy by Congress* (New York, 1979), 13–33.

25. A good discussion of Lyndon Johnson's vulnerability to public and congressional opinion, especially as reflected in the press, is Kathleen J. Turner, *Lyndon Johnson's Dual War: Vietnam and the Press* (Chicago, 1985), chaps. 6–8.

26. "Kissinger's Critique," *Economist,* Feb. 3, 1979, 17.

27. Gerard Smith, *Doubletalk: The Story of the First Strategic Arms Limitation Talks* (Garden City, N.Y., 1980), 29. Smith reiterated his views when interviewed by the author, Apr. 12, 1983. On this point, see also Melvin Laird, "A Strong Start in a Difficult Decade: Defense Policy in the Nixon-Ford Years," *International Security* 10 (Fall 1985): 5–26; and Henry Kissinger, *White House Years* (Boston, 1979), 1486.

28. Henry Kissinger, *For the Record: Selected Statements, 1977–1980* (Boston, 1981), 137.

29. Breslauer, *Khrushchev and Brezhnev as Leaders,* 137–78.

30. According to Fedor Burlatsky, *Khrushchev and the First Russian Spring*

(London, 1991), 220–21, Brezhnev was actually quite hostile to the Kosygin reforms, which he found complicated and irrelevant. For a helpful analysis of the bargaining among the oligarchs in the first post-Khrushchev years, see Richard D. Anderson Jr., *Public Politics in an Authoritarian State: Making Foreign Policy in the Brezhnev Years* (Ithaca, N.Y., 1993), chap. 4.

31. Gertrude Schroeder, "Soviet Economic Reforms at an Impasse," *Problems of Communism* 20 (July–Aug. 1971): 36–46.

32. Wolfe, *Soviet Power and Europe,* chap. 15.

33. Abraham Rothberg, *The Heirs of Stalin: Dissidence and the Soviet Regime, 1953–1970* (Ithaca, N.Y., 1972), chaps. 12–19.

34. John Dornberg, *Brezhnev: The Masks of Power* (New York, 1974), chap. 16.

35. Gertrude Schroeder, "Consumption in the USSR: A Survey," *Studies on the Soviet Union* 10 (1970): 1–38.

36. M. Elizabeth Denton, "Soviet Consumer Policy: Trends and Prospects," in U.S. Congress, Joint Economic Committee, *Soviet Economy in a Time of Change,* 96th Cong., 1st sess. (Washington, 1979), 1:767–73.

37. Gertrude Schroeder, "Consumer Problems and Prospects," *Problems of Communism* 22 (Mar.–Apr. 1973): 10–24.

38. Imogene Edwards, "Automotive Trends in the USSR," in Morris Bornstein and Daniel R. Fusfield, eds., *The Soviet Economy: A Book of Readings* (Homewood, Ill., 1974).

39. Gregory Grossman, "The Soviet Economy Before and After the Twenty-fifth Congress," in Alexander Dallin, ed., *The Twenty-fifth Party Congress of the CPSU: Assessment and Context* (Stanford, Calif., 1977).

40. Schroeder, "Consumer Problems," 16–19.

41. Ibid., 12.

42. Robert F. Miller, "Khrushchev and the Soviet Economy: Management by Reorganization," in R. F. Miller and F. Feher, eds., *Khrushchev and the Communist World* (London, 1984).

43. Werner G. Hahn, *The Politics of Soviet Agriculture, 1960–1970* (Baltimore, 1972), chaps. 8–11, Postscript.

44. Martin McCauley, *Khrushchev and the Development of Soviet Agriculture: The Virgin Land Programme, 1953–1964* (New York, 1976), chap. 5.

45. Roy D. Laird, "The Political Economy of Soviet Agriculture under Brezhnev," in Donald R. Kelley, ed., *Soviet Politics in the Brezhnev Era* (New York, 1980).

46. Valerie Bunce, *Do New Leaders Make a Difference? Executive Succession and Public Policy under Capitalism and Socialism* (Princeton, N.J., 1981), 206–8. For a highly critical discussion of Brezhnev's efforts, see Keith Bush, *Soviet Agriculture: Ten Years under New Management,* Radio Liberty Research Paper (Munich, Aug. 21, 1974).

47. Douglas B. Diamond and Constance B. Krueger, "Recent Developments in Output and Productivity in Soviet Agriculture," in U.S. Congress, Joint Economic Committee, *Soviet Economic Prospects for the Seventies,* 93d Cong., 1st sess. (Washington, 1973).

48. Marianne Armstrong, "The Campaign Against Parasites," in Peter H. Juviler and Henry W. Morton, eds., *Soviet Policy-Making: Studies of Communism in Transition* (New York, 1967), 163–82; Walter D. Connor, *Deviance in Soviet Society: Crime, Delinquency, and Alcoholism* (New York, 1972), 35–189; and Louise Shelley, "Crime and Delinquency in the Soviet Union," in Jerry G. Pankhurst and Michael Paul Sacks, eds., *Contemporary Soviet Society: Sociological Perspectives* (New York, 1980).

49. *Problems of the Younger Generation in the Soviet Union,* Radio Liberty Dispatch (Munich, Mar. 9, 1970).

50. Walter D. Connor, "Mass Expectations and Regime Performance," in Seweryn Bialer, ed., *The Domestic Context of Soviet Foreign Policy* (Boulder, Colo., 1980).

51. Marshall S. Shatz, *Soviet Dissent in Historical Perspective* (Cambridge, Eng., 1980), chap. 5. See also Aleksander M. Nekrich, "The Socio-Political Effects of Khrushchev: His Impact on Soviet Intellectual Life," in Miller and Feher, *Khrushchev and the Communist World.*

52. Wolfe, *Soviet Power,* 248–49.

53. Shatz, *Soviet Dissent,* chaps. 6, 7. For a participant's perspective, see Ludmilla Alexeyeva and Paul Goldberg, *The Thaw Generation: Coming of Age in the Post-Stalin Era* (Boston, 1990), chaps. 5–10.

54. Timothy J. Colton, "The Impact of the Military on Soviet Society," in Bialer, *Domestic Context,* 119–28.

55. Wolfgang Berner et al., eds., *The Soviet Union, 1973: Domestic Policy, Economics, Foreign Policy* (New York, 1975), x–xi. See, in addition, Georgi Arbatov, *The System: An Insider's Life in Soviet Politics* (New York, 1992), 142–52.

56. Rasma Karklins, *Ethnic Relations in the USSR: The Perspective from Below* (Boston, 1986), chaps. 1–3.

57. Hélène Carrère d'Encausse, *Decline of an Empire: The Soviet Socialist Republics in Revolt* (New York, 1979), 48, chaps. 2, 3.

58. Jeremy Azrael, "The 'Nationality Problem' in the USSR: Domestic Pressures and Foreign Policy Constraints," in Bialer, *Domestic Context.*

59. Gail W. Lapidus, "Ethnonationalism and Political Stability: The Soviet Case," *World Politics* 36 (July 1984): 555–80. The extreme sensitivity of the Brezhnev elite to ethnic pressures is highlighted by the way in which the Ukrainian nationalism of party leader Petr Shelest, revealed so openly in his book of 1970, entitled *Our Soviet Ukraine,* became an important factor in his removal from regional office and from the Politburo in 1972 and 1973. On this, see Carrère d'Encausse, *Decline of an Empire,* 215–17.

60. On the other hand, some argue that one of the reasons the Soviets crushed the Dubček regime in 1968 was the Politburo's fear that Czechoslovak nationalism might excite the Ukrainians; Grey Hodnett and Peter J. Potichny, *The Ukraine and the Czechoslovak Crisis* (Canberra, 1970), 77–89.

61. Dale R. Herspring, *The Soviet High Command, 1967–1989: Personalities and Politics* (Princeton, N.J., 1990), 51–74.

62. Wolfe, *Soviet Power,* 428. Michael MccGwire argues that the new Soviet

emphasis on conventional capability and force projection was also a response to changes in Western military doctrine, especially NATO's espousal of "flexible response." MccGwire, *Military Objectives in Soviet Foreign Policy* (Washington, 1987), 22–35.

63. David Holloway, *The Soviet Union and the Arms Race* (New Haven, Conn., 1983), 43–64. See also William T. Lee and Richard F. Staar, *Soviet Military Policy since World War II* (Stanford, Calif., 1986), 61–78.

64. Morton Schwartz, *The Foreign Policy of the USSR: Domestic Factors* (Encino, Calif., 1975), chap. 2.

65. Holloway, *Soviet Union and the Arms Race,* chap. 6.

66. Center for Strategic and International Studies, *New Trends in Kremlin Policy* (Washington, 1970), 47–55.

67. Sidney I. Ploss, *The Soviet Political Process: Aims, Techniques, and Examples of Analysis* (Waltham, Mass., 1971), 278–79.

68. Joseph S. Berliner and Franklyn Holzman, "The Soviet Economy: Domestic and International Issues," in William E. Griffith, ed., *The Soviet Empire: Expansion and Détente* (Lexington, Mass., 1976), 85–86.

69. See the chapter "Comparative Growth of the Soviet Economy," in U.S. Congress, Joint Economic Committee, *Soviet Economic Performance: 1966–1967,* 90th Cong., 2d sess. (Washington, 1968). For slightly different figures, see R. A. Clark and D.J.I. Matko, *Soviet Economic Facts, 1917–1981* (London, 1988), 7–15.

70. Joseph S. Berliner, "Economic Reform in the USSR," in Joseph W. Strong, ed., *The Soviet Union under Brezhnev and Kosygin* (New York, 1971), 53–54.

71. Emily Clark Brown, "Continuity and Change in the Soviet Labor Market," in Bornstein and Fusfeld, *Soviet Economy.*

72. Abraham Katz, *The Politics of Economic Reform in the Soviet Union* (New York, 1972), chap. 8. Helpful discussions of the Kosygin reforms and their problems are in David A. Dyker, *The Future of the Soviet Economic Planning System* (Armonk, N.Y., 1985), 46–63; and Ed A. Hewett, *Reforming the Soviet Economy: Equality versus Efficiency* (Washington, 1988), 227–45.

73. Hans Jurgen Wagner, *The Statistical Report for 1969,* Radio Liberty Dispatch (Munich, Jan. 28, 1970).

74. Brezhnev, in effect, had been able to take back for defense and agriculture what he earlier had lost to the "reformers." See Hahn, *Politics of Soviet Agriculture,* 189–99.

75. Gertrude E. Schroeder, "Soviet Technology: System vs. Progress," *Problems of Communism* 19 (Sept.–Oct. 1970): 19–29. Such modifications, of course, were introduced in part by friends of the reforms.

76. Brezhnev's "secret" statement to the plenum, which generated considerable internal backlash, was ultimately published in Leonid I. Brezhnev, *Ob osnovnyk voprosakh ekonomicheskoi politiki KPSS na sovremennom etape: Rechi i doklady* (Moscow, 1979), 1:451–63. For analysis, see Christian Duevel, *Brezhnev's Secret Report,* Radio Liberty Dispatch (Munich, Jan. 29, 1970); and Harry Gelman, *The Brezhnev Politburo and the Decline of Détente* (Ithaca, N.Y., 1984), 126–31.

77. Dornberg, *Brezhnev,* 252–53.

78. Michel Tatu, "Kremlinology: The 'Mini Crisis' of 1970," *Interplay* 3 (Oct. 1970): 13–19.

79. Paul Cocks, "Science Policy and Soviet Development Strategy," in Dallin, *The Twenty-fifth Congress of the CPSU,* 40–42. The text is in Brezhnev, *Ob osnovnykh voprosakh,* 1:502–12.

80. Herbert S. Levine, "Soviet Economic Development, Technological Transfer, and Foreign Policy," in Bialer, *Domestic Context,* 180–83.

81. Katz, *Politics of Economic Reform,* chaps. 5, 6.

82. Marshall I. Goldman, *Détente and Dollars: Doing Business with the Soviets* (New York, 1975), 27–34. Philip Hanson, *Trade and Technology in Soviet-Western Relations* (New York, 1981), 106–16, contends that Kosygin was a vigorous advocate of importing Western technology as early as the Khrushchev years but that Brezhnev became an advocate only gradually.

83. Schroeder, "Soviet Technology," 21–24.

84. Wolfe, *Soviet Power,* 246–47.

85. A. D. Sakharov, V. F. Turchin, and R. A. Medvedev to Soviet leaders, March 19, 1970, translated in *Survey* (Summer 1970): 160–70. The serious lag in Soviet computer hardware and software is demonstrated in detail by Martin Cave, "Computer Technology," in Ronald Amann, Julian Cooper, and R. W. Davis, eds., *The Technological Level of Soviet Industry* (New Haven, Conn., 1977).

86. Brezhnev, *Ob osnovnykh voprosakh,* 1:359–67, published in *Pravda,* Mar. 30, 1968.

87. Hanson, *Trade and Technology,* 94–97.

88. Cited in Levine, "Soviet Economic Development," 189–90.

89. Paul Marer, "The Economics of Eastern Europe and Soviet Foreign Policy," in Bialer, *Domestic Context.* See also Michael Kaser, *Comecon: Integration Problems of the Planned Economies,* 2d ed. (London, 1967).

90. Vladimir Sobell, *The Red Market: Industrial Cooperation and Specialization in Comecon* (Aldershot, Eng., 1984), chap. 1. William M. Reisinger, *Energy and the Soviet Bloc: Alliance Politics after Stalin* (Ithaca, N.Y., 1992), 21–25.

91. *Izvestiya,* Mar. 27, 1970.

92. Richard Bolling and John Bowles, *America's Competitive Edge: How to Get Our Country Moving Again* (New York, 1982), chaps. 1, 2.

93. Ibid., 5, 41.

94. On the unforeseen consequences of continued Cold War spending, see, in particular, Lloyd Dumas, *The Overburdened Economy: Uncovering the Causes of Chronic Unemployment, Inflation, and National Decline* (Berkeley, 1986), chap. 11; and Robert Kuttner, *The End of Laissez Faire: National Purpose and the Global Economy after the Cold War* (New York, 1991), chap. 2.

95. Bowling and Bowles, *Competitive Edge,* 42, cite statistics from the United States Department of Commerce.

96. Robert Reich, *The Next American Frontier* (New York, 1983), 260–67.

97. Michael Dertouzos, Richard Lester, and Robert Solow, *Made in America: Regaining the Productive Edge* (Cambridge, Mass., 1989), chaps. 2–8.

98. Nasrollah S. Fatemi, *While the United States Slept* (New York, 1982), 88–89.

99. Robert Solomon, *The International Monetary System, 1945–1981*, rev. ed. (New York, 1982), 21–26, 49–57, 109–13.

100. Bolling and Bowles, *Competitive Edge*, 46–54, 79–98, 157–77; and John M. Blair, *The Control of Oil* (New York, 1976), chaps. 1–12.

101. Fatemi, *While the United States Slept*, 28.

102. Solomon, *Monetary System*, 26.

103. David P. Calleo, *The Imperious Economy* (Cambridge, Mass., 1982), chap. 1.

104. Ibid., chap. 2. An excellent discussion of the general situation is in Fred L. Block, *The Origins of International Economic Disorder: A Study of United States International Monetary Policy from World War I to the Present* (Berkeley, Calif., 1977), chaps. 6, 7.

105. Solomon, *Monetary System*, 100–109.

106. Robert A. Pastor, *Congress and the Politics of U.S. Foreign Economic Policy, 1929–1976* (Berkeley, Calif., 1980), 123–35.

107. Joanne Gowa, *Closing the Gold Window: Domestic Politics and the End of Bretton Woods* (Ithaca, N.Y., 1983), chaps. 5, 6.

108. Joan E. Spero, *The Politics of International Economic Relations*, 2d ed. (New York, 1981), 33–52. On the Bretton Woods system, see Gowa, *Closing the Gold Window*, 33–59.

109. Solomon, *Monetary System*, chaps. 12, 13.

110. Michael Mastanduno, *Economic Containment: CoCom and the Politics of East-West Trade* (Ithaca, N.Y., 1992), chap. 3.

111. Ibid., chap. 4. For a contemporary assessment, see Philip D. Grub and Karil Hollick, eds., *American–East European Trade: Controversy, Progress, Prospects* (Washington, 1969).

112. U.S. Congress, Senate Committee on Banking and Currency, *Hearings on East-West Trade*, 90th Cong., 2d sess. (Washington, 1969), 149–62, 296–306, 993–1133. On Nixon's efforts to restrain congressional enthusiasm for liberalizing export controls, see William J. Long, "The Executive, Congress and Interest Groups in U.S. Export Control Policy," in Gary K. Bertsch, ed., *Controlling East-West Trade and Technology Transfer: Power, Politics, and Policies* (Durham, N.C., 1988).

113. Cited in "Arthur Burns to Richard Nixon, April 12, 1969," Box 70, CO 158 (U.S.S.R.), Country Files, Central Files, Richard M. Nixon Papers, National Archives, College Park, Md.

114. Kissinger, *White House Years*, 153.

115. Stans remembers that he asked Nixon several times in 1969 and 1970 to be allowed to travel to Russia for the purpose of discussing an expansion of trade; Maurice Stans, interviewed by the author, July 21, 1992.

116. Cited in "Peter Flanigan to Henry Kissinger, November 23, 1970," Box 71, CO 158 (U.S.S.R.), Country Files, Central files, Nixon Papers.

117. Kissinger, *White House Years*, 153–55, 179–80.

Chapter 3. New Military Parity and the Decline of Bipolarity

1. Alan Milward, *War, Economy, and Society, 1939–1945* (Berkeley, Calif., 1977), 63–74.

2. Greg Herken, *The Winning Weapon: The Atomic Bomb in the Cold War, 1945–1950* (New York, 1982), chaps. 10–14.

3. Holloway, *Soviet Union and the Arms Race,* 15–23; Vasily Yemelyanov, "The Making of the Soviet Bomb," *Bulletin of the Atomic Scientists* 43 (Dec. 1987): 39–41.

4. Malcolm Mackintosh, *Juggernaut: A History of the Soviet Armed Forces* (New York, 1967), chap. 13.

5. Wolfe, *Soviet Power,* chap. 3.

6. Samuel P. Huntington, *The Common Defense: Strategic Programs in National Politics* (New York, 1961), 1–63.

7. Gaddis, *Strategies,* chap. 4. See also Ernest R. May, ed., *American Cold War Strategy: Interpreting NSC 68* (Boston, 1993).

8. Wolfe, *Soviet Power,* 10–11.

9. See Robert W. Clawson and Lawrence S. Kaplan, eds., *The Warsaw Pact: Political Purpose and Military Means* (Wilmington, Del., 1982), 27–63, 111–62.

10. Lee and Staar, *Soviet Military Policy,* 18–22. See also Robert A. Kilmarx, *A History of Soviet Air Power* (New York, 1962), 227–53; and David Woodward, *The Russians at Sea: A History of the Russian Navy* (New York, 1966), chap. 19.

11. McGeorge Bundy, *Danger and Survival: Choices about the Bomb in the First Fifty Years* (New York, 1988), 236–350. See also Dwight D. Eisenhower, *Mandate for Change, 1953–1956* (New York, 1965), 533–48.

12. Gaddis, *Strategies,* chaps. 5, 6.

13. Jerome H. Kahan, *Security in the Nuclear Age: Developing U.S. Strategic Arms Policy* (Washington, 1975), 32–47.

14. Ibid., 28.

15. Allen Dulles, *The Craft of Intelligence* (New York, 1963), 162–63.

16. Edmund Beard, *Developing the ICBM: A Study in Bureaucratic Politics* (New York, 1976), chap. 7. See also Herbert York, *Race to Oblivion: A Participant's View of the Arms Race* (New York, 1970), chaps. 5–7.

17. Raymond L. Garthoff, *Soviet Strategy in the Nuclear Age* (New York, 1958), 170–95.

18. Robert P. Berman and John C. Baker, *Soviet Strategic Forces: Requirements and Responses* (Washington, 1982), 45–50. Breslauer, *Khrushchev and Brezhnev,* 69–70, suggests that Khrushchev may also have been attempting to "marginally deescalate the arms race in order to improve the prospects of striking a deal with the USA."

19. Lincoln P. Bloomfield, Walter C. Clemens, Jr., and Franklyn Griffiths, *Khrushchev and the Arms Race: Soviet Interest in Arms Control and Disarmament, 1954–1964* (Cambridge, Mass., 1966), 96–99, 229–32.

20. Raymond J. Swider, Jr., *Soviet Military Reform in the Twentieth Century: Three Case Studies* (Westport, Conn., 1992), 123–46; and Thomas M. Nichols,

The Sacred Cause: Civil-Military Conflict over Soviet National Security, 1917–1992 (Ithaca, N.Y., 1993), 64–84.

21. Wolfe, *Soviet Power,* 184–88.

22. Robert W. Herrick, *Soviet Naval Strategy: Fifty Years of Theory and Practice* (Annapolis, Md., 1968), chap. 7.

23. Gaddis, *Strategies,* chap. 7; and Janne E. Nolan, *Guardians of the Arsenal: The Politics of Nuclear Strategy* (New York, 1989), 61–77.

24. Ball, *Politics and Force Levels,* chaps. 2–5; and Deborah Shapley, *Promise and Power: The Life and Times of Robert McNamara* (Boston, 1993), 104–11.

25. Ball, *Politics and Force Levels,* chaps. 6–9. Shapley, *Promise and Power,* 139–45, 190–95, emphasizes the extent to which the Cuban missile crisis was instrumental in pushing McNamara toward "assured destruction." See also Nolan, *Guardians,* 77–85.

26. Under the impact of the new nuclear factor, Khrushchev and the Soviet leadership were rethinking their ideas about war during this period, abandoning notions of an inevitable military conflict with the capitalist powers. At the same time, they were loath to relinquish opportunities to exploit increasing Western difficulties with the Third World, particularly since the Chinese were using anti-Western militancy as a litmus test of loyalty to the Communist movement. Hence Khrushchev talked much of aiding "national liberation struggles," but afraid of escalation and lacking the ability to project nonnuclear military power, he generally turned to arms sales and foreign aid as substitutes for intervention. On this, see McGwire, *Military Objectives,* 22–42. Beschloss, *Crisis Years,* 60–65, argues that Khrushchev's speech of January 6, 1961, promising to assist the "sacred" struggles of colonial peoples, was taken much too seriously by the new Kennedy administration.

27. Robert P. Haffa, Jr., *The Half War: Planning U.S. Rapid Deployment Forces to Meet a Limited Contingency, 1960–1983* (Boulder, Colo., 1984), 17–38.

28. The most detailed treatment of the October crisis is Beschloss, *Crisis Years,* 374–575; but see also James G. Blight, Bruce J. Allyn, and David A. Welch, *Cuba on the Brink: Castro, the Missile Crisis, and the Soviet Collapse* (New York, 1993).

29. Bruce Miroff, *Pragmatic Illusions: The Presidential Politics of John F. Kennedy* (New York, 1976), 82–100.

30. Roman Kolkowicz, *The Dilemma of Superpower: Soviet Policy and Strategy in Transition* (Arlington, Va., 1967), 10. McGwire, *Military Objectives,* 361–62, qualifies this by arguing that "the watershed [in Soviet defense policy] had occurred more than a year earlier, when decisions were taken in response to the Kennedy defense buildup."

31. Holloway, *Soviet Union and the Arms Race,* 43–44, 128.

32. Wolfe, *Soviet Power,* 434–41; and Lee and Staar, *Soviet Military Policy,* 66–70.

33. Nichols, *Sacred Cause,* 94–100. McGwire, *Military Objectives,* 42–59, contends that in December 1966, in a decision of truly historic proportions, the Soviets altered their basic military strategy to accord with the object of keeping future wars limited and nonnuclear. Such a decision implied the need for a sus-

tained buildup in the number and quality of Soviet ground forces, navy personnel, and frontal aviation forces. At the same time (according to Franklyn Griffiths, "The Soviet Experience of Arms Control," *International Journal* 44 [Spring 1989]: 304–64), "it made negotiated limitations on strategic intercontinental forces increasingly appropriate" (332).

34. Shapley, *Promise and Power,* 192–201. See also Robert S. McNamara, *The Essence of Security: Reflections in Office* (New York, 1968), which, as Desmond Ball, *Politics and Force Levels,* points out, gives the impression that McNamara had favored assured destruction from the beginning (204).

35. Ball, *Politics and Force Levels,* chap. 7.

36. Ted Greenwood, *Making the MIRV: A Study of Defense Decision Making* (Cambridge, Mass., 1975), 101–5; Charles R. Morris, *Iron Destinies, Lost Opportunities: The Arms Race between the USA and the USSR, 1945–1987* (New York, 1988), 246–57.

37. Haffa, *Half War,* 30–33.

38. William P. Mako, *U.S. Ground Forces and the Defense of Central Europe* (Washington, 1983), 20–23.

39. Richard A. Hunt and Richard H. Schultz, Jr., eds., *Lessons from an Unconventional War: Reassessing U.S. Strategies for Future Conflicts* (New York, 1982), 143–90.

40. Shapley, *Promise and Power,* 390–92. This is not meant to imply that McNamara had previously been uninterested in arms control. On this, see Bernard J. Firestone, *The Quest for Nuclear Stability: John F. Kennedy and the Soviet Union* (Westport, Conn., 1982), 56–70.

41. Morton Halperin, "The Decision to Deploy the ABM: Bureaucratic and Domestic Politics in the Johnson Administration," *World Politics* 25 (Oct. 1972): 62–95; and Greenwood, *Making the MIRV,* 123–39.

42. Fred Kaplan, *The Wizards of Armageddon* (New York, 1983), 343–48.

43. McNamara, *Essence of Security,* 60–67.

44. See, for example, George F. Kennan, "Polycentrism and Western Policy," *Foreign Affairs* 42 (Jan. 1964): 171–83.

45. Alastair Buchan, *The End of the Postwar Era: A New Balance of World Power* (New York, 1974), chaps. 1–4.

46. William Diebold, Jr., *The United States and the Industrial World: American Foreign Economic Policy in the 1970s* (New York, 1972), chaps. 2, 3, 6, 7.

47. Seyom Brown, *New Forces in World Politics* (Washington, 1974), 13–20.

48. Richard Lowenthal, *World Communism: The Disintegration of a Secular Faith* (New York, 1964), 232–67; and Harold C. Deutsch, "The Western Crisis of the Sixties," in Robert H. Beck et al., *The Changing Structure of Europe: Economic, Social, and Political Trends* (Minneapolis, Minn., 1970).

49. Wilfrid L. Kohl, *French Nuclear Diplomacy* (Princeton, N.J., 1971), chap. 1.

50. Edward A. Kolodziej, *French International Policy under de Gaulle and Pompidou: The Politics of Grandeur* (Ithaca, N.Y., 1974), chap. 1.

51. Michael M. Harrison, *The Reluctant Ally: France and Atlantic Security* (Baltimore, 1981), chap. 2.

52. Elliot R. Goodman, *The Fate of the Atlantic Community* (New York,

1974), 82–93. See also Charles de Gaulle, *Memoirs of Hope: Renewal and Endeavor* (New York, 1971), 37–269.

53. Kolodziej, *French International Policy*, 292–334. See also Philip Cerny and Joylon Howorth, "National Independence and Atlanticism: the Dialectic of French Policies," in Kenneth Dyson, ed., *European Détente: Case Studies in the Politics of East-West Relations* (London, 1986).

54. Harrison, *Reluctant Ally*, 115–63; Frank Costigliola, *France and the United States: The Cold Alliance since World War II* (New York, 1992), chap. 4.

55. Kolodziej, *French International Policy*, 341–75. See also the memoirs of French Foreign Minister Maurice Couve de Murville, *Une Politique Étrangère, 1958–1969* (Paris, 1971), 191–233. For basic documentation, see Documentation française, *Les Relations Franco-Sovietiques, 1958–1966* (Paris, 1966).

56. Kolodziej, *French International Policy*, 391–93.

57. Wolfe, *Soviet Power*, 407–22.

58. Kohl, *French Nuclear Diplomacy*, 145–50. See also Ole Holsti, P. Terrence Hopmann, and John D. Sullivan, *Unity and Disintegration in International Alliances: Comparative Studies* (New York, 1973), 176–227.

59. Terence Prittie, *Adenauer: A Study in Fortitude* (London, 1972), 307.

60. Helga Haftendorn, *Security and Détente: Conflicting Priorities in German Foreign Policy* (New York, 1985), 159–72; Wolfram F. Hanrieder, *Germany, America, Europe: Forty Years of German Foreign Policy* (New Haven, Conn., 1989), 170–86. The essential documentation is in Boris Meissner, ed., *Die Deutsche Ostpolitik 1961–1970: Kontinuität und Wandel* (Cologne, 1970), 63–160.

61. Hanrieder, *Germany, America, Europe*, 186–94; and Meissner, *Ostpolitik*, 161–63.

62. Walter F. Hahn, "West Germany's Ostpolitik: The Grand Design of Egon Bahr," *Orbis* 16 (Winter 1973): 859–81. See also Willy Brandt, *People and Politics: The Years 1960–1975* (Boston, 1976), 151–71.

63. Gerhard Wettig, *Community and Conflict in the Socialist Camp: The Soviet Union, East Germany, and the German Problem, 1965–1972* (London, 1975), 33–41; and N. Edwina Moreton, *East Germany and the Warsaw Alliance: The Politics of Détente* (Boulder, Colo., 1978), 51–75.

64. Angela Stent, *From Embargo to Ostpolitik: The Political Economy of West German–Soviet Relations, 1955–1980* (Cambridge, Eng., 1981), 131–53.

65. Brandt, *People and Politics*, 169–70. On East German efforts to discourage Soviet interest in improving relations with Bonn, see Michael J. Sodaro, *Moscow, Germany, and the West from Khrushchev to Gorbachev* (Ithaca, N.Y., 1990), 88–134.

66. Terence Prittie, *Willy Brandt: Portrait of a Statesman* (London, 1974), 197–225. Brandt's attitudes at the time were spelled out in Willy Brandt, *A Peace Policy for Europe* (New York, 1969).

67. Ulam, *Expansion and Coexistence*, 748–67. For eyewitness, if sometimes suspect, testimony, see Arkady Shevchenko, *Breaking with Moscow* (New York, 1985), 169.

68. Stent, *Embargo to Ostpolitik*, 158–60, 163–69; Arnulf Baring, *Machtwechsel: Die Ära Brandt-Scheel* (Stuttgart, 1982), 229–44.

69. Lawrence L. Whetten, *Germany's Ostpolitik: Relations between the Federal Republic and the Warsaw Pact Countries* (London, 1971), 93–127; Werner Link, "Aussen- und Deutschland Politik in der Ära Brandt, 1969–1974," in Karl Dietrich Bracher, Wolfgang Jager, and Werner Link, *Republik in Wandel, 1969–1974: Die Ära Brandt* (Stuttgart, 1986); Meissner, *Ostpolitik,* 380–90.

70. The phrases are from Article I of the treaty. See Whetten, *Germany's Ostpolitik,* 224.

71. Ibid., 127–51. The memoir literature includes Brandt, *People and Politics,* 323–45; Baring, *Machtwechsel,* 332–49; and Helmut Allardt, *Moskauer Tagebuch: Beobachtungen, Notizen, Erlèbnisse* (Frankfurt, 1980), chaps. 28–37.

72. Stent, *Embargo to Ostpolitik,* 162, 174; Brandt, *People and Politics,* 286–305; Kissinger, *White House Years,* 405–12, 529–34, 823–33.

73. Brandt, *People and Politics,* 288. See also Douglas Brinkley, *Dean Acheson: The Cold War Years, 1953–1971* (New Haven, Conn., 1992), 291–96.

74. Josef Korbel, *Détente in Europe: Real or Imaginary?* (Princeton, N.J., 1972), 194. For the French reaction, which became decidedly more hostile over time, see Haig Simonian, *The Privileged Partnership: Franco-German Relations in the European Community, 1969–1984* (Oxford, Eng., 1985), 94–100, 117–20.

75. Brandt, *People and Politics,* 284; and Kissinger, *White House Years,* 409–12, 529–34.

76. Zbigniew Brzezinski, *The Soviet Bloc: Unity and Conflict,* rev. ed. (Cambridge, Mass., 1967), chap. 6; and Wolfe, *Soviet Power,* chaps. 2, 3.

77. William Zimmerman, "Soviet Relations with Yugoslavia and Romania, " in Sarah M. Terry, ed., *Soviet Policy in Eastern Europe* (New Haven, Conn., 1984); and A. Doak Barnett, *China and the Major Powers in East Asia* (Washington, 1977), 24–27.

78. A. Ross Johnson, *The Transformation of Communist Ideology: The Yugoslav Case, 1945–1953* (Cambridge, Mass., 1972), 65–220.

79. Joseph L. Nogee and Robert H. Donaldson, *Soviet Foreign Policy since World War II,* 3d ed. (New York, 1988), 222–25.

80. Brzezinski, *Soviet Bloc,* 176–80, 185–93.

81. Robert L. Hutchings, *Soviet–East European Relations: Consolidation and Conflict, 1968–1980* (Madison, Wis., 1983), 18–19.

82. Brzezinski, *Soviet Bloc,* 239–68; Nikita S. Khrushchev, *Khrushchev Remembers: The Last Testament* (Boston, 1974), 196–207.

83. Brzezinski, *Soviet Bloc,* 210–38; Nikita S. Khrushchev, *Khrushchev Remembers* (Boston, 1970), 415–29.

84. Richard C. Thornton, *China: The Struggle for Power, 1917–1972* (Bloomington, Ind., 1973), 234–41. See also Kazuko Mori, "Sino-Soviet Relations: From Confrontation to Cooperation," *Japan Review of International Affairs* 2 (Spring–Summer 1988): 44–47

85. Chang, *Friends and Enemies,* 184–213; Harrison E. Salisbury, *The New Emperors: China in the Era of Mao and Deng* (New York, 1992), 152–59, 191–93; Khrushchev, *Last Testament,* 235–75.

86. Barnett, *China and the Major Powers,* 39–41. The most comprehensive account of the doctrinal differences is Donald S. Zagoria, *The Sino-Soviet Conflict,*

1956–1961 (Princeton, N.J., 1962). The essential documentation is in Peter Jones and Sian Kevill, comp., *China and the Soviet Union, 1949–1984* (London, 1985).

87. Barnett, *China and the Major Powers*, 45–47; William E. Griffith, *The Sino-Soviet Rift* (Cambridge, Mass., 1964), 33–161.

88. Nogee and Donaldson, *Soviet Foreign Policy*, 237–38. See also Tai Sung An, *The Sino-Soviet Territorial Dispute* (Philadelphia, 1973).

89. U.S. Congress, Joint Economic Committee, *People's Republic of China: An Economic Assessment*, 92d Cong., 2d sess. (Washington, 1972), 347–51.

90. Barnett, *China and the Major Powers*, 48–49. See also, in general, David Mozingo, *China's Foreign Policy and the Cultural Revolution* (Ithaca, N.Y., 1970).

91. Hutchings, *Soviet-East European Relations*, 20–34. For an economic overview, see J. F. Brown, *Eastern Europe and Communist Rule* (Durham, N.C., 1988). For military-political considerations, see Christopher D. Jones, *Soviet Influence in Eastern Europe: Political Autonomy and the Warsaw Pact* (New York, 1981).

92. Reisinger, *Energy and the Soviet Bloc*, 45–52.

93. Peter R. Prifti, "Albania," in Adam Bromke and Teresa Rakowska-Harmstone, eds., *The Communist States in Disarray, 1965–1971* (Minneapolis, Minn., 1972). For the views of the Albanian leader, see Enver Hoxha, *The Khrushchevites: Memoirs* (Tirana, Albania, 1980).

94. Wolfe, *Soviet Power*, 303–8, 352–59. See also, in general, Laurence S. Graham, *Romania: A Developing Socialist State* (Boulder, Colo., 1982).

95. Bennett Kovrig, *Communism in Hungary: From Kun to Kadar* (Stanford, Calif., 1979), chaps. 14–16; and H. Gordon Skilling, *Czechoslovakia's Interrupted Revolution* (Princeton, N.J., 1976), chaps. 7–20.

96. Karen Dawisha, *The Kremlin and the Prague Spring* (Berkeley, Calif., 1985), 341–66; R. Craig Nation, *Black Earth, Red Star: A History of Soviet Security Policy, 1917–1991* (Ithaca, N.Y., 1992), 245–55.

97. Robert G. Sutter, *Chinese Foreign Policy after the Cultural Revolution, 1966–1977* (Boulder, Colo., 1978), 3–105; and Sutter, *China Watch: Sino-American Reconciliation* (Baltimore, 1978), chaps. 5–7.

98. Hutchings, *Soviet–East European Relations*, chap. 2. See also Vernon V. Aspaturian, "East European Relations with the USSR," in Peter A. Toma, ed., *The Changing Face of Communism in Eastern Europe* (Tucson, Ariz., 1970); and Adam Bromke, "Polycentrism in Eastern Europe," in Bromke and Rakowska-Harmstone, *Communist States in Disarray*.

Chapter 4. Seeking America's Escape from Vietnam

1. For a discussion of the ideological traditions, see Nelson and Olin, *Why War?* 8–91. See also Alexander L. George, "The Causal Nexus between Cognitive Beliefs and Decision Making Behavior," in Lawrence S. Falkowski, ed., *Psychological Models in International Politics* (Boulder, Colo., 1979).

2. On this, see Roger D. Master, *The Nation Is Burdened* (New York, 1967).

3. A. James Reichley, *Conservatives in an Age of Change: The Nixon and Ford Administrations* (Washington, 1981), 98–129.

4. Jerry Hough, *Russia and the West: Gorbachev and the Politics of Reform* (New York, 1988), 137-42.

5. Illustrative of such reactions is York, *Race to Oblivion*, 147-69.

6. Charles DeBenedetti, "On the Significance of Citizen Peace Activism: America, 1961-1975," *Peace and Change* 9 (Summer 1983): 6-20. However, see Paul Boyer, "From Activism to Apathy: The American People and Nuclear Weapons, 1963-1980," *Journal of American History* 70 (Mar. 1984): 821-44. On the reactions of decision makers, see, for example, Glenn T. Seaborg, *Kennedy, Khrushchev, and the Test Ban* (Berkeley, Calif., 1981), 175-231.

7. Firestone, *Quest for Nuclear Stability*, 38-147; and Stevenson, *Rise and Fall of Détente*, chap. 5.

8. Lyndon Baines Johnson, *The Vantage Point: Perspectives on the Presidency, 1963-1969* (New York, 1971), 465-67; Glenn T. Seaborg, *Stemming the Tide: Arms Control in the Johnson Years* (Lexington, Mass., 1987), 39-49.

9. W. W. Rostow, *The Diffusion of Power: An Essay in Recent History* (New York, 1972), 377-84; Seaborg, *Stemming the Tide*, chaps. 12-15, 27, 28.

10. Johnson, *Vantage Point*, 467.

11. Ibid., 464. The agreement was signed in November 1966.

12. Mastanduno, *Economic Containment*, 135-36.

13. Johnson, *Vantage Point*, 470-72. The "building bridges" phrase was first used by Johnson in a speech at Virginia Military Institute, May 23, 1964.

14. Mastanduno, *Economic Containment*, 136-40; Philip J. Funigiello, *American-Soviet Trade in the Cold War* (Chapel Hill, N.C., 1988), 153-73.

15. Funigiello, *American-Soviet Trade*, 173-76.

16. Seaborg, *Stemming the Tide*, 201-26, 391-401.

17. Ibid., 214, 449-51.

18. Paul B. Stares, *The Militarization of Space: U.S. Policy, 1945-1984* (Ithaca, N.Y., 1985), 101-5.

19. George Quester, *The Politics of Nuclear Proliferation* (Baltimore, 1973), 14-32. See also Seaborg, *Stemming the Tide*, chaps. 27, 28.

20. Kahan, *Security in the Nuclear Age*, 117-41. What Americans knew is carefully traced in Lawrence Freedman, *U.S. Intelligence and the Soviet Strategic Threat*, 2d ed. (Houndmills, Eng., 1986), 97-128.

21. Shapley, *Promise and Power*, 389-92. Robert S. McNamara, interviewed by the author, Mar. 29, 1985.

22. Halperin, "Decision to Deploy the ABM," 83-88. See also Johnson, *Vantage Point*, 479-85; and Seaborg, *Stemming the Tide*, chaps. 31, 32.

23. Thomas W. Wolfe, "Soviet Interests in SALT," in William R. Kintner and Robert Pfaltzgraff, Jr., eds., *SALT: Implications for Arms Control in the 1970s* (Pittsburgh, 1973). On American decisions to build and test MIRV, see Herbert York, *The Origins of MIRV*, SIPRI Research Report 9 (Stockholm, Aug. 1973), 7-23.

24. Johnson, *Vantage Point*, 485-91; and Seaborg, *Stemming the Tide*, 431-43.

25. Theodore H. White, *The Making of the President, 1968* (New York, 1969), chaps. 5-12.

26. Edward W. Knappman, ed., *Presidential Election, 1968* (New York, 1970), 170–71, 184, 194, 199, 209.

27. Ibid., 152–53, 184, 189, 206–9; and Lester A. Sobel, ed., *Kissinger and Détente* (New York, 1975), 50–51.

28. White, *Making of the President, 1968,* 462–70.

29. Joan Hoff-Wilson, "Richard M. Nixon: The Corporate Presidency," in Fred I. Greenstein, ed., *Leadership in the Modern Presidency* (Cambridge, Mass., 1988).

30. Robert S. Litwak, *Détente and the Nixon Doctrine: American Foreign Policy and the Pursuit of Stability, 1969–1976* (Cambridge, Eng., 1984), 64–73; and Kissinger, *White House Years,* 38–48. Richard Helms, interviewed by the author, Apr. 13, 1983.

31. On Nixon's personality, see Barber, *Presidential Character,* 299–388. For a good indication of Nixon's strong hierarchical tendencies (and First and Second World focus), see his "Memorandum to H. R. Haldeman, John Erlichman, and Henry Kissinger of March 2, 1970," in which he writes that

> in the future all that I want brought to my attention [in the field of foreign policy] are the following items:
>
> 1. East-West relations.
> 2. Policy toward the Soviet Union.
> 3. Policy toward Communist China.
> 4. Policy toward Eastern Europe, provided it really affects East-West relations at the highest level.
> 5. Policy toward Western Europe, but only where NATO . . . and . . . major countries are affected.

Staff Member and Office Files, Special Files, Nixon Papers.

32. Dana Ward, "Kissinger: A Psychohistory," *History of Childhood Quarterly* 2 (1975): 291–92.

33. Walter Isaacson, *Kissinger: A Biography* (New York, 1992), 17–32. See also the excellent study by Stephen G. Walker, "Cognitive Maps and International Realities: Henry A. Kissinger's Approach to World Politics," in Dan Caldwell, ed., *Henry Kissinger: His Personality and Policies* (Durham, N.C., 1983).

34. Henry Brandon, *The Retreat of American Power* (New York, 1972), 23–45; Kissinger, *White House Years,* 112–94; Richard Nixon, *RN: The Memoirs of Richard Nixon* (New York, 1978), 343–47.

35. Litwak, *Détente and the Nixon Doctrine,* 48–64. An early indication of this view is Richard M. Nixon, "Asia after Vietnam," *Foreign Affairs* 46 (Oct. 1967): 111–25.

36. William G. Hyland, *Mortal Rivals: Superpower Relations from Nixon to Reagan* (New York, 1987), 20. In any case, Kissinger attempted privately to reassure the Soviets of Nixon's reasonableness even before Nixon was elected; see Oleg Kalugin, *The First Directorate: My 32 Years in Intelligence and Espionage against the West* (New York 1994), 110–12.

37. Richard J. Whalen, *Catch the Falling Flag: A Republican's Challenge to His*

Party (Boston, 1972), 283–94; and Melvin Small, *Johnson, Nixon, and the Doves* (New Brunswick, N.J., 1988), 162, 166.

38. Seymour M. Hersh, *The Price of Power: Kissinger in the Nixon White House* (New York, 1983), 51, 77–78. See also Allan E. Goodman, *The Lost Peace: America's Search for a Negotiated Settlement of the Vietnam War* (Stanford, Calif., 1978), 78–99. An indication of Nixon's optimism can be seen in his remarks to his cabinet on March 20, 1969, regarding Vietnam. The president "stated flatly that war will be over by next year, but that it must be understood that next four to five months will be very tough, because we have to take public position that outlook is tough, etc., while we negotiate in private." H. R. Haldeman, *The Haldeman Diaries: Inside the Nixon White House* (New York, 1994), 42.

39. Marvin Kalb and Bernard Kalb, *Kissinger* (Boston, 1974), 124–26. This is supposed to have occurred on January 23, 1969, although apparently the offer was not formally endorsed by the administration until April 1 in National Security Decision Memorandum 9. It was made public by Nixon on May 14, 1969, in his first presidential address on Vietnam.

40. William Shawcross, *Sideshow: Kissinger, Nixon, and the Destruction of Cambodia* (New York, 1981), 91–95; Nixon, *RN,* 380–82; and Kissinger, *White House Years,* 239–54.

41. Garthoff, *Détente and Confrontation,* 77–82; and Kissinger, *White House Years,* 138–47. Kissinger was still vigorously pushing this line as late as early July, when he met with Dobrynin on the eve of the latter's departure for a stay in Moscow. Nixon, he assured Dobrynin, was prepared to ratify the status quo of a divided Berlin and Germany as well as "take into account the special interests of the Soviet Union in Eastern Europe." Interestingly, Dobrynin took it upon himself to practice "reverse linkage," expressing "the hope that the Nixon government would act much more actively towards Bonn" in achieving the ratification of the non-proliferation treaty; "Anatoly Dobrynin to A. Gromyko, July 12, 1969," *Cold War International History Project Bulletin* (Washington, Fall 1993), 63–67.

42. Ross Terrill, *800,000,000* (New York, 1972), 144–45.

43. Sutter, *China Watch,* 63–90; and Kissinger, *White House Years,* 167–82. On the armed clashes, see Gerald Segal, *Defending China* (Oxford, Eng., 1985), 176–96.

44. Kalb and Kalb, *Kissinger,* 100–114; and Kissinger, *White House Years,* 130–47. Gerard Smith, interviewed by the author, Apr. 12, 1983.

45. Kissinger, *White House Years,* 262, 272, 285–88; and Nixon, *RN,* 292–93.

46. Goodman, *Lost Peace,* 86–89.

47. Nixon, *RN,* 392–93; and Kissinger, *White House Years,* 272–77.

48. Litwak, *Détente and the Nixon Doctrine,* 120–26; Nixon, *RN,* 394–97; and Kissinger, *White House Years,* 220–25. For a Soviet view, see Jurii Davydov, ed., *Doktrina Niksona* (Moscow, 1972).

49. Kissinger, *White House Years,* 274–77, 282–86. Note especially Kissinger's "Memorandum to the President of September 10, 1969," in ibid., 1480–81.

50. Nixon, *RN,* 398–407; and Kissinger, *White House Years,* 159–62, 277–88.

51. Hersh, *Price of Power,* chap. 10.

52. Gaddis, *Strategies,* 276–83; Richard Nixon, *The Nixon Presidential Press*

Conferences (New York, 1978), 4–5; and Nixon, *RN,* 415. National Security Study Memorandum 3, "Military Posture," Jan. 21, 1969, was designed to address the sufficiency question.

53. Alain C. Enthoven and K. Wayne Smith, *How Much Is Enough? Shaping the Defense Program, 1961–1969* (New York, 1971), 208.

54. Freedman, *U.S. Intelligence,* 101–17. Seaborg, *Stemming the Tide,* 437, notes that in the American draft treaty for SALT of 1968, "there were to be no numerical restrictions on MIRVs; the Joint Chiefs insisted on this."

55. Freedman, *U.S. Intelligence,* 118–52; Nixon, *RN,* 415–17; and Kissinger, *White House Years,* 204–10.

56. Aaron Wildavsky, "The Politics of ABM," *Commentary* (Nov. 1969): 55–63. George Rathjens, interviewed by the author June 7, 1988.

57. Laird's testimony before Senate and House committees in the spring of 1969 is in reels 1 and 2 of "Public Statements by the Secretaries of Defense, Part 4: The Nixon and Ford Administrations," Microform Collections. For Richard Helms's more cautious point of view, which nearly cost him his job, see Thomas Powers, *The Man Who Kept the Secrets: Richard Helms and the CIA* (New York, 1979), 211–12. For a critical analysis, see Freedman, *U.S. Intelligence,* 137–52. Evidence of how very deeply Nixon was involved in the fight over the ABM is provided by "Haldeman's Handwritten Notes, April 27, 1969."

58. Frye, *Responsible Congress,* 55–66. Alton Frye, interviewed by the author, Mar. 21, 1985.

59. Nixon wrote on his "News Summary of May 31, 1969," "I have decided to move ahead on MIRV testing regardless of Senatorial opposition. Inform all hands so that there will be one Administration line." News Summaries, Box 30, President's Office Files, Special Files, Nixon Papers. The Senate's vote of the next year is discussed in Platt, *U.S. Senate and Strategic Arms Policy,* 13–14.

60. Kissinger, *White House Years,* 540; and Smith, *Doubletalk,* 161. Melvin Laird argues, in retrospect, that "MIRVs were the only feasible option available for response to an expanding Soviet threat, given the hostile attitude of many members of Congress toward defense spending." Laird, "Strong Start," 11.

61. Smith, *Doubletalk,* 154–78; and Garthoff, *Détente and Confrontation,* 158–61. This point was amplified by Gerard Smith, interviewed by the author, Apr. 12, 1983; and Raymond Garthoff, interviewed by author, Mar. 20, 1985.

62. Small, *Johnson, Nixon, and the Doves,* 173–92.

63. Burstein and Freudenberg, "Changing Public Policy."

64. Kissinger, *White House Years,* 214. According to Laird, "Strong Start," 9, the Nixon administration was attempting to pursue "major modernization programs for all three legs of the strategic Triad (land-based missiles, bombers, and submarines)."

65. On Nixon's European trip, see Nixon, *RN,* 370–75; and Kissinger, *White House Years,* 73–111. For a critical view, see J. Robert Schaetzel, *The Unhinged Alliance: America and the European Community* (New York, 1975), 48–53.

66. Whetten, *Germany's Ostpolitik,* 93–151. For added discussion and bibliography, see chap. 3.

67. Kissinger, *White House Years,* 405–12.

68. The phrase is Kissinger's (ibid., 412). On American anxiety about Bonn's *Ostpolitik*, see ibid., 410–12; Henry Kissinger, *Years of Upheaval* (Boston, 1982), 143–48; 154–59; Garthoff, *Détente and Confrontation*, 125–27; and Brandt, *People and Politics*, 278–96. Kenneth Rush underlined the tension and even hostility involved when interviewed by the author, Mar. 28, 1985. Nixon's attitude is revealed in a marginal note he made on a news summary of December 30, 1970, reporting that George Ball had expressed fear of West Germany's new policy toward the Soviet Union: "Good for him!" "News Summary of December 30, 1970."

69. As Kissinger puts it, "The cumulative impact of all the bureaucratic indiscipline, with media and Congressional pressures added, was that we had to abandon our attempt to use the opening of the SALT talks as a lever for other negotiations" (*White House Years*, 138). See also Garthoff, *Détente and Confrontation*, 146–52.

70. Garthoff, *Détente and Confrontation*, 151. For Kissinger's analysis of Soviet stonewalling during the summer of 1969, see *White House Years*, 144–45, 159–62; and Hyland, *Mortal Rivals*, 41–42. As late as September, however, Kissinger was still attempting to link issues, warning Dobrynin that lack of help on Vietnam made progress on arms control unlikely. See Isaacson, *Kissinger*, 246–49.

71. Thomas W. Wolfe, *The SALT Experience* (Cambridge, Mass., 1979), 29–36; Kissinger, *White House Years*, 147–49; and Smith, *Doubletalk*, 108–12.

72. Isaacson, *Kissinger*, 249–50.

73. Kissinger, *White House Years*, 149; and Smith, *Doubletalk*, 75–80.

74. Smith, *Doubletalk*, 80–88.

75. Garthoff, *Détente and Confrontation*, 152–54. Raymond Garthoff, interviewed by the author, Mar. 20, 1985.

76. Kissinger, *White House Years*, 541. The directive was National Security Decision Memorandum 49. On the preparations, see Smith, *Doubletalk*, 116–20; and Garthoff, *Détente and Confrontation*, 154–59.

77. Kissinger, *White House Years*, 541–42.

78. Ibid., 543.

79. Ibid., 543–44.

80. Desmond Ball, *Déjà Vu: The Return of Counterforce to the Nixon Administration* (Los Angeles, 1975), 19; and Smith, *Doubletalk*, 119–20, 173–74.

81. Garthoff, *Détente and Confrontation*, 160–62.

82. Kissinger, *White House Years*, 545; and Smith, *Doubletalk*, 124–25. See also Raymond Garthoff, "BMD and East-West Relations," in Ashton B. Carter and David N. Schwartz, eds., *Ballistic Missile Defense* (Washington, 1984).

83. Kissinger, *White House Years*, 549. The American proposal of Aug. 4 has also frequently been termed Option E.

84. Kissinger, *White House Years*, 550. "My preferred position," Kissinger writes, "was to maintain the deployment [of the ABMs] both sides were actually building" (548). He believes that the Russians assumed that, if they were patient, they could get the U.S. Congress to do their work for them (scuttling the American ABM) without having to give something up for it. The probability is, however, that

it was the administration's insistence on coupling an offensive and defensive agreement (without giving up MIRV) that led Moscow to go slow.

85. Stephen Ambrose, *Nixon: The Triumph of a Politician, 1962–1972* (New York, 1989), 299-304; Hersh, *Price of Power,* 118–31; Nixon, *RN,* 398–403; and Kissinger, *White House Years,* 282–305.

86. Ambrose, *Triumph,* 305–13; and Nixon, *RN,* 404–10. See also Raymond Price, *With Nixon* (New York, 1977), 152–57; and William Safire, *Before the Fall: An Inside View of the Pre-Watergate White House* (Garden City, N.Y., 1975), 178. The speech is in *Public Papers of the President, Richard Nixon 1969* (Washington, 1969), 901–9.

87. Goodman, *Lost Peace,* 102–4; Nixon, *RN,* 410–4; Kissinger, *White House Years,* 307–8.

88. Small, *Johnson, Nixon, and the Doves,* 190–98. See also Heineman, "Silent Majority," 416–20.

89. Hersh, *Price of Power,* 168–74; and Kissinger, *White House Years,* 448–57.

90. Shawcross, *Sideshow,* 128–60; and Ambrose, *Triumph,* 343–63. Nixon presents his view of what happened in *No More Vietnams* (New York, 1985), 116–28.

91. Brandon, *Retreat,* 146–47.

92. Tad Szulc, *The Illusion of Peace: Foreign Policy in the Nixon Years* (New York, 1978), 337–41; and Kissinger, *White House Years,* 968–80.

93. John W. Garver, *China's Decision for Rapprochement with the United States, 1968–1971* (Boulder, Colo., 1982), 84–148. For the American side, see Nixon, *RN,* 547; Kissinger, *White House Years,* 698–99, 1487; and Garthoff, *Détente and Confrontation,* 252–57.

94. Kissinger, *White House Years,* 552.

95. Ibid., 554–58; and Garthoff, *Détente and Confrontation,* 198–204.

96. Indeed, Kissinger writes of September and October 1970 as the "autumn of crises," *White House Years,* 594–652. Similar views are found in Nixon, *RN,* 483–90; and Kalb and Kalb, *Kissinger,* 186–212. For interpretations that play down the gravity of these events, see Szulc, *Illusion of Peace,* 321–31, 364–66; Hersh, *Price of Power,* 234–56; and Garthoff, *Détente and Confrontation,* 87–100. See also Isaacson, *Kissinger,* 285–315, which presents a day-by-day analysis emphasizing the responsibility of Kissinger for inflaming matters.

97. On the German negotiations, see Brandt, *People and Politics,* 323–65. On the American reaction, see Nixon, *RN,* 793–97; Kissinger, *White House Years,* 532–34; and Hyland, *Mortal Rivals,* 28–33. Always indefatigable, Nixon shortly after the autumn election was busy integrating his summit plans into a "new international game plan." It "now fits with politics," he observed. "Hold [the] summit until *we* want a big story and [until] it will be very big—with results." "Haldeman Handwritten Notes, November 7, 1970."

98. Richard Nixon, *U.S. Foreign Policy for the 1970s: A New Strategy for Peace* (Washington, 1970).

99. Kissinger, *White House Years,* 410.

100. Nixon, *RN,* 497. Just how little confidence Nixon possessed about Rus-

sian intentions one can see from a memorandum he wrote to Henry Kissinger on November 30, 1970, part of which reads: "With regard to Soviet policy hardening . . . it may be that Harriman, and other Kremlinologists who talk rather freely with people in Washington who get the word back to Moscow . . . may be encouraging the Moscow leaders to wait out the '72 election on the theory that having any kind of détente between now and '72 would come up against a very tough bargainer and might help him get reelected, whereas waiting after '72 might reduce his chances of getting re-elected and thereby increase the chance for them to make a better deal after '72 than before." Box 229, Haldeman Chronological File, Special Files, Nixon Papers.

Chapter 5. Finding America's Way to Détente

1. Kissinger, *White House Years*, 798.
2. Elmo R. Zumwalt, Jr., *On Watch: A Memoir* (New York, 1976), 319. "After Kissinger's outburst on the train [coming back from the Army-Navy game], I knew he *had* to have a deal with the Russians." Elmo Zumwalt, interviewed by the author, Mar. 24, 1988.
3. On Nixon's China policy during 1969 and 1970, see Garthoff, *Détente and Confrontation*, 242–53; and Kissinger, *White House Years*, 167–84. As for the rumors of nuclear war, the administration was in fact gravely concerned. By the summer of 1969, Nixon was convinced the Soviets were preparing for an all-out attack on China. John Robert Greene, *The Limits of Power: The Nixon and Ford Administrations* (Bloomington, Ind., 1992), 109. Not coincidentally, Moscow was watching American reactions carefully. See also chap. 6, n. 33; and Bundy, *Danger and Survival*, 532–35.
4. Sutter, *China Watch*, 96–99; and Kissinger, *White House Years*, 188–94.
5. Kissinger, *White House Years*, 697.
6. Ibid., 698–99.
7. Garver, *China's Decision*, chaps. 3, 4. See also Salisbury, *New Emperors*, 289–95.
8. Hersh, *Price of Power*, 366–67; and Kissinger, *White House Years*, 698–701.
9. Franz Schurmann, *The Foreign Politics of Richard Nixon: The Grand Design* (Berkeley, Calif., 1987), 137; and Kissinger, *White House Years*, 708–10. The second annual presidential report on foreign policy (issued February 25, 1971) was used to continue the "signaling" to Beijing. See Richard M. Nixon, *U.S. Foreign Policy for the 1970s: Building for Peace* (Washington, 1971), 105–9.
10. Szulc, *Illusion of Peace*, 398–400; and Kissinger, *White House Years*, 712.
11. Kissinger, *White House Years*, 714.
12. Garthoff, *Détente and Confrontation*, 258–60.
13. Ambrose, *Triumph*, 450–54. The quotation is from Kissinger, *White House Years*, 765.
14. Haldeman, *Haldeman Diaries*, 359, 368–69; and Kissinger, *White House Years*, 765–84. Note that Kissinger continued his practice of personally informing the Chinese of developments in Soviet-American relations even as late as his visits

to Beijing as Secretary of State in November 1974 and October 1975; see Richard H. Solomon, *U.S.-PRC Political Negotiations, 1967–1984: An Annotated Chronology* (Santa Monica, 1985), 14–60.

15. Brown, *Eastern Europe*, 166–73.

16. William Hyland, interviewed by the author, Apr. 14, 1983. See also Hyland, *Mortal Rivals*, 33–34.

17. Kissinger, *White House Years*, 798.

18. See, for example, Kalb and Kalb, *Kissinger*, 213–14.

19. Kissinger, *White House Years*, 801–3.

20. Garthoff, *Détente and Confrontation*, 178–80; Smith, *Doubletalk*, 222–35. For a view more sympathetic to Kissinger, see John Newhouse, *Cold Dawn: The Story of SALT* (New York, 1973), 203–19.

21. David M. Keithly, *Breakthrough in the Ostpolitik: The 1971 Quadripartite Agreement* (Boulder, Colo., 1986), 112.

22. Honore M. Catudal, Jr., *The Diplomacy of the Quadripartite Agreement on Berlin: A New Era in East-West Politics* (Berlin, 1978), 139–41.

23. Catudal, *Quadripartite Agreement*, 141–45, 152–53; and Hyland, *Mortal Rivals*, 32–33.

24. Kissinger, *White House Years*, 800.

25. Ibid., 804, 807.

26. Egon Bahr, interviewed by the author, July 1, 1982.

27. Kenneth Rush, interviewed by the author, Mar. 28, 1985. See also Kissinger, *White House Years*, 827–28; and John P. Leacocos, "Kissinger's Apparat," *Foreign Policy* 5 (Winter 1971–72): 2–27.

28. A. James McAdams, *East Germany and Détente: Building Authority after the Wall* (Cambridge, Eng., 1985), 110–18.

29. Kissinger, *White House Years*, 798–99.

30. Ibid., 811–12.

31. Joan Hoff-Wilson, "'Nixingerism,' NATO, and Détente," *Diplomatic History* 13 (Fall 1989): 501–25.

32. Kissinger, *White House Years*, 813. The context is in Laurance, "Changing Role of Congress."

33. Ambrose, *Nixon*, 417–21; Kissinger, *White House Years*, 987–1010; and Nixon, *RN*, 298–99.

34. Small, *Johnson, Nixon, and the Doves*, 213–18.

35. William C. Berman, *William Fulbright and the Vietnam War: The Dissent of a Political Realist* (Kent, Ohio, 1988), 140–44; and Kissinger, *White House Years*, 1012.

36. Hersh, *Price of Power*, 315.

37. Ernest R. May and Janet Fraser, eds., *Campaign '72: The Managers Speak* (Cambridge, Mass., 1973), 32.

38. Alan S. Blinder, *Economic Policy and the Great Stagflation* (New York, 1979), 26–27; Susan Strange, "The Dollar Crisis 1971," *International Affairs* 48 (Apr. 1972): 191–215.

39. Nixon was so eager to bring Connally into his administration that he asked Haldeman to tell him that he, Nixon, "feels urgently you are *desperately* needed

in this position now and another position [the presidency?] in [the] future."
"H. R. Haldeman Handwritten Notes, December 4, 1970." See also Haldeman, *Haldeman Diaries*, 215–16; and Safire, *Before the Fall*, 497–508. On the Council on International Economic Policy and the new game plan, see Herbert Stein, *Presidential Economics: The Making of Economic Policy from Roosevelt to Reagan and Beyond* (New York, 1984), 160–68.

40. Solomon, *Monetary System*, 185–87. See also chap. 2, above.

41. Undated presidential news summary (probably from Nov. 1970), Safire, *Before the Fall*, plate 15. Nixon minuted on the summary, "K—We must get *all* hands in line on this. Discuss with Peterson and Ehrlichman." Stans subsequently toned down his public statements. Maurice Stans, interviewed by the author, July 21, 1992.

42. Dom Bonafede, "Peterson Unit Helps Shape Tough International Economic Policy," *National Journal* 13 (Nov. 1971): 2238–48.

43. "Peter Peterson to Richard Nixon, July 7, 1971," President's Handwriting Files, President's Office Files, Special Files, Nixon Papers. Peterson added that "more or less complete liberalization [of American trade with Eastern Europe] would *add* by 1975 about $1 billion to exports and something like $400 million to our balance of trade."

44. Kissinger, *White House Years*, 840. This is verified in "Peter Peterson to [Congressman] Olin Teague, November 16, 1971," Box 18, Trade Files, Central Files, Nixon Papers.

45. James Trager, *The Great Grain Robbery* (New York, 1975), 9–11.

46. Roger B. Porter, *The US–USSR Grain Agreement* (Cambridge, Eng., 1984), 11–12; and Hersh, *Price of Power*, 343–48.

47. Joseph Halow, *U.S. Grain: The Political Commodity* (Lanham, Md., 1989), 36–37.

48. Smith, *Doubletalk*, 222–25.

49. Freedman, *U.S. Intelligence*, 159–64. On the public pressure, see Kissinger, *White House Years*, 806, 812, 816.

50. Freedman, *U.S. Intelligence*, 164–68.

51. Garthoff, *Détente and Confrontation*, 171–73.

52. Smith, *Doubletalk*, 131, 211–18.

53. Kissinger, *White House Years*, 810–19.

54. Wolfe, *SALT Experience*, 103–6.

55. Smith, *Doubletalk*, 228–29.

56. Kissinger, *White House Years*, 813–19.

57. Garthoff, *Détente and Confrontation*, 179–82, 91. But see also Isaacson, *Kissinger*, 326–27.

58. Kissinger, *White House Years*, 819–23.

59. See "John Scali to Richard Nixon, May 26, 1971," President's Handwriting Files.

60. Garthoff, *Détente and Confrontation*, 212.

61. Sodaro, *Moscow, Germany and the West*, 207–10.

62. Catudal, *Diplomacy*, 166–71; and Brandt, *People and Politics*, 292–93.

63. Moreton, *East Germany and the Warsaw Alliance,* 188.

64. Nixon, *RN,* 524.

65. Kissinger, *White House Years,* 837–38.

66. Ibid., 828.

67. Kenneth Rush, interviewed by the author, Mar. 28, 1985. Egon Bahr is more generous to Kissinger. "It was so crucial to give up all the talk about legal rights in Berlin—to let that lie—and to try to regulate practical matters. Henry saw this. He got the point. The other Americans were much slower to understand, and the French were very legalistic." Egon Bahr, interviewed by the author, July 1, 1982.

68. McAdams, *East Germany and Détente,* 114–21. On Andrei Gromyko's attitudes, see Shevchenko, *Breaking with Moscow,* 169; on Brezhnev's, see Dornberg, *Brezhnev,* 213. Note also Georgi Arbatov's remarks in an interview in 1989: "Kissinger thinks it was China that played the decisive role in getting us to feel the need to preserve our relationship with the U.S.A. But Berlin actually played a much bigger role, almost a decisive one. Having the East German situation settled was most important to us, and we did not want to jeopardize that." Isaacson, *Kissinger,* 422–23.

69. "Briefing Book of March 2, 1971," Box 166, Foreign Affairs Files, President's Personal Files, Special Files, Nixon Papers.

70. Press conference of Oct. 12, 1971, in Nixon, *Presidential Press Conferences,* 212.

71. Nixon, *RN,* 524.

72. Catudal, *Diplomacy,* 178–83; and Kissinger, *White House Years,* 755–63, 837.

73. Nixon, *Presidential Press Conferences,* 191.

74. Garthoff, *Détente and Confrontation,* 197–98, 263, 1130.

75. The texts of the two agreements are in Smith, *Doubletalk,* 517–23. See also Andrew Bennett, "The Accidents Measures Agreement," in Albert Carnesale and Richard N. Haass, eds., *Superpower Arms Control: Setting the Record Straight* (Cambridge, Mass., 1987).

76. Smith, *Doubletalk,* 294–95.

77. Ambrose, *Triumph,* 478.

78. Hersh, *Price of Power,* 346–48. Much, if not all, of the arrangement is spelled out in "Peter Flanigan to Richard Nixon, November 3, 1971," Box 68, Charles Colson Files, Staff Member Files, Special Files, Nixon Papers. See also "John C. Whitaker to Richard Nixon, November 2, 1971," Box 18, Trade Files, Central Files, Nixon Papers.

79. Sobel, *Kissinger and Détente,* 88.

80. Maurice Stans, interviewed by the author, July 21, 1992.

81. Garthoff, *Détente and Confrontation,* 105–6, 303. See also "Press Conference of Secretary of Agriculture Earl Butz in Moscow, April 12, 1972," Box 12, Peter Flanigan Files, Staff Member Files, Special Files, Nixon Papers.

82. Brandon, *Retreat,* 227–46.

83. Christopher Van Hollen, "The Tilt Policy Revisited: Nixon-Kissinger Geopolitics and South Asia," *Asian Survey* 20 (Apr. 1980): 339–61. Kissinger's ver-

sion, *White House Years,* 842–94, is very suspect. So is Richard C. Thornton's, *The Nixon-Kissinger Years: Reshaping America's Foreign Policy* (New York, 1989), 105–9.

84. Kissinger, *White House Years,* 848, 853.

85. Robert Jackson, *South Asian Crisis: India, Pakistan, and Bangladesh: A Political and Historical Analysis of the 1971 War* (New York, 1975), 224–28. Nixon offers a relatively brief discussion in *RN,* 525–28.

86. The president's pro-Pakistani bias had been made known to senior policy makers as early as July 1971, but the public did not become aware of it until December. See Van Hollen, "Tilt Policy Revisited," 346–57.

87. Nixon, *RN,* 527; and Kissinger, *White House Years,* 900–901.

88. Garthoff, *Détente and Confrontation,* 304–5. See also Zumwalt, *On Watch,* 360–69.

89. Nixon, *RN,* 529; and Kissinger, *White House Years,* 910.

90. Kissinger, *White House Years,* 912. Haldeman records (Dec. 15, 1971) that "there was some discussion [with Nixon] about the threat in [Kissinger's] backgrounder that we would call off the Soviet summit. . . . The P[resident] told [Ron] Ziegler to cool that on the grounds that the issue hasn't reached that point and that it might later if the Russians don't act to stop the cannibalizing there." Haldeman, *Haldeman Diaries,* 385.

91. Nixon, *RN,* 529–30; and Kissinger, *White House Years,* 913–18. Gandhi's comments were made in an interview with Jonathan Power in the *Washington Post,* Dec. 30, 1979.

92. Kissinger, *White House Years,* 897. See also Haldeman, *Haldeman Diaries,* 380–83.

93. Hersh, *Price of Power,* 465–66.

94. Ambrose, *Triumph,* 488–91; and Haldeman, *Haldeman Diaries,* 387.

95. "Haldeman Handwritten Notes, January 13, 1972." Relations between the president and Kissinger were particularly strained in the three weeks following Christmas 1971. Haldeman, *Haldeman Diaries,* 388–94; Hersh, *Price of Power,* 473–76; and Isaacson, *Kissinger,* 383–95.

96. Goodman, *America's Search for a Negotiated Settlement,* 107–11.

97. Szulc, *Illusion of Peace,* 386–87.

98. Ibid., 390–92; and Isaacson, *Kissinger,* 331–32. For the text of the May 31 proposal, see Kissinger, *White House Years,* 1488–89.

99. Szulc, *Illusion of Peace,* 392–94, 487–97; and Goodman, *America's Search,* 111–15. For the text of the Oct. 11, 1971, proposal, see Kissinger, *White House Years,* 1489–90.

100. Goodman, *America's Search,* 115–17. Thornton, *Nixon-Kissinger Years,* 99–100, 118–25, contends that, after Kissinger proposed a cease-fire in place in May 1971, the Soviet Union abandoned earlier restraint and actually connived with North Vietnam to facilitate a successful invasion from the North in the spring of 1972. The more probable explanation for the expansion of both Soviet and Chinese military and economic assistance to North Vietnam during 1971 and 1972 is that Moscow and Beijing were locked in competition with each other for influence in Hanoi; on this, see Hemen Ray, *China's Vietnam War* (Kalkaji, India,

1983), 51–56; and Ramesh Thakur and Carlyle A. Thayer, *Soviet Relations with India and Vietnam* (Houndmills, Eng., 1992), 116–19.

101. Kissinger, *White House Years*, 1042–43.

102. Hersh, *Price of Power*, 480–88; and Nixon, *RN*, 584–86.

103. Hersh, *Price of Power*, 489–92.

104. Ambrose, *Triumph*, 517–24.

105. Garthoff, *Détente and Confrontation*, 287–88.

106. Gelman, *Brezhnev Politburo*, 120. See also *The Soviet Union's Hard Look at China*, Radio Liberty Dispatch (Munich, Apr. 12, 1972).

107. Szulc, *Illusion of Peace*, 521–25; and Kissinger, *White House Years*, 1074–87.

108. Garthoff, *Détente and Confrontation*, 275.

109. John W. Garver, "Sino-Vietnamese Conflict and the Sino-American Rapprochement," *Political Science Quarterly* 96 (Fall 1981): 445–64.

110. Goodman, *America's Search*, 117–19.

111. Hersh, *Price of Power*, 503–10. See also Haldeman; *Haldeman Diaries*, 436–37.

112. Nixon, *RN*, 589.

113. Kissinger, *White House Years*, 1108–20.

114. Nixon, *RN*, 589–90.

115. Kissinger, *White House Years*, 1135–37, 1148, 1154–64.

116. Nixon, *RN*, 588–91.

117. Garthoff, *Détente and Confrontation*, 183–86.

118. Kissinger, *White House Years*, 1146–47.

119. Tad Szulc, "Behind the Vietnam Cease-Fire Agreement," *Foreign Policy* 15 (Summer 1974): 21–69; and Hersh, *Price of Power*, 512–13.

120. Kissinger, *White House Years*, 1147.

121. Ibid., 1150.

122. Garthoff, *Détente and Confrontation*, 179–85; Kissinger, *White House Years*, 1128–31, 1148–54; Smith, *Doubletalk*, 352–72; and Zumwalt, *On Watch*, 403–5.

123. John Newhouse, *War and Peace in the Nuclear Age* (New York, 1989), 231, 444. Laird's intention, of course, had been to induce the Russians to agree to an SLBM limit. He did not know when he suggested the idea in January that the upper limit on Soviet SLBMs would be 950.

124. Garthoff, *Détente and Confrontation*, 175–77; and Kissinger, *White House Years*, 1148–50.

125. Alexander L. George, "The Basic Principles Agreement of 1972: Origins and Expectations," in Alexander George, ed., *Managing U.S.-Soviet Rivalry: Problems of Crisis Prevention* (Boulder, Colo., 1983), 107–10; and Garthoff, *Détente and Confrontation*, 110–13, 330–31.

126. Hersh, *Price of Power*, 531–35; and Kissinger, *White House Years*, 1133–36.

127. Joseph Alsop, "A View of the Summit," *Washington Post*, May 24, 1972.

128. Hersh, *Price of Power*, 514–19; and Kissinger, *White House Years*, 1158–64.

129. "Kissinger to Alexander Haig, April 24, 1972," as cited in Kissinger, *White House Years,* 1163.

130. Szulc, *Illusion of Peace,* 547.

131. Kissinger, *White House Years,* 1169–76.

132. Haldeman, *Haldeman Diaries,* 450–55. Kissinger's description of his role in this matter (*White House Years,* 1174–79) is rather misleading, implying that he first acquiesced in Nixon's decision to cancel the summit and later opposed it. In truth, Nixon's immediate reaction had been to cancel the summit (diary entry of May 3), but he quickly decided to put off the decision. Nixon, *RN,* 600–601.

133. Szulc, *Illusion of Peace,* 551–56.

134. Kissinger, *White House Years,* 1193–94.

135. Garthoff, *Détente and Confrontation,* 325–26; Kissinger, *White House Years,* 1202–14; and Nixon, *RN,* 609–11.

136. Kissinger, *White House Years,* 1133.

137. Garthoff, *Détente and Confrontation,* 339; Zumwalt, *On Watch,* 391–94. These agreements are reproduced in Charles E. Timberlake, ed., *Détente: A Documentary Record* (New York, 1978), 1–13.

138. Kissinger, *White House Years,* 1216–42 (the quotation is on 1230). See also Smith, *Doubletalk,* 407–40.

139. Garthoff, *Détente and Confrontation,* 189–91, 196–97. As Robert Schulzinger notes, the fact of signing the SALT agreement was more important to Kissinger than the contents; see Robert D. Schulzinger, *Henry Kissinger: Doctor of Diplomacy* (New York, 1989), 65–66.

140. Garthoff, *Détente and Confrontation,* 186–97; Kissinger, *White House Years,* 1216–21, 1230–41; and Smith, *Doubletalk,* 410–31.

141. Garthoff, *Détente and Confrontation,* 188–90; Kissinger, *White House Years,* 1235–41; and Smith, *Doubletalk,* 431–33. The relatively harmonious resolution of this matter should not obscure the fact that the Joint Chiefs and Secretary Laird were dismayed in April by Kissinger's acceptance of high (and unequal) limits on submarine-launched ballistic missiles, i.e., what Admiral Elmo Zumwalt called "the appalling SLBM numbers" (*On Watch,* 403). The only way the Joint Chiefs could reconcile themselves to the Soviet limits (950 SLBMs plus modernization) was to insist that the Trident and other American strategic programs be further accelerated (they had already been accelerated in late 1971; see Newhouse, *War and Peace,* 228–31). Zumwalt (*On Watch,* 407) is severe in judging the end result: "it was the unconscionable [i.e., excessive] numbers in the SALT agreements . . . that virtually froze us into five more years of high spending on US strategic forces." For Kissinger's astonishing attempts to justify his figures, particularly in the period between his Moscow trip and the summit, see Hersh, *Price of Power,* 539–41; and Garthoff, *Détente and Confrontation,* 185–89.

142. Garthoff, *Détente and Confrontation,* 194–95; Kissinger, *White House Years,* 1236–41; and Smith, *Doubletalk,* 413–17. Kissinger's memoirs confuse the issue by suggesting that the American delegation in Helsinki had proposed a unilateral U.S. declaration on *silo* dimensions, when in actuality (and at Kissinger's direction) it had proposed such a declaration only for *missile* volume. Kissinger is saying in effect that, by specifying a limit of 10–15% in the increase of silo dimen-

sions, he had obtained a Soviet commitment that the delegation could not obtain, but in truth the delegation (as Smith wired him) simply preferred the wording of the revised Russian draft, namely that "the size of land-based ICBM silo launchers will not be increased."

143. Garthoff, *Détente and Confrontation*, 191–94; Kissinger, *White House Years*, 1218–19, 1231, 1239, 1241; and Smith, *Doubletalk*, 413–23. The unfortunate aspect of their decision, of course, was that the unilateral definition of "light" and "heavy" missiles implied limitations on change that did not exist when American authorities already knew that the successor ICBM to the SS-11 would be larger than the SS-11. Kissinger himself was later tempted, in testifying before Congress, to suggest that such limitations on the Russians existed. See Garthoff, *Détente and Confrontation*, 172–73.

Note that the reason the Americans did not fight harder for a general rule prohibiting increases in missile size was that such a limit might have impeded the modernization of Minuteman.

144. Nixon, *RN*, 616. The texts of the ABM Treaty and Interim Agreement are in Timberlake, *Détente*, 14–29.

145. The most comprehensive and thoughtful discussion of the basic principles and what they meant to each side is in Garthoff, *Détente and Confrontation*, 326–35. The text of the Declaration of Basic Principles is in Timberlake, *Détente*, 28–29.

146. Kissinger, *White House Years*, 1208.

147. Ibid., 1131–32, 1250, 1254; and Nixon, *RN*, 618. The quotations are from Kissinger's postsummit (May 29) press conferences in Moscow and Kiev. Box 6, John Scali Files, Staff Member Files, Special Files, Nixon Papers.

148. Garthoff, *Détente and Confrontation*, 326.

149. See V. F. Petrovsky, "The Role and Place of Soviet-American Relations in the Contemporary World," *Voprosy istorii* 10 (Oct. 1978), cited in Garthoff, *Détente and Confrontation*, 332–34.

150. See S. Beglov, "An Important Step in the Realization of the Peace Program," *Sovetskaya Rossiya*, June 20, 1972, cited in Garthoff, *Détente and Confrontation*, 332. Regarding the "bargain" on CSCE and MBFR, see Kissinger, *White House Years*, 401, 412–16, 947–49, 966–67, 1208, 1249–50. See also the "President's Briefing Book for June 9, 1972," Box 22, Patrick Buchanan Files, Staff Member Files, Special Files, Nixon Papers.

151. Kissinger, *White House Years*, 1222–29; and Nixon, *RN*, 613–14.

152. Szulc, *Illusion of Peace*, 571–73; Nixon, *RN*, 617; and Kissinger, *White House Years*, 1251.

153. See, for example, Kissinger, *White House Years*, 1133–34, 1269–73. In Kissinger's press conference in Kiev on May 29, 1972, he is quoted as saying, "We never expected to get a trade agreement here. We never even attempted to negotiate a trade agreement here." Box 6, Scali Files.

154. "Peter Flanigan to Richard Nixon, March 7, 1972," Box 10, Peter Flanigan Files. This package was being developed in response to National Security Decision Memorandum 151, "Next Steps with Respect to US–Soviet Trading Relationships," issued on February 15, 1972, over the joint signatures of Henry

Kissinger and Peter G. Peterson. "Documents of the National Security Council, 1947–1977" (five reels), Microform Collections. This NSDM in turn supplemented a Kissinger memorandum of January 31, 1972, to the Departments of State, Commerce, and Agriculture stressing the need for more Soviet trade; U.S. Congress, Senate Government Operations Committee, *Russian Grain Transactions*, 93 Cong. 1 sess. (Washington, 1973), 1:15. The work was buttressed by such CIA studies as "Potential for Soviet Trade with the United States in Industrial Raw Materials" (Dec. 1971). "CIA Research Reports: The Soviet Union, 1946–1976" (five reels), Microform Collections.

155. Flanigan wrote: "The meeting of union leaders on which implementation of a maritime agreement depends is scheduled for Thursday [May 25] in the U.S. Negotiation of outstanding differences with the Soviets is scheduled for Thursday and Friday in Moscow. If a satisfactory solution is reached, the exchange of notes can be announced on Saturday [May 27] as an element of the commercial package." "Peter Flanigan to Richard Nixon, May 23, 1972," Box 66, Trip Files, Subject Files, Central Files, Nixon Papers. On May 25, Haldeman recorded his expectation that the "Ag[ricultural] deal and Lend-Lease [agreement would be signed on] Sat[urday]." "Haldeman Handwritten Notes." Yet on May 27 in Moscow, Kissinger told William Safire, "There'll be a grain deal when [Peter] Peterson gets here [in July]. The maritime deal was screwed up by the unions, and that must be handled first before we can conclude the grain deal." Safire, *Before the Fall*, 454. What Kissinger was really saying was that the union leaders had refused to go along with his plan to abandon the requirement that half of all exports to the Soviets be carried in American-flagged ships. Isaacson, *Kissinger*, 428. Thus the Nixon administration was having trouble with the unions much later than Seymour Hersh suggests. Hersh, *Price of Power*, 346–48.

156. "Peter Flanigan to Richard Nixon, May 23, 1972." Flanigan disclosed that Nikolai Patolichev (Soviet minister of foreign trade) had informed the Americans on May 23 that "he [Patolichev] had reported with approval our proposal that the USSR buy $750 million of grain over 3 years with CCC financing but had gotten no instructions from 'the top.' . . . You [Nixon] might wish to stimulate . . . [acceptance] in your discussions with Secretary Brezhnev. The announcement of the grain purchase agreement would be on Saturday." See also Kissinger, *White House Years*, 1269.

157. See the detailed attachments, "Flanigan to Nixon, March 7, 1972."

158. On the first issue, see Peter G. Peterson, *U.S.–Soviet Commercial Relationships in a New Era* (Washington, 1972), 18–19. On the second, see Trager, *Great Grain Robbery*, 72–73. Regarding the lend-lease dispute, see "Flanigan to Nixon, May 23, 1972."

159. The president's "Briefing Book of June 9, 1972."

160. Goldman, *Détente and Dollars*, 204–5. The text of the agreement is in Timberlake, *Détente*, 53–56.

161. Kissinger, *White House Years*, 1271.

162. The texts of the commercial agreements and a helpful White House press release are in Timberlake, *Détente*, 48–71.

163. Sobel, *Kissinger and Détente,* 141–43. The second and fourth of these agreements are in Timberlake, *Détente,* 37–39, 43–47.

164. "Patrick Buchanan to Richard Nixon, Sept. 28, 1972," Box 62, Trade Files, Central Files, Nixon Papers. For context, see Goldman, *Détente and Dollars,* 193–224; and Halow, *U.S. Grain,* 39–66.

165. Paula Stern, *Water's Edge: Domestic Politics and the Making of American Foreign Policy* (Westport, Conn., 1979), 18–52.

166. Kissinger, *White House Years,* 1272.

167. Anwar el-Sadat, *In Search of Identity: An Autobiography* (New York, 1978), 228–31; and Kissinger, *White House Years,* 1276–1300.

168. Goodman, *America's Search,* 123–64.

169. *Izvestiya,* Sept. 4, 1972.

Chapter 6. Brezhnev and Squaring the Circle

1. Sodaro, *Moscow, Germany, and the West,* 43–79. See also Richter, *Khrushchev's Double Bind,* chap. 8.

2. Gelman, *Brezhnev Politburo,* 80–81; MccGwire, *Military Objectives,* 13–66; and Herspring, *Soviet High Command,* 40–48. For an insightful analysis of the bargaining that went on among Soviet leaders in this period, especially among Brezhnev, Kosygin, Suslov, Podgorny, and Shelepin, see Anderson, *Public Politics,* 87–165.

3. Breslauer, *Khrushchev and Brezhnev,* 137–44. See also Dornberg, *Brezhnev,* 189–91.

4. Jan Adam, *Economic Reforms in the Soviet Union and Eastern Europe since the 1960s* (Houndmills, Eng., 1989), 40–54. Kosygin's speech is in M. E. Sharpe, ed., *Reform of Soviet Economic Management* (New York, 1966), 3–46.

5. Gelman, *Brezhnev Politburo,* 87–92. For the revealing observations of a highly placed intellectual, see Burlatsky, *Khrushchev,* 243–48.

6. Sodaro, *Moscow, Germany, and the West,* 80–82.

7. Wolfe, *Soviet Power,* 308–15. Anderson, *Public Politics,* 181–87, argues that the "Bucharest Line" was a bargain among the four core Politburo members (Brezhnev, Kosygin, Suslov, Podgorny) in the face of a "sectarian" (i.e., hard-line and purist) challenge from Shelepin during 1966–67 regarding foreign policy. Sodaro *Moscow, Germany, and the West,* 88–103, underlines the ambivalences in the Soviet position.

8. Sodaro, *Moscow, Germany, and the West,* 84–88.

9. Ulam, *Expansion and Coexistence,* 719–22. See also Richard K. Herrmann, *Perceptions and Behavior in Soviet Foreign Policy* (Pittsburgh, 1985), 50–74.

10. Wolfe, *Soviet Power,* 313, 325–32.

11. Sodaro, *Moscow, Germany, and the West,* 103–7. See also Brandt, *People and Politics,* 169–75, 183–87. Anderson, *Public Politics,* 188–94, contends that, after Shelepin's fall and the Six-Day War in 1967, the coalition among Brezhnev, Kosygin, Suslov, and Podgorney broke down, creating a situation that "presaged reversals on all the foreign policy issues." Documentation is in German Federal

Republic, Presse und Informationsamt, *Die Politik der Gewaltverzichts* (Bonn, 1968), 8–31.

12. Wolfe, *Soviet Power,* 267.

13. Quester, *Politics of Nuclear Proliferation,* 33–55; and Seaborg, *Stemming the Tide,* chaps. 21–28.

14. Seaborg, *Stemming the Tide,* 413–30. See also Johnson, *Vantage Point,* 481–85.

15. Dina R. Spechler, "Soviet Policy in the Middle East: The Crucial Change," in Paul Marantz and Blema Steinberg, eds., *Superpower Involvement in the Middle East* (Boulder, Colo., 1985).

16. Wolfe, *Soviet Power,* 250–51. See also Ludmilla Alexeyeva, *Soviet Dissent: Contemporary Movements for National, Religious, and Human Rights* (Middletown, Conn., 1985), 267–82.

17. Christian Duevel, *Brezhnev Exhorts "Monolithic Unity" and "Iron Discipline,"* Radio Liberty Dispatch (Munich, Apr. 3, 1968); Burlatsky, *Khrushchev,* 248–56.

18. Georgi Arbatov, *Zatianuvsheesia Vyzdorovlenie* (Moscow, 1991), 151. This passage does not appear in the English version (Arbatov, *The System*).

19. Ibid., 134; and Burlatsky, *Khrushchev,* 210–29. See also Jerry Hough, "The Brezhnev Era: The Man and the System," *Problems of Communism* 25 (Mar.–Apr. 1976): 1–17. Brezhnev had high regard for scientific judgment, and indeed it was during his tenure that the think tanks of the Academy of Science were given the resources to flourish. According to Oleg Bykov of the Institute for the Study of the World Economy and International Relations (IMEMO), Brezhnev on occasion during group discussions would turn to Nikolai Inozemtzev, director of IMEMO, with the question, "Well, comrade, what does *science* say?" Oleg Bykov, interviewed by the author, Oct. 23, 1990.

20. Gelman, *Brezhnev Politburo,* 72–78; and Anderson, *Public Politics,* 166–94. See also Leonard Schapiro, "The General Department of the CC of the CSPU," *Survey* (Summer 1965): 53–65.

21. Dornberg, *Brezhnev,* 205–6.

22. Gelman, *Brezhnev Politburo,* 71–104; Dornberg, *Brezhnev,* 198–280; and Serge Petroff, *The Red Eminence: A Biography of Mikhail A. Suslov* (Clifton, N.J., 1988), 160–86. See also Arbatov, *The System,* 121–22. Richter, *Khrushchev's Double Bind,* chap. 9, offers a very perceptive comparison of Brezhnev's and Kosygin's foreign policy ideas during the early years, contrasting Brezhnev's emphasis on military power with Kosygin's belief in the centrality of economic relations. Kosygin tended to be more optimistic than the general secretary about U.S.-Soviet relations.

23. Breslauer, *Khrushchev and Brezhnev,* 137–52; and Hahn, *Politics of Soviet Agriculture,* 189–206.

24. Breslauer, *Khrushchev and Brezhnev,* 137–78. Many of Brezhnev's speeches are in Leonid Brezhnev, *Leninskim Kursom,* vol. 1 (Moscow, 1970); and Brezhnev, *Ob osnovnykh voprosakh.* Kosygin's are in A. N. Kosygin, *A. N. Kosygin: izbrannye rechi i stat'i* (Moscow, 1974).

25. Dornberg, *Brezhnev,* 219–22.

26. Arbatov, *The System,* 141.

27. Jiri Valenta, "Soviet Decisionmaking on Czechoslavakia, 1968," in Jiri Valenta and William C. Potter, eds., *Soviet Decisionmaking for National Security* (London, 1984). Dawisha, *Kremlin,* 341–66, places greater emphasis on the elements of agreement among the Soviet leaders. See also Mark Kramer, "New Sources on the 1968 Soviet Invasion of Czechoslovakia," *Cold War International History Project Bulletin* 2, (Fall 1992): 1, 4–13.

28. Nation, *Black Earth, Red Star,* 251–54. For East Germany's highly idiosyncratic reaction, see Sodaro, *Moscow, Germany, and the West,* 123–34.

29. Johnson, *Vantage Point,* 485–89.

30. Hutchings, *Soviet–East European Relations,* 44–58.

31. Harry Gelman, *The Soviet Far East Buildup and Soviet Risk-Taking against China* (Santa Monica, 1982), 28–52.

32. Thomas W. Robinson, "The Sino-Soviet Border Conflict," in Stephen S. Kaplan et al., *Diplomacy of Power: Soviet Armed Forces as a Political Instrument* (Washington, 1981). See also Segal, *Defending China,* 176–96.

33. Richard Wich, *Sino-Soviet Crisis Politics: A Study of Political Change and Communication* (Cambridge, Mass., 1980), 97–192. According to Shevchenko, *Breaking with Moscow,* 165–66, the Politburo even put out informal feelers in Washington to see if the United States would endorse punitive military action against China. He believes it was Ambassador Dobrynin's discovery of the Nixon administration's hostility to the idea that dissuaded the Politburo from approving an attack. See chap. 5, n. 3, above.

34. Wich, *Sino-Soviet Crisis Politics,* 193–230; Garver, *China's Decision,* 71–79.

35. Georgi Arbatov, "American Foreign Policy at the Threshold of the 1970s," *USA: Economics, Politics, Ideology (Jan. 1970),* translated and published in *U.S. Joint Publications Research Service,* Jan. 20, 1970, 24–26; and Arbatov, *The System,* 172–75.

36. Kissinger, *White House Years,* 113–14, 143–44. Anatoly Dobrynin, interviewed by the author, Oct. 26, 1990.

37. Leonid Brezhnev, *O vneshnei politike KPSS i sovetskogo gosudarstva: Rechi i stat'i* (Moscow, 1978), 85.

38. Sobel, *Kissinger and Détente,* 62–63.

39. Garthoff, *Détente and Confrontation,* 73, 132. Kissinger, *White House Years,* 145, contends that the Soviets were awaiting the end of the Senate's ABM debate. There is also the possibility that they were waiting for Chinese agreement to take up bilateral talks.

40. Kissinger, *White House Years,* 145, 523–24.

41. Ibid., 138, 144. Dobrynin, interviewed by author.

42. Thomas W. Wolfe, "Soviet Approaches to SALT," *Problems of Communism* 19 (Sept.–Oct. 1970): 1–10.

43. Stent, *Embargo to Ostpolitik,* 159; and McAdams, *East Germany and Détente,* 96–97.

44. Dornberg, *Brezhnev,* 238, 258.

45. Sodaro, *Moscow, Germany, and the West,* 149–51.

46. Brandt, *People and Politics,* 194–95.

47. Egon Bahr, interviewed by the author, July 1, 1982.

48. Georgi Arbatov, interviewed by the author, May 19, 1991. See also, Arbatov, *The System,* 171–72.

49. Arbatov, interviewed by author. According to Anderson, *Public Politics,* 204–10, Brezhnev was placing himself in a median position between the grand strategies of his rivals. He designed his East-West program to be more acceptable to Podgorny and Suslov than was Kosygin's by giving somewhat higher priority to security goals than did Kosygin.

50. Kissinger, *White House Years,* 410.

51. John Erickson, "The Soviet Union and European Détente," in Dyson, *European Détente,* 180–81. For the debate going on within the Soviet camp, see Sodaro, *Moscow, Germany, and the West,* 152–65.

52. Link, "Aussen- und Deutschland Politik," 181.

53. Stent, *Embargo to Ostpolitik,* 166–69; and Sodaro, *Moscow, Germany, and the West,* 146–49, 169–74. This agreement, with the Thyssen Pipe Works, had been under discussion since the previous May.

54. Allardt, *Moskauer Tagebuch,* chaps. 28, 29.

55. The April speech was published in *Pravda,* Apr. 14, 1970. On the negotiations, see Whetten, *Germany's Ostpolitik,* 142–43.

56. Tatu, "Kremlinology"; and Whetten, *Germany's Ostpolitik,* 141–51.

57. Baring, *Machtwechsel,* 272–314.

58. Brandt, *People and Politics,* 323–45.

59. Dornberg, *Brezhnev,* 242–44; and Gelman, *Brezhnev Politburo,* 125–26.

60. John Hardt, "Plan and Economy," in Norton T. Dodge, ed., *Analysis of the USSR's 24th Party Congress and 9th Five Year Plan* (Mechanicsville, Md., 1971), 43–46.

61. Schroeder, "Soviet Economic Reforms at an Impasse," 45–46. See also chap. 2, n. 76, above.

62. Breslauer, *Khrushchev and Brezhnev,* 180–84, 189–91. See also Sidney I. Ploss, "Politics in the Kremlin," *Problems of Communism* 19 (May–June 1970): 1–14.

63. See chap. 2, n. 85, above.

64. Dornberg, *Brezhnev,* 244–48; and Breslauer, *Khrushchev and Brezhnev,* 194–99.

65. Brandt, *People and Politics,* 325–44.

66. Kissinger, *White House Years,* 508–9.

67. Ibid., 560–75, 593. For a persuasive argument that Soviet policy vis-à-vis Egypt should be seen as more benign than Nixon and Kissinger believed at the time, see George W. Breslauer, *Soviet Strategy in the Middle East* (Boston, 1990), 23–60.

68. Kissinger, *White House Years,* 582–91.

69. Hersh, *Price of Power,* 226–33; and Kissinger, *White House Years,* 551–57, 788–93.

70. Garthoff, *Détente and Confrontation,* 199–204; and Kissinger, *White House Years,* 554.

71. Hersh, *Price of Power,* chaps. 19, 20; and Kissinger, *White House Years,*

chaps. 15, 16. See also Raymond Garthoff, "Handling the Cienfuegos Crisis," *International Security* 8 (Summer 1983): 46–66.

72. Kissinger, *White House Years*, 793–94 (my italics).

73. Hersh, *Price of Power*, 300–303. The Soviet actions are discussed in Garthoff, *Détente and Confrontation*, 206–7; Freedman, *U.S. Intelligence*, 13–19, 164–67; and Catudal, *Quadripartite Agreement*, 124–30. For evidence of Soviet ambivalence with regard to both the United States and West Germany, see Sodaro, *Moscow, Germany, and the West*, 193–202; and Anderson, *Public Politics*, 210–16.

74. Kissinger, *White House Years*, 797–98.

75. Catudal, *Quadripartite Agreement*, 139–45; and Kissinger, *White House Years*, 800–812.

76. Robert L. Paarlberg, *Food Trade and Foreign Policy: India, the Soviet Union, and the United States* (Ithaca, N.Y., 1985), 79–84.

77. Kissinger, *White House Years*, 801–4.

78. Catudal, *Quadripartite Agreement*, 147–49; and Kissinger, *White House Years*, 807–8.

79. Kissinger, *White House Years*, 814.

80. Peter M. E. Volten, *Brezhnev's Peace Program: A Study of Soviet Domestic Political Process and Power* (Boulder, Colo., 1982), 66–87; quotation is on 66–67. See also Breslauer, *Khrushchev and Brezhnev*, 184–87.

81. Benjamin Zook, "Continuity and Change in Soviet Foreign Policy," in Dodge, *24th Party Congress;* and Volten, *Brezhnev's Peace Program*, 58–72. Brezhnev's report to the congress is in Leo Gruliow et al., eds., *Current Soviet Policies VI: The Documentary Record of the 24th Congress of the Communist Party of the Soviet Union* (Columbus, Ohio, 1973), 7–38. An indication of how the parts of Brezhnev's program fit together is given by B. Piguchin, "The Ninth Five-Year Plan and International Economic Cooperation," *International Affairs* (Moscow) 18 (Feb. 1972): 7–14.

82. Dornberg, *Brezhnev*, 256–58.

83. Ibid., 257–58. See also Herspring, *Soviet High Command*, 106–8.

84. Volten, *Brezhnev's Peace Program*, 72–75, 124–29, 276.

85. Paul A. Smith, Jr., "Brezhnev and Dissent: Implications of the 24th Party Congress," in Dodge, *24th Party Congress*. Anderson, *Public Politics*, 200–201, notes that another way in which Brezhnev reassured the conservatives in this speech was with a cautious statement regarding arms control. Sodaro, *Moscow, Germany, and the West*, 204–7, points out that the theme of intercapitalist contradictions (i.e., conflicts between Western Europe and the United States that could be exploited) was still very much in evidence.

86. Garthoff, *Détente and Confrontation*, 114–17.

87. Smith, *Doubletalk*, 222–32. Anderson, *Public Politics*, 198–204, argues, however, that Soviet arms control policy now became a second area (in addition to general East-West relations) in which Brezhnev differentiated himself from Kosygin and increased his appeal to the more fearful Suslov and Podgorny. He did this by insisting on replacing Kosygin's principle of "no unilateral advantages" with an emphasis on "equal security," thereby creating a rationale for a variety of one-sided

U.S. concessions to compensate for alleged U.S. strategic advantages. The ultimate results of this policy, of course, were the agreements of May 1972 that conceded the U.S.S.R. higher limits on SLBMs and ICBMs than those assigned the United States.

88. Garthoff, *Détente and Confrontation*, 167–72; and Kissinger, *White House Years*, 817–20.

89. Freedman, *U.S. Intelligence*, 166–67.

90. Sodaro, *Moscow, Germany, and the West*, 207–12. See also Moreton, *East Germany and the Warsaw Alliance*, 179–90.

91. Catudal, *Quadripartite Agreement*, 168–69.

92. Ibid., 173. Brezhnev's speech is reprinted in *Neues Deutschland*, June 17, 1971.

93. Kissinger, *White House Years*, 829. Kenneth Rush, interviewed by the author, Mar. 28, 1985.

94. Kissinger, *White House Years*, 830. Note, however, that Kissinger did not release Rush to finish the negotiations until Aug. 9.

95. Sodaro, *Moscow, Germany, and the West*, 212–15.

96. Brandt, *People and Politics*, 345–55.

97. Ibid., 354–55. Anatoly Dobrynin recalls that "we never needed the China factor to be attracted by a deal with West Germany." Dobrynin, interviewed by the author.

98. The announcement is detailed in Kissinger, *White House Years*, 837–39.

99. Ibid., 837.

100. Smith, *Doubletalk*, 280–97. The quotation is on 295.

101. Hersh, *Price of Power*, 334–48; Sobel, *Kissinger and Détente*, 87–88; and Kissinger, *White House Years*, 839–40.

102. Dornberg, *Brezhnev*, 262.

103. Volten, *Brezhnev's Peace Program*, 72–75.

104. Ibid., 124; and Boris Meissner, "Die Sowjetunion zwishen den XXIV und XXV Parteikongress der KPdSU," *Osteuropa* 11 (Nov. 1975): 899–915; quotation is on 900). According to Anderson, *Public Politics*, 217–34, Brezhnev won over Suslov to his policies by a combination of threat (allowing junior Politburo members to intrude into Suslov's specialty of relations with European Communists) and reward (agreeing in the fall of 1971 to allow Suslov to formulate a policy to diminish ethnic autonomy within the Soviet Union). With Podgorny, Brezhnev employed a reverse tack, offering first the reward (approval in May 1971 of Podgorny's desire for a less pro-American line in Vietnam and for building an Arab coalition around Egypt) and later the threat (using tension with Sadat in Dec. 1971 to reclaim control of Middle Eastern policy and to free Sadat for a more aggressive policy toward Israel). Brezhnev and Kosygin would presumably have preferred negotiating a Middle Eastern peace settlement with the United States but were precluded from that possibility by Kissinger's unwillingness to include them.

105. Dornberg, *Brezhnev*, 264. William B. Husband notes that December 1971 was the point at which the Soviet specialist literature first reflected a pronounced optimism about the prospects for international cooperation. "Soviet Perceptions of U.S. 'Positions of Strength' Diplomacy in the 1970s," *World Politics* 31 (July 1979): 507.

106. Ibid., 262–64. See also Christian Duevel, *A USSR State Council?* Radio Liberty Dispatch (Munich, Nov. 22, 1971).

107. Kissinger, *White House Years*, 866–94; quotation is on 867. For context, see Robert C. Horn, *Soviet-Indian Relations: Issues and Influence* (New York, 1982), 49–76. For an open-minded view of Soviet policy, see William J. Barnds, "Moscow and South Asia," *Problems of Communism* 21 (May–June 1972): 12–31.

108. Van Hollen, "Tilt Policy Revisited," 350–61. See also Garthoff, *Détente and Confrontation*, chap. 8.

109. Hersh, *Price of Power*, 467–64; and Pran Chopra, *India's Second Liberation* (Cambridge, Mass., 1974), 212–13.

110. Arbatov, *The System*, 195.

111. L. I. Brezhnev, *Selected Speeches and Writings on Foreign Affairs* (Oxford, Eng., 1979), 259. We know from Brezhnev's behavior at subsequent summits with Nixon that he did worry deeply about the possibility that the United States might enter into secret military arrangements with China; on this, see Garthoff, *Détente and Confrontation*, 374, 478.

112. *The Soviet Union's Hard Look at China,* Radio Liberty Dispatch (Munich, Apr. 12, 1972).

113. Brezhnev, *Selected Speeches*, 260. See also Anderson, *Public Politics*, 211–22.

114. Kissinger, *White House Years*, 1099–1108.

115. Szulc, *Illusion of Peace,* 531–58; and Kissinger, *White House Years,* 1108–23.

116. Hersh, *Price of Power*, 507.

117. Jonathan Haslam, *The Soviet Union and the Politics of Nuclear Weapons in Europe, 1969–1987: The Problem of the SS-20* (Houndmills, Eng., 1989), 42–43. Brezhnev even showed Georgi Arbatov telegrams he had received from regional party secretaries urging him to call off the summit. Arbatov, interviewed by Walter Isaacson, cited in Isaacson, *Kissinger*, 422.

118. Arbatov, *The System*, 183–85; and Isaacson, *Kissinger*, 422.

119. Dornberg, *Brezhnev*, 265–66.

120. Arbatov, *The System*, 184. The close interconnection between the summit and events in Germany is underlined by the fact that during the Central Committee meeting on May 19 (called because "I do not want to take all the blame [for the Politburo decision of May 10]," as Brezhnev told Georgi Arbatov) Brezhnev requested a recess so that participants could learn of the results of the vote in the West German Bundesrat. "If things had gone the other way in Bonn," Arbatov asserts, "Brezhnev and the Central Committee would have decided to cancel the summit." Isaacson, *Kissinger*, 422–23. See also Shevchenko, *Breaking with Moscow,* 211–13.

121. Stent, *Embargo to Ostpolitik,* 186–90.

122. Kissinger, *White House Years*, 1212–14, 1249–50.

123. Szulc, *Illusion of Peace,* 544–45.

124. Hersh, *Price of Power,* 518.

125. Kissinger, *White House Years*, 1133.

126. Ibid., 1126–27, 1131–32. According to Garthoff, *Détente and Confrontation,* 326–35, a great deal of Moscow's preparatory work for the negotiations was done by the Foreign Ministry, whose new Department for Planning Foreign Policy Measures (UPVM) authored seven of the ten basic Soviet position papers.

127. Kissinger, *White House Years,* 1128–34.

128. Ibid., 1124.

129. Garthoff, *Détente and Confrontation,* 175–77; Kissinger, *White House Years,* 1148–49; and Smith, *Doubletalk,* 364–69.

130. Garthoff, *Détente and Confrontation,* 183–86; and Kissinger, *White House Years,* 1149–50.

131. Coit D. Blacker, "The Kremlin and Détente: Soviet Conceptions, Hopes, and Expectations," in Alexander L. George et al., eds., *Managing U.S.-Soviet Rivalry: Problems of Crisis Prevention* (Boulder, Colo., 1983); and Kissinger, *White House Years,* 1150–51.

132. Hersh, *Price of Power,* 531; and Safire, *Before the Fall,* 435–36.

133. Garthoff, *Détente and Confrontation,* 334–35. How seriously Brezhnev took the declarations of principle can be judged from the numerous agreements of this kind that Moscow entered into in the period 1966–79. See John Van Oudenaren, *Détente in Europe: The Soviet Union and the West since 1953* (Durham, N.C., 1991), 78–80.

134. Gelman, *Brezhnev Politburo,* 132. Gerard Smith, interviewed by the author, Apr. 12, 1983.

135. Smith, *Doubletalk,* 453–64.

136. Garthoff, *Détente and Confrontation,* 188–96.

137. Ibid., 341–43. Kosygin's and Brezhnev's eagerness for trade was illuminated by an argument they had on the subject with Podgorny at the summit. Kissinger, *White House Years,* 1213–16. Kissinger made his own interest evident as early as Maurice Stans's visit to Moscow in November 1971. Maurice Stans, interviewed by the author, July 21, 1992.

138. Garthoff, *Détente and Confrontation,* 342. Preparatory talks for the conference on European security and cooperation began in Helsinki in November 1972. The preparatory phase for talks on mutual and balanced force reductions opened in Vienna January 31, 1973.

139. The Soviet–West German treaty was ratified by the Bundestag on May 17, 1972, by a vote of 248 to 10, with 238 abstentions; it was ratified by the Bundesrat two days later. It came into force on May 24. The Berlin agreement was put into effect on June 3, 1972, after travel regulations had been worked out by the two German states. According to Sodaro, *Moscow, Germany, and the West,* 225–26, Kremlin policy makers borrowed elements from both the Europeanist and Americanist orientations of their advisers and opted decisively for linking détente in Europe with détente with the United States.

140. Sobel, *Kissinger and Détente,* 137–45. See also Bowker and Williams, *Superpower Détente,* 79–85.

141. Sobel, *Kissinger and Détente,* 148; and Stent, *Embargo to Ostpolitik,* 191–95.

142. Kissinger, *White House Years,* chap. 30.

143. Ibid., 1269–71. For further discussion, see Goldman, *Détente and Dollars;* and Halow, *U.S. Grain.*

144. Dornberg, *Brezhnev,* 267–69; and Breslauer, *Khrushchev and Brezhnev,* 201–7.

145. Volten, *Brezhnev's Peace Program,* 116–32; and Breslauer, *Khrushchev and Brezhnev,* 208–19.

Epilogue: From Détente to the Gorbachev Revolution

1. Nixon subsequently argued that "we should think of détente as a complement to containment rather than as a substitute for it. Containment, the task of resisting Russian expansionism, must remain the *sine qua non* of US foreign policy." Nixon, *The Real War,* 286.

2. See R. Judson Mitchell, "A New Brezhnev Doctrine: The Restructuring of International Relations," *World Politics* 30 (Apr. 1978): 366–90.

3. Garthoff, *Détente and Confrontation,* 360–537. See also Coit Blacker, "The Soviets and Arms Control: The SALT Negotiations, November 1972–March 1976," in Michael Mandelbaum, ed., *The Other Side of the Table: The Soviet Approach to Arms Control* (New York, 1990).

4. Bowker and Williams, *Superpower Détente,* 97–167; Stern, *Water's Edge,* 54–193. Jackson-Vanik's co-sponsor was Rep. Charles Vanik (R-Ill.). The Clark Amendment was authored by Senator Dick Clark (D-Iowa).

5. Nixon, *No More Vietnams,* 165–211.

6. Garthoff, *Détente and Confrontation,* 377.

7. The (Senator Adlai [D-Ill.]) Stevenson Amendment limited the amount of credit the Soviet Union could receive to $300 million over four years.

8. Mastanduno, *Economic Containment,* 156–67.

9. Arbatov, *The System,* 215.

10. Marshall Goldman, *The Enigma of Soviet Petroleum: Half Empty or Half Full?* (London, 1980), 88–111; and Simon Bromley, *American Hegemony and World Oil: The Industry, the State System, and the World Economy* (Cambridge, Eng., 1991), 189–96.

11. Herspring, *Soviet High Command,* chaps. 4, 5.

12. The information about Brezhnev's health is from Georgi Arbatov, interviewed by the author, May 19, 1991.

13. Breslauer, *Khrushchev and Brezhnev,* 220–29. Brezhnev's speech to the Party Congress was published in *Pravda,* Feb. 25, 1976.

14. Bowker and Williams, *Superpower Détente,* 167–84, 206–55; and Froman, *Idea of Détente,* 74–95.

15. Garthoff, *Détente and Confrontation,* chap. 28; Froman, *Idea of Détente,* 96–117; and Lou Cannon, *President Reagan: The Role of a Lifetime* (New York, 1991), chap. 13. See also Cynthia Roberts, "Limited Adversaries, Limited Arms Control: Changing Soviet Interests and Prospects for Enhanced Security Cooperation," in Mandelbaum, *The Other Side of the Table.*

16. Richard Ned Lebow and Janice Gross Stein, *We All Lost the Cold War* (Princeton, 1994).

BIBLIOGRAPHY

Unpublished Primary Materials

Archival Sources

Press Files. Institute for the Study of the World Economy and International Relations (IMEMO), 1969–73. Moscow.

Richard M. Nixon Papers. Nixon Presidential Materials Project. National Archives. College Park, Maryland (formerly Alexandria, Virginia). The Central Files include (1) Staff Member and Office Files and (2) Subject Categories. The Special Files include (1) President's Office Files, (2) President's Personal Files, (3) Staff Member Files (Patrick Buchanan, Charles Colson, John Ehrlichman, Peter Flanigan, H. R. Haldeman, Alexander Haig, Egil Krogh, Peter Peterson, John A. Scali, Herbert Stein, Gordon Strachan, John Whitaker, David Young, and Ronald Ziegler), and (4) Confidential Files

Microform Collections, University Publications of America, Frederick, Maryland

"CIA Research Reports: The Soviet Union, 1946–1976." Five reels.

"Daily Diary of President Johnson, 1963–1969." Fourteen reels.

"Documents of the National Security Council, 1947–1977." Five reels, four supplements.

"The Lyndon B. Johnson National Security Files: USSR and Eastern Europe, 1963–1969." One reel.

"Minutes and Documents of the Cabinet Meetings of President Johnson." Seventeen reels.

"Nuclear Weapons, Arms Control, and the Threat of Thermonuclear War: Special Studies, 1969–1981." Seventeen reels.

"Public Statements by the Secretaries of Defense." Pt. 3: "The Kennedy and Johnson Administrations." Nineteen reels. Pt. 4: "The Nixon and Ford Administrations." Twenty-five reels. "The Soviet Union: Special Studies, 1970–1980." Nine reels.

Published Primary Materials

Executive Documents

Central Intelligence Agency. *Estimating Soviet Defense Spending in Rubles, 1970–1975*. Washington, 1976.

Johnson, Lyndon. *Public Papers of the President: Lyndon B. Johnson, 1964–1968*. Washington, 1966–70.

———. *The Johnson Presidential Press Conferences*. 2 vols. New York, 1978.

Nixon, Richard. *Economic Report of the President to the Congress, 1969–1972*. Washington, 1969–72.

———. *U.S. Foreign Policy for the 1970s: A New Strategy for Peace; A Report to the Congress*. Washington, 1970.

———. *Public Papers of the President: Richard M. Nixon, 1969–1972*. Washington, 1971–74.

———. *U.S. Foreign Policy for the 1970s: Building the Peace; A Report to the Congress*. Washington, 1971.

———. *U.S. Foreign Policy for the 1970s: The Emerging Structure of Peace; A Report to the Congress*. Washington, 1972.

———. *U.S. Foreign Policy for the 1970s: Shaping a Durable Peace; A Report to the Congress*. Washington, 1973.

———. *The Nixon Presidential Press Conferences*. New York, 1978.

Timberlake, Charles E. *Détente: A Documentary Record*. New York, 1978.

Solomon, Richard H. *U.S.-PRC Political Negotiations, 1967–1984: An Annotated Chronology*. (Santa Monica, 1985), 14–60.

Congressional Documents

House Committee on Foreign Affairs. *Hearings: ABM, MIRV, SALT, and the Strategic Arms Race*. 91st Cong., 1st sess. Washington, 1969.

———. *Hearings: Diplomatic and Strategic Impact of Multiple Warhead Missiles*. 91st Cong., 1st sess. Washington, 1969.

———. *Détente: Prospects for Increased Trade with Warsaw Pact Countries*. 93d Cong., 2d sess. Washington, 1974.

Joint Economic Committee. *Soviet Economic Performance: 1966–1967*. 90th Cong., 2d sess. Washington, 1968.

———. *Soviet Economy and National Security*. 91st Cong., 1st sess. Washington, 1969.

———. *People's Republic of China: An Economic Assessment*. 92d Cong., 2d sess. Washington, 1972.

———. *Soviet Economic Prospects for the Seventies*. 93d Cong., 1st sess. Washington, 1973.

———. *Hearings: Allocation of Resources in the Soviet Union and China—1975*. 94th Cong., 1st sess. Washington, 1975.

———. *Soviet Economy in a New Perspective*. 94th Cong., 2d sess. Washington, 1976.

———. *Soviet Economy in a Time of Change*. 96th Cong., 1st sess. Washington, 1979.

Senate Committee on Armed Services. *Military Implications of the Treaty on the Limitation of Anti-Ballistic Missile Systems and the Interim Agreement on the Limitation of Strategic Offensive Arms.* 92d Cong., 2d sess. Washington, 1972.
Senate Committee on Foreign Relations. *Hearings: Strategic and Foreign Policy Implications of ABM Systems, Anti-Submarine Warfare, Multiple Independently Targeted Reentry Vehicles (MIRV).* 91st Cong., 1st sess. Washington, 1969.
———. *Strategic Arms Limitations Agreements.* 92d Cong., 2d sess. Washington, 1972.
———. *Nomination of Henry A. Kissinger to Be Secretary of State.* 93d Cong., 1st sess. Washington, 1973.
———. *Détente.* 93d Cong., 2d sess. Washington, 1974.
———. *US-USSR Strategic Policies.* 93d Cong., 2d sess. Washington, 1974.
Senate Committee on Government Operations. *Russian Grain Transactions: Hearings before the Permanent Subcommittee on Investigations.* 93d Cong., 1st sess. Washington, 1973.

Foreign Documents

French Embassy. *Major Addresses, Statements, and Press Conferences of General Charles de Gaulle, May 19, 1958–January 31, 1964.* New York. n.d.
German Federal Republic, Auswärtiges Amt. *Die Auswärtige Politik der Bundesrepublik Deutschland.* Cologne, 1972.
German Federal Republic, Presse und Informationsamt. *Die Politik der Gerwaltverzichts.* Bonn, 1968.
———. *Bundeskanzler Brandt: Reden und Interviews (II).* Bonn, 1973.
Radio Liberty Committee, Central Research Department.
Radio Liberty Dispatches. Munich, 1969–72.
Radio Liberty Research Papers. Munich, 1969–74.

Speeches, Statements, and Autobiographies of Participants

Abrasimov, Pyotr. *West Berlin: Yesterday and Today.* Dresden, 1981.
Alexeyeva, Ludmilla, and Paul Goldberg. *The Thaw Generation: Coming of Age in the Post-Stalin Era.* Boston, 1990.
Allardt, Helmut. *Politik vor und hinter den Kulissen: Erfahrungen eines Diplomaten zwischen Ost und West.* Düsseldorf, 1979.
———. *Moskauer Tagebuch: Beobachtungen, Notizen, Erlebnisse.* Frankfurt, 1980.
Arbatov, Georgi. *The War of Ideas in Contemporary International Relations.* Moscow, 1973.
———. *The System: An Insider's Life in Soviet Politics.* New York, 1992.
Arbatov, Georgi, and Willem Oltmans. *The Soviet Viewpoint.* New York, 1981.
Ball, George W. *Diplomacy for a Crowded World: An American Foreign Policy.* Boston, 1976.
———. *The Past Has Another Pattern: Memoirs.* New York, 1982.

Beam, Jacob D. *Multiple Exposure: An American Ambassador's Unique Perspective on East West Issues.* New York, 1978.

Birrenbach, Kurt. *Meine Sondermissionen: Rückblick auf zwei Jahrzehnte bundesdeutscher Aussenpolitik.* Düsseldorf, 1984.

Brandt, Willy. *A Peace Policy for Europe.* New York, 1969.

————. *Peace: Writings and Speeches of the Nobel Peace Prize Winner 1971.* Bonn, 1971.

————. *People and Politics: The Years 1960—1975.* Boston, 1976.

Brezhnev, Leonid Ilyich. *Leninskim kursom.* 7 vols. Moscow, 1970.

————. *On the Policy of the Soviet Union and the International Situation.* Garden City, N.Y., 1973.

————. *O vneshnei politike KPSS i sovetskogo gosudarstva: Rechi i stat'i.* 3d ed. Moscow, 1978.

————. *Ob osnovnykh voprosakh ekonomicheskoi politiki KPSS na sovremennom etape: Rechi i doklady.* 2 vols. Moscow, 1979.

————. *Peace, Détente, and Soviet-American Relations.* New York, 1979.

————. *Selected Speeches and Writings on Foreign Affairs.* Oxford, Eng., 1979.

————. *Peace, Détente, Cooperation.* New York, 1981.

Brown, George. *In My Way.* London, 1971.

Burlatsky, Fedor. *Khrushchev and the First Russian Spring.* London, 1991.

Colson, Charles W. *Born Again.* Old Tappen, N.J., 1976.

Couve de Murville, Maurice. *Une Politique Étrangère, 1958–1969.* Paris, 1971.

de Gaulle, Charles. *Discours et messages.* Paris, 1970.

————. *Lettres, notes, et carnets.* 12 vols. Paris, 1980–88.

Eagleton, Thomas E. *War and Presidential Power: A Chronicle of Congressional Surrender.* New York, 1974.

Ehrlichman, John. *Witness to Power: The Nixon Years.* New York, 1982.

Gromyko, Andrei. *Only for Peace: Selected Speeches and Writings.* Oxford, Eng., 1979.

————. *Memories.* London, 1989.

Gromyko, Andrei, and B. N. Ponomarev. *Soviet Foreign Policy, 1917–1980.* 4th ed. Moscow, 1980.

Haig, Alexander, Jr. *Inner Circles; How America Changed the World: A Memoir.* New York, 1992.

Haldeman, H. R. *The Ends of Power.* New York, 1978.

————. *The Haldeman Diaries: Inside the Nixon White House.* New York, 1994.

Healey, Denis. *The Time of My Life.* London, 1989.

Hoxha, Enver. *The Khrushchevites: Memoirs.* Tirana, Alb., 1980.

Hyland, William G. *Mortal Rivals: Superpower Relations from Nixon to Reagan.* New York, 1987.

Javits, Jacob K. *Javits: The Autobiography of a Public Man.* Boston, 1981.

Johnson, Lyndon B. *The Vantage Point: Perspectives of the Presidency, 1963–1969.* New York, 1971.

Johnson, U. Alexis. *The Right Hand of Power.* Englewood Cliffs, N.J., 1984.

Kalugin, Oleg. *The First Directorate: My 32 years in Intelligence and Espionage against the West.* New York, 1994.

Khrushchev, Nikita S. *For Victory in Peaceful Competition with Capitalism.* New York, 1960.
————. *To Avert War, Our Prime Task.* Moscow, 1963.
————. *Khrushchev Remembers.* Boston, 1970.
————. *Khrushchev Remembers: The Last Testament.* Boston, 1974.
————. *Khrushchev Remembers: The Glasnost Tapes.* Boston, 1990.
Kissinger, Henry. *The Troubled Partnership.* New York, 1965.
————. *American Foreign Policy.* New York, 1977.
————. *White House Years.* Boston, 1979.
————. *For the Record: Selected Statements, 1977–1980.* Boston, 1981.
————. *Years of Upheaval.* Boston, 1982.
Kosygin, A. N. *A. N. Kosygin: izbrannye rechi i stat'i.* Moscow, 1974.
————. *Selected Speeches and Writings.* Oxford, Eng., 1981.
McNamara, Robert S. *The Essence of Security: Reflections in Office.* New York, 1968.
Moersch, Karl. *Kursrevision: Deutsche Politik nach Adenauer.* Frankfurt, 1978.
Nixon, Richard. *RN: The Memoirs of Richard Nixon.* New York, 1978.
————. *The Real War.* New York, 1980.
————. *Leaders: Profiles and Reminiscences of Men Who Have Shaped the Modern World.* New York, 1982.
————. *No More Vietnams.* New York, 1985.
————. *1999: Victory without War.* New York, 1988.
————. *In the Arena: A Memoir of Victory, Defeat, and Renewal.* New York, 1990.
Peterson, Peter G. *U.S.-Soviet Commercial Relations in a New Era.* Washington, 1972.
Pompidou, Georges. *Entretiens et Discours, 1968–1974.* 2 vols. Paris, 1975.
Rostow, W. W. *The Diffusion of Power: An Essay in Recent History.* New York, 1972.
Rusk, Dean. *As I Saw It.* New York, 1990.
Safire, William. *Before the Fall: An Inside View of the Pre-Watergate White House.* Garden City, N.Y., 1975.
Schlesinger, James R., et al. *Defending America.* New York, 1977.
Schmidt, Helmut. *Strategie des Gleichgewichts: Deutsche Friedenspolitik und die Weltmächte.* Stuttgart, 1969.
————. *Men and Powers: A Political Retrospective.* New York, 1989.
Seaborg, Glenn T. *Kennedy, Khrushchev, and the Test Ban.* Berkeley, Calif., 1981.
————. *Stemming the Tide: Arms Control in the Johnson Years.* Lexington, Mass., 1987.
Seaborg, Glenn T., with Benjamin S. Loeb. *The Atomic Energy Commission under Nixon: Adjusting to Troubled Times.* New York, 1993.
Shevchenko, Arkady N. *Breaking with Moscow.* New York, 1985.
Smith, Gerard. *Doubletalk: The Story of SALT I.* New York, 1980.
Stein, Herbert. *Presidential Economics.* New York, 1984.
Weit, Erwin. *At the Red Summit: Interpreter behind the Iron Curtain.* New York, 1973.

Whalen, Richard J. *Catch the Falling Flag: A Republican's Challenge to His Party.* Boston, 1972.
Wilson, Harold. *The Labour Government, 1964–1970: A Personal Record.* London, 1971.
York, Herbert F. *Race to Oblivion: A Participant's View of the Arms Race.* New York, 1970.
Zumwalt, Elmo R., Jr. *On Watch.* New York, 1976.

Secondary Literature

Inasmuch as only 2 million of the 40 million pages of material in the Nixon Papers (and among these almost none from the National Security Council files) have been opened to the public, and because the Soviet archives from the Brezhnev years remain largely inaccessible, historians of Soviet-American relations in this period are still very much dependent on what governments have chosen to publish and participants have chosen to say and write. For that reason I have listed the specifics of these sources above as completely as possible.

As for the memoir literature, the American side is particularly rich. Dominating in detail and comprehensiveness, of course, although often marred by special pleading, are the recollections of National Security Adviser Henry Kissinger, *White House Years* (Boston, 1979), and *Years of Upheaval* (Boston, 1982), the first volume of which focuses on the years 1969–72. Also crucial for our purposes are President Nixon's perspectives in *RN: The Memoirs of Richard Nixon* (New York, 1978) and in later offerings like *The Real War* (New York, 1980), despite the former president's tendency to ignore certain subjects altogether. Secretary of Defense Melvin Laird has given us only an article ("A Strong Start in a Difficult Decade: Defense Policy in the Nixon-Ford Years" *International Security* 10 [Fall 1985]: 5–26), but we do have the candid and critical memoirs of SALT negotiator Gerard Smith, *Doubletalk: The Story of SALT I* (New York, 1980), and Chairman of the Joint Chiefs of Staff Admiral Elmo Zumwalt, *On Watch* (New York, 1976), as well as the surprisingly independent thoughts of Nixon's speechwriter William Safire, *Before the Fall: An Inside View of the Pre-Watergate White House* (Garden City, N.Y., 1975).

Of special note are the impressive memoir-histories of SALT delegate Raymond Garthoff, *Détente and Confrontation: American-Soviet Relations from Nixon to Reagan* 2d ed. (Washington, 1994); NSC staff member William Hyland, *Mortal Rivals: Superpower Relations from Nixon to Reagan* (New York, 1987); and Herbert Stein, *Presidential Economics* (New York, 1984). Garthoff's book, in particular, is objective, exhaustive, and indispensable. For the Lyndon Johnson administration, the most significant retrospectives are those of Johnson himself, *The Vantage Point: Perspectives of the Presidency, 1963–1969* (New York, 1971); National Security Adviser Walter W. Rostow, *The Diffusion of Power: An Essay in Recent History* (New York, 1972); and Chairman of the Atomic Energy Commission Glenn T. Seaborg, *Stemming the Tide: Arms Control in the Johnson Years* (Lexington, Mass., 1987).

Among West European autobiographies, the most focused on détente is Willy

Brandt, *People and Politics: The Years 1960–1975* (Boston, 1976). But Harold Wilson, *The Labour Government, 1964–1970: A Personal Record* (London, 1971), is also revealing. For the inner workings of the German government, the remembrances of State Secretary Karl Moersch, *Kursrevision: Deutsche Politik nach Adenauer* (Frankfurt, 1978), and Ambassador to Russia Helmut Allardt, *Moskauer Tagebuch: Beobachtungen, Notizen, Erlebnisse* (Frankfurt, 1980), are especially helpful. The only comparable French commentary is Foreign Minister Maurice Couve de Murville, *Une Politique Étrangère, 1958–1969* (Paris, 1971).

The Russians are better represented in memoirs than one might expect. Foreign Minister Andrei Gromyko, *Memories* (London, 1989), is disappointing, but one can glean a great deal of information from the works of two highly placed intellectuals; see Fedor Burlatsky, *Khrushchev and the First Russian Spring* (London, 1991), and Georgi Arbatov, *The System: An Insider's Life in Soviet Politics* (New York, 1992). Arkady Shevchenko, *Breaking with Moscow* (New York, 1985), the disclosure of a prominent defector, is important but sometimes suspect. Rich and rewarding for the period before 1964 are the memoirs of Nikita Khrushchev, now in three volumes: *Khrushchev Remembers* (Boston, 1970), *Khrushchev Remembers: The Last Testament* (Boston, 1974), and *Khrushchev Remembers: The Glasnost Tapes* (Boston, 1990).

The first synthetic accounts of foreign relations in the Nixon years were produced by journalists who were active at the time. Some of these were individuals with close ties to the administration, like Henry Brandon, *The Retreat of American Power* (New York, 1972); John Newhouse, *Cold Dawn: The Story of SALT* (New York, 1973); and Marvin Kalb and Bernard Kalb, *Kissinger* (Boston, 1974). Others were independent and critical observers, like Tad Szulc, *The Illusion of Peace: Foreign Policy in the Nixon Years* (New York, 1978); William Shawcross, *Sideshow: Kissinger, Nixon, and the Destruction of Cambodia* (New York, 1981); and Seymour Hersh, *The Price of Power: Kissinger in the Nixon White House* (New York, 1983). Though somewhat superseded now, these studies still contain valuable information and perspectives derived from interviews and proximity to the event. Hersh's volume, particularly, offers the reader marvelous insight into the manipulations of Kissinger as national security adviser.

Toward the end of the 1970s historians and political scientists began to make their own contributions to the understanding of Soviet-American rapprochement. Among the earliest scholarly monographs was Coral Bell, *The Diplomacy of Détente: The Kissinger Era* (London, 1977), which remains useful. Noteworthy for its attention to context is Seyom Brown, *The Crises of Power: An Interpretation of United States Foreign Policy during the Kissinger Years* (New York, 1979). Focused and carefully analytical is Robert Litwak, *Détente and the Nixon Doctrine: American Foreign Policy and the Pursuit of Stability, 1969–1976* (Cambridge, Eng., 1984). Franz Schurmann, *The Foreign Policies of Richard Nixon: The Grand Design* (Berkeley, Calif., 1987); and Richard Thornton, *The Nixon-Kissinger Years: Reshaping American Foreign Policy* (New York, 1989), are interesting but somewhat idiosyncratic. Two of the more clearheaded discussions of détente are found in Stanley Hoffman, *Primacy or World Order: American Foreign Policy since the Cold War* (New York, 1978); and John Lewis Gaddis, *Strategies of*

Containment: A Critical Appraisal of Postwar American National Security Policy (New York, 1982).

A number of biographies are important. Michael Beschloss, *The Crisis Years: Kennedy and Khrushchev, 1960–1963* (New York, 1991), tells us much that is new about the early 1960s. Deborah Shapley, *Promise and Power: The Life and Times of Robert McNamara* (Boston, 1993), is also revealing, especially on LBJ's foreign policy. But one should not overlook such earlier discussions as Philip Geyelin, *Lyndon Johnson and the World* (New York, 1966); and Doris Kearns, *Lyndon Johnson and the American Dream* (New York, 1976). In understanding Nixon's attitudes, we get help from Fawn Brodie, *Richard Nixon: The Shaping of His Character* (New York, 1981); James David Barber, *The Presidential Character* (Englewood Cliffs, N.J., 1972); and Stephen Ambrose's three-volume *Nixon* (New York, 1987–91), which includes much fresh material from the presidential papers. The numerous studies of Henry Kissinger attest to his central role in Nixon's government. Aside from Hersh, the most notable for our purposes are Stephen Graubard, *Kissinger: Portrait of a Mind* (New York, 1973); Dan Caldwell's edited volume, *Henry Kissinger: His Personality and Politics* (Durham, 1983); Robert D. Schulzinger, *Henry Kissinger: Doctor of Diplomacy* (New York, 1989); and Walter Isaacson, *Kissinger: A Biography* (New York, 1992). The last two books have mined a number of underutilized sources.

Among monographs dealing with the Soviet side of détente, the classic studies are Thomas W. Wolfe, *Soviet Power and Europe, 1945–1970* (Baltimore, 1970); Adam Ulam, *Expansion and Coexistence: Soviet Foreign Policy, 1917–1973* (New York, 1974); Adam Ulam, *Dangerous Relations: The Soviet Union in World Politics, 1970–1982* (New York, 1983); Peter Volten, *Brezhnev's Peace Program: A Study of Soviet Domestic Political Process and Power* (Boulder, Colo., 1982); and Harry Gelman, *The Brezhnev Politburo and the Decline of Détente* (Ithaca, N.Y., 1984). These have recently been supplemented by James Richter, *Khrushchev's Double Bind: International Pressures and Domestic Coalition Politics* (Baltimore, 1994); and Richard D. Anderson, Jr., *Public Politics in an Authoritarian State: Making Foreign Policy during the Brezhnev Years* (Ithaca, N.Y., 1993).

For the political-economic background, the outstanding work is George Breslauer's comparative analysis, *Khrushchev and Brezhnev as Leaders* (London, 1982). Valuable as well are Michel Tatu, *Power in the Kremlin: From Khrushchev to Kosygin* (London, 1969); and edited volumes by Paul Cocks et al., *The Dynamics of Soviet Politics* (Cambridge, Mass., 1976); and Donald R. Kelley, *Politics in the Brezhnev Era* (New York, 1980). As for biographies, the best by far is John Dornberg, *Brezhnev; The Masks of Power* (New York, 1974), which includes much information not readily available. Serge Petroff, *The Red Eminence: A Biography of Mikhail Suslov* (Clifton, N.J., 1988), is surprisingly thin. The official Soviet interpretation of the period is reflected in the second volume of A. A. Gromyko and B. N. Ponomarev, *Soviet Foreign Policy, 1917–1980*, 4th ed. (Moscow, 1981).

A special reference should be made to analyses of détente itself, both in the general sense and in its manifestation during the Nixon-Brezhnev years. The phenomenon is the subject of Stephen R. Rock, *Why Peace Breaks Out: Great Power Rapprochement in Historical Perspective* (Chapel Hill, N.C., 1989), but most discussions tend to focus on specific Cold War developments. Perhaps the most provocative are Richard W. Stevenson, *The Rise and Fall of Détente: Relaxations of Tension in US-Soviet Relations, 1953–1984* (Houndmills, Eng., 1985); and Mike Bowker and Phil Williams, *Superpower Détente: A Reappraisal* (London, 1988), both of which are historical and comparative in approach. Impressive also is Michael B. Froman, *The Development of the Idea of Détente: Coming to Terms* (New York, 1991). Paul Herman, Jr., *Thinking about Peace: The Conceptualization and Conduct of U.S.-Soviet Détente* (Lanham, Md., 1987), is an attempt to be more scientific and less impressionistic. For studies of the related Soviet concept of peaceful coexistence, see Dale Terence Lahey, "Soviet Ideological Development of Coexistence: 1917–1929," *Canadian Slavonic Papers* 6 (1964); Nikita Khrushchev, "On Peaceful Coexistence," *Foreign Affairs* 38 (Oct. 1959); and G. D. Vernon, "Controlled Conflict: Soviet Perceptions of Peaceful Coexistence," *Orbis* 23 (1979).

The contributions of other major powers to the making of détente are discussed in a number of scholarly studies. The role of France has not yet been addressed directly, but much can be learned from Edward A. Kolodziej, *French International Policy under de Gaulle and Pompidou: The Politics of Grandeur* (Ithaca, N.Y., 1974); Philip Cerny, *The Politics of Grandeur: Ideological Aspects of de Gaulle's Foreign Policy* (Cambridge, 1980); Michael Harrison, *The Reluctant Ally: France and Atlantic Security* (Baltimore, 1981); and Frank Costigliola, *France and the United States: The Cold Alliance since World War II* (New York, 1992).

West German *Ostpolitik* has attracted more scholarly attention than has French policy. The most substantial work in English is Helga Haftendorn, *Security and Détente: Conflicting Priorities in German Foreign Policy* (New York, 1985); but one should not overlook Lawrence L. Whetten's volume, *Germany's Ostpolitik: Relations between the Federal Republic and the Warsaw Pact Countries* (London, 1971), a model of description and analysis; and Angela Stent, *From Embargo to Ostpolitik: The Political Economy of West German–Soviet Relations, 1955–1980* (Cambridge, 1981), which underlines the importance of economic factors. Among several monographs in the German language, the most rewarding are Arnulf Baring, *Machtwechsel: Die Ära Brandt-Scheel* (Stuttgart, 1982); and Karl Dietrich Bracher et al., *Republik im Wandel, 1969–1974: Die Ära Brandt* (Stuttgart, 1986). Relatively little has been done on British activity in relation to East-West ties, except for surveys like Elisabeth Barker, *Britain in a Divided Europe, 1945–1970* (London, 1971); and F. S. Northedge, *Descent from Power: British Foreign Policy, 1945–1973* (London, 1974).

On the fissiparous tendencies within the Communist world and their role in facilitating détente, there is a wide range of excellent writing, particularly on the Chinese and East German situations. To understand the part China played, one must begin with Donald S. Zagoria, *The Sino-Soviet Conflict, 1956–1961* (Princeton, 1962); or A. Doak Barnett, *China and the Major Powers in East Asia* (Washington, 1977), and then turn to the studies of David Mozingo, *China's Foreign Policy and the Cultural Revolution* (Ithaca, N.Y., 1970); and Robert G. Sutter, *Chinese Foreign Policy after the Cultural Revolution, 1966–1977* (Boulder, Colo., 1978). On the Chinese-American-Soviet interrelationship, the most penetrating investigations are Robert G. Sutter, *China Watch: Sino-American Reconciliation* (Baltimore, 1978); James W. Garver, *China's Decision for Rapprochement with the United States, 1968–1971* (Boulder, Colo., 1982); and more generally, Gordon H. Chang, *Friends and Enemies: The United States, China, and the Soviet Union, 1948–1972* (Stanford, Calif., 1990).

The East German factor has been blessed with at least four fine historical monographs: Gerhard Wettig, *Community and Conflict in the Socialist Camp: The Soviet Union, East Germany, and the German Problem, 1965–1972* (London, 1975); Edwina Moreton, *East Germany and the Warsaw Alliance: The Politics of Détente* (Boulder, Colo., 1978); A. James McAdams, *East Germany and Détente: Building Authority after the Wall* (Cambridge, Eng., 1985); and especially Michael J. Sodaro, *Moscow, Germany, and the West from Khrushchev to Gorbachev* (Ithaca, N.Y., 1990), which puts as much emphasis on Moscow as on East Berlin. Even so, these should be placed in the context of such books as Robert L. Hutchings, *Soviet–East European Relations: Consolidation and Conflict, 1968–1980* (Madison, Wis., 1983); Sarah M. Terry, *Soviet Policy in Eastern Europe* (New Haven, Conn., 1984); and William M. Reisinger, *Energy and the Soviet Bloc: Alliance Politics after Stalin* (Ithaca, N.Y., 1992). Two particularly crucial incidents are discussed in Wayne Vucinich's edited work, *At the Brink of War and Peace: The Tito-Stalin Split in Historical Perspective* (New York, 1982); Jiri Valenta, *Soviet Intervention in Czechoslovakia, 1968: Anatomy of Decision* (Baltimore, 1979); and Karen Dawisha, *The Kremlin and the Prague Spring* (Berkeley, Calif., 1985).

The role of public attitudes in influencing foreign policy in both the United States and the Soviet Union during détente can often be assessed only indirectly. The impact of the Vietnam War on the American public is discussed in general in such volumes as William O'Neill, *Coming Apart: An Informal History of America in the 1960s* (Chicago, 1971); and Alexander Kendrick, *The Wound Within: America in the Vietnam Years, 1945–1974* (Boston, 1974). The resulting shifts in public opinion are traced by Louis Harris, *The Anguish of Change* (New York, 1973); Ben J. Wattenberg, *The Real America: A Surprising Examination of the State of the Union* (Garden City, N.Y., 1974); and Ole Holsti and James Rosenau, *American Leadership in World Affairs: Vietnam and the Breakdown of Consensus* (Boston, 1984). The peace movement is the focus of Nancy Zaroulis and Gerald Sullivan, *Who Spoke Up? American Protest against the War in Vietnam, 1963–1975* (Garden City, N.Y., 1984); and Charles DeBenedetti with Charles Chatfield, *An American Ordeal: The Anti-War Movement in the Vietnam Era* (Syracuse, N.Y., 1990). To comprehend the relation of these phenomena to presidential decisionmaking, one can turn for help to studies like Kathleen Turner, *Lyndon Johnson's Dual War: Vietnam and the Press* (Chicago, 1985); and especially Melvin Small, *Johnson, Nixon, and the Doves* (New Brunswick, N. J., 1988).

The effects on Congress are easier to measure and have been explored in articles by Paul Burstein and William Freudenberg. "Changing Public Policy: The Impact of Public Opinion, Antiwar Demonstrations, and War Costs on Senate Voting on Vietnam War Motions," *American Journal of Sociology* 84 (July 1978); and Arnold Kanter, "Congress and the Defense Budget: 1960–1970," *American Political*

Science Review 66 (March 1972). See also Alan Platt, *The U.S. Senate and Strategic Arms Policy, 1969–1977* (Boulder, Colo., 1978); and Alton Frye, *A Responsible Congress: The Politics of National Security* (New York, 1975).

For the Russian public, there is much less material available to the scholar. One can get some inkling of opinion, of course, in such examinations of political dissent as Abraham Rothberg, *The Heirs of Stalin: Dissidence and the Soviet Regime, 1953–1970* (Ithaca, N.Y., 1972); Frederick C. Barghoorn, *Détente and the Democratic Movement in the USSR* (New York, 1976); and Ludmilla Alexeyeva and Paul Goldberg, *The Thaw Generation: Coming of Age in the Post-Stalin Era* (Boston, 1990). But both majority feelings and the reactions of the elite remain largely hidden from scholarly view. To appraise these, one must lean heavily on studies of secondary social phenomena, like Walter D. Connor, *Deviance in Soviet Society: Crime, Delinquency, and Alcoholism* (New York, 1972); and Seweryn Bialer, ed., *The Domestic Context of Soviet Foreign Policy* (Boulder, Colo., 1980). One can also obtain assistance from investigations of the nationality problem, such as Hélène Carrère d'Encausse, *Decline of an Empire: The Soviet Socialist Republics in Revolt* (New York, 1979); and Rasma Karklins, *Ethnic Relations in the USSR: The Perspective from Below* (Boston, 1986).

When one takes up military issues, the essential text on the American side is John Lewis Gaddis, *Strategies of Containment,* cited above, but there are other surveys that present significant material, including Jerome H. Kahan, *Security in the Nuclear Age: Developing U.S. Strategic Arms Policy* (Washington, 1975); Lawrence Freedman, *The Evolution of Nuclear Strategy* (New York, 1981); Charles R. Morris, *Iron Destinies, Lost Opportunities: The Arms Race between the USA and the USSR, 1945–1987* (New York, 1988); Michael M. Boll, *National Security Planning: Roosevelt through Reagan* (Lexington, Ky., 1988); and Janne E. Nolan, *Guardians of the Arsenal: The Politics of Nuclear Strategy* (New York, 1989). For details on specific weapons, see Desmond Ball, *Politics and Force Levels: The Strategic Missile Program of the Kennedy Administration* (Berkeley, Calif., 1980); Ted Greenwood, *Making the MIRV: A Study of Defense Decision Making* (Cambridge, Mass., 1975); and Ernest J. Yanarella, *The Missile Defense Controversy* (Lexington, Mass., 1977).

In examining the military factor in Soviet attitudes, one cannot dispense with David Holloway, *The Soviet Union and the Arms Race* (New Haven, Conn., 1983), for carefulness and balance; but this should be supplemented with the older work of Thomas W. Wolfe, *The Military Dimension in the Making of Soviet Foreign and Defense Policy* (Santa Monica, Calif., 1977); and the newer volume by Michael MccGwire, *Military Objectives in Soviet Foreign Policy* (Washington, 1987). Military capabilities per se are the subject of Robert A. Kilmarx, *A History of Soviet Air Power* (New York, 1962); David Woodward, *The Russians at Sea: A History of the Russian Navy* (New York, 1966); and William T. Lee and Richard F. Staar, *Soviet Military Policy since World War II* (Stanford, Calif., 1986).

What Americans think about Soviet capabilities is disclosed in John Prados, *The Soviet Estimate: US Intelligence Analysis and Russian Military Strength* (New York, 1982). The continuing internal struggle over the shape and role of Soviet armed forces is chronicled in Dale R. Herspring, *The Soviet High Command,*

1967–1989 (Princeton, N.J., 1990); Raymond J. Swider, Jr., *Soviet Military Reform in the Twentieth Century: Three Case Studies* (Westport, Conn., 1992); and Thomas M. Nichols, *The Sacred Cause: Civil-Military Conflict over Soviet National Security, 1917–1992* (Ithaca, N.Y., 1993).

Economic matters, both domestic and international, have received a great deal of attention from specialists. To understand America's increasing uncompetitiveness, one can examine a number of insightful works, including Seymour Melman, *Our Depleted Society* (New York, 1965); David Calleo, *The Imperious Economy* (Cambridge, Mass., 1982); Robert Reich, *The Next American Frontier* (New York, 1983); Lloyd Dumas, *The Overburdened Economy: Uncovering the Causes of Chronic Unemployment, Inflation, and National Decline* (Berkeley, Calif., 1986); and Robert Kuttner, *The End of Laissez Faire: National Purpose and the Global Economy after the Cold War* (New York, 1991).

To see how this uncompetitiveness, in turn, created problems for the international economic system, one can refer to William Diebold, Jr., *The United States and the Industrial World: American Foreign Economic Policy in the 1970s* (New York, 1972); Fred L. Block, *The Origins of International Economic Disorder: A Study of United States International Monetary Policy from World War I to the Present (Berkeley, 1977); Joan Edelman Spero, The Politics of International Economic Relations* (New York, 1981); and Robert Solomon, *The International Monetary System, 1945–1981* (New York, 1982).

For commentary on the economic situation as Richard Nixon found it and affected it, see especially Alan S. Blinder, *Economic Policy and the Great Stagflation* (New York, 1979); Joanne Gowa, *Closing the Gold Window: Domestic Politics and the End of Bretton Woods* (Ithaca, N.Y., 1983); and Edward R. Tufte, *Political Control of the Economy* (Princeton, N.J., 1978), as well as the memoirs of William Safire and Herbert Stein.

On economic relations with the Communist world, there are recent and excellent books by Philip J. Funigiello, *American-Soviet Trade in the Cold War* (Chapel Hill, 1988); and Michael Mastanduno, *Economic Containment: CoCom and the Politics of East-West Trade* (Ithaca, N.Y., 1992). But Thomas A. Wolf, *U.S. East-West Trade Policy: Economic Warfare versus Economic Welfare* (Lexington, Mass., 1973); Marshall I. Goldman, *Détente and Dollars: Doing Business with the Soviets* (New York, 1975); Philip Hanson, *Trade and Technology in Soviet-Western Relations* (New York, 1981); and Robert A. Pastor, *Congress and Politics of U.S. Foreign Economic Policy, 1929–1976* (Berkeley, Calif., 1982), remain useful.

The development and achievements of the Soviet economy are surveyed in such studies as Alec Nove, *An Economic History of the U.S.S.R.* (London, 1969); Ronald Amann et al., eds., *The Technological Level of Soviet Industry* (New Haven, Conn., 1977); and Frederick J. Fleron Jr., ed., *Technology and Communist Culture* (New York, 1977), as well as the excellent periodic publications of the U.S. Congress, Joint Economic Committee (see above). For Nikita Khrushchev's attempts to improve productivity, consult Robert Miller's chapter in R. F. Miller and F. Feher, eds., *Khrushchev and the Communist World* (London, 1984). For the growing difficulties of the 1960s and the so-called Kosygin reforms, see in particular Gertrude Schroeder, "Soviet Economic Reforms at an Impasse," *Problems of Communism* 20 (July-Aug. 1971); Abraham Katz, *The Politics of Economic Reform in the Soviet Union* (New York, 1972); David A. Dyker, *The Future of the Soviet Economic Planning System* (Armonk, N.Y., 1985); Ed A. Hewett, *Reforming the Soviet Economy: Equality versus Efficiency* (Washington, 1988); and Jan Adam, *Economic Reforms in the Soviet Union and Eastern Europe since the 1960s* (London, 1989).

On the agricultural dimension of the challenge, see Martin McCauley, *Khrushchev and the Development of Soviet Agriculture: The Virgin Land Programme, 1953–1964* (New York, 1976); and Werner Hahn, *The Politics of Soviet Agriculture, 1960–1970* (Baltimore, 1972). On economic relations among the Communist powers, the most comprehensive discussions are in Michael Kaser, *Comecon: Integration Problems of the Planned Economies* (London, 1967); and Vladimir Sobell, *The Red Market: Industrial Cooperation and Specialization in Comecon* (Aldershot, Eng., 1984).

INDEX

Library of Congress Cataloging-in-Publication Data

Nelson, Keith L.
　The making of détente : Soviet-American relations in the shadow of Vietnam /
Keith L. Nelson.
　　　p.　　cm.
　Includes bibliographical references (p.　　).
　ISBN 0-8018-4883-0 (hc : acid-free paper)
　1. United　States—Foreign　relations—Soviet　Union.　2. Soviet　Union—Foreign
relations—United States.　3. Detente.　I. Title.
E183.8.S65N45　1995
327.73047—dc20　　94-34423